S0-AYI-959

TAHOE BENEATH THE SURFACE

TAHOE

BENEATH THE SURFACE

*The Hidden Stories of
America's Largest Mountain Lake*

SCOTT LANKFORD

HEYDAY, BERKELEY, CALIFORNIA
SIERRA COLLEGE PRESS, ROCKLIN, CALIFORNIA

©2010 by Scott Lankford

All rights reserved. No portion of this work may be reproduced or transmitted in any form or by any means, electronic or mechanical, including photocopying and recording, or by any information storage or retrieval system, without permission in writing from Heyday.

Material in chapter 15 from *Wa She Shu: A Washoe Tribal History* is used by permission of the Inter-Tribal Council of Nevada.

Quotations from *China Men*, by Maxine Hong Kingston, copyright ©1977, 1978, 1979, 1980 by Maxine Hong Kingston. Used by permission of Alfred A. Knopf, a division of Random House, Inc.

Quotes from Gary Kaufman's website, www.vistagallery.com/html/twister_story.html, are also used with permission.

Library of Congress Cataloging-in-Publication Data
Lankford, Scott, 1957-
  Tahoe beneath the surface : the hidden stories of America's largest mountain lake / Scott Lankford.
    p. cm.
  ISBN 978-1-59714-139-0 (alk. paper)
   1. Tahoe, Lake (Calif. and Nev.)—History—Anecdotes. 2. Tahoe, Lake, Region (Calif. and Nev.)—History—Anecdotes. 3. Tahoe, Lake, Region (Calif. and Nev.)—Environmental conditions—Anecdotes. 4. Tahoe, Lake, Region (Calif. and Nev.)—Intellectual life—Anecdotes. 5. Authors, American—Tahoe, Lake, Region (Calif. and Nev.)—Biography—Anecdotes. 6. Indians of North America—Tahoe, Lake, Region (Calif. and Nev.)—Biography—Anecdotes. 7. Tahoe, Lake, Region (Calif. and Nev.)—Biography—Anecdotes. 8. American literature—Tahoe, Lake, Region (Calif. and Nev.)—History and criticism. I. Title.
  F868.T2L364 2010
  979.4'38—dc22

                            2010022318

Cover Art: *Lake Tahoe from Maggies Peaks* ©2005 by Tom Killion (tomkillion.com)
Maps: Ben Pease, Pease Press Cartography
Cover Design: Lorraine Rath
Interior Design/Typesetting: Rebecca LeGates
Printing and Binding: Thomson-Shore, Dexter, MI

This book was copublished by Heyday and Sierra College Press.
Orders, inquiries, and correspondence should be addressed to:
      Heyday
      P. O. Box 9145, Berkeley, CA 94709
      (510) 549-3564, Fax (510) 549-1889
      www.heydaybooks.com

10 9 8 7 6 5 4 3 2 1

I see the clear waters of Lake Tahoe—I see forests of majestic pines,
Or, crossing the great desert, the alkaline plains, I behold enchanting
mirages of waters and meadows;
Marking through these, and after all, in duplicate slender lines,
Bridging the three or four thousand miles of land travel,
Tying the Eastern to the Western sea...

—*Walt Whitman*

CONTENTS

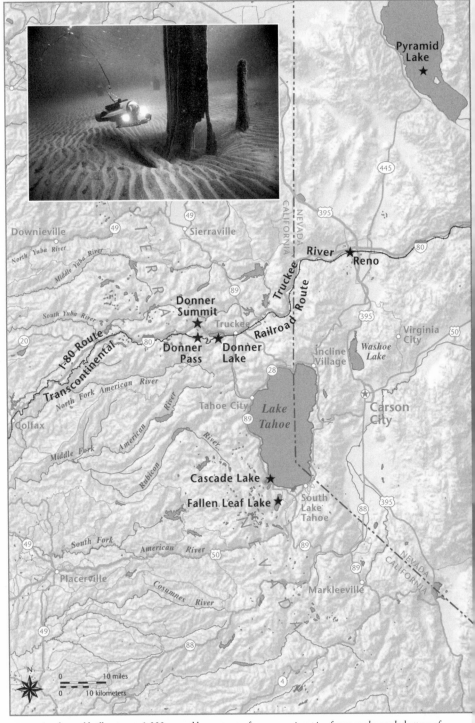

A submersible illuminates 6,000-year-old tree stumps from an ancient pine forest on the sandy bottom of Lake Tahoe, California. Photograph by Emory Kristof. Reprinted with permission of National Geographic

one

JACQUES COUSTEAU

Diving beneath the Surface

Legend has it that the corpses of those drowned in Lake Tahoe never rise. Instead they are said to float deep beneath the surface in a perpetual state of liquid limbo—eyes wide open, arms outstretched, and fully clothed. Some old-time Lakers even claim that when Jacques Cousteau, the French inventor of SCUBA, first plunged into the unexplored depths of Lake Tahoe what he found down there astonished him: dozens of fully-clothed Victorian corpses—a sight so appalling that Cousteau allegedly fled straight to the surface, never to return. Sacré bleu.

Armed with modern SCUBA gear, satellites, and even deep-sea submersibles, a small army of scientists have long since plumbed the hidden depths of Tahoe's underwater cliffs and canyons—and found no floating human corpses down there after all. Nor is there any record of Cousteau's alleged visit. Instead what scientists found down there seems equally shocking: fossil evidence of phantom forests up to six thousand years old, formed when droughts dropped the level of the lake far below its present horizon. Evidence, in short, of catastrophic climate change.

Diving further still, using deep-sea submarines, scientists have located the wrecked remains of Tahoe's lost *Titanics*—luxurious little passenger steamers claimed by Sierra snowstorms, scuttled by their bankrupt owners, or blown to smithereens by exploding boilers during Tahoe's Gilded Age (a term first coined by the best-known of all Tahoe authors, Mark Twain).

As Twain himself discovered, myths and magic abound beneath the surface of the Tahoe deep—including stories of a Loch Ness monster affectionately known as Tahoe Tessie and of the long-haired, mermaidlike beings called Water Babies, still believed by the local Washoe Indians to be among the lake's most ancient, dangerous, and seductive denizens. Perhaps that's why early pioneers claimed that anyone attempting to swim in Lake Tahoe would quickly sink like a stone. As one Washoe elder warned back in the 1940s, "Washoe people don't swim in Big Water. Water Baby get."

Scientifically speaking, there may be some truth behind the old myth that the bodies of those who drown in Lake Tahoe never rise: the same dearth of microorganisms which helps give Tahoe its legendary crystal clarity also helps shield human corpses from the out-gassing bacterial wastes which might otherwise send them rocketing back toward the surface like ghostly balloons. Yet these days, it seems far more likely that any organic detritus—human corpses included—would be quickly nibbled into nothingness by the millions of freshwater crayfish recently introduced into the lake's fragile ecosystem, where they spread like a plague beneath the surface.

Peer beneath the surface of Time itself, and you will find that there were far earlier, far deeper, far wider mountain lakes to reckon with than Lake Tahoe: vast inland oceans that made Tahoe look like a pond by comparison. Pleistocene Lake Lahontan, scientists say, once covered much of present-day northwestern Nevada, fed by melting continental glaciers at the end of the last Ice Age—and leaving behind a bathtub ring still visible across the flanks of Nevada's desiccated mountainsides. In an era when saber-toothed tigers, woolly mammoths, and camels still roamed the Great Basin, Tahoe shivered bravely beneath perpetual snows, its shores gouged by glaciers whose tracks are still clearly etched in granite. Alone among all these lost glaciers and vanished inland oceans, Tahoe has survived to claim the title of the last true Mountain Sea.

So beware, tenderfoot, you have been warned: peer too deeply beneath the mirrored surface of Lake Tahoe, breathe some life into those old lake legends, and the secrets that you'll find hidden in its depths may amaze you. Or frighten you. Or both. For in the end that's the deepest magic of them all, the inky sorcery upon which all human literature is founded: that language gives us the power to shatter time; and writing the means by which the voices of those long dead may speak from beyond the grave. Time out of mind, the corpses of our ancestors confront us—eyes wide open, arms outstretched, and fully clothed.

It's a fact seldom noted, except by me, that Lake Tahoe transformed America, not just once but many times over—from our earliest Ice Age civilizations all the way forward to the strangely tangled fates of the Kennedys, Frank Sinatra, Jack Ruby, and Marilyn Monroe. Somewhere in between, Tahoe helped to conquer California, launch the Republican Party, and ignite the Western Indian wars. The nearby town of Truckee helped to trigger some of the bloodiest race riots in our nation's history. And although Lake Tahoe never became a national park, John Muir's battle to save it ultimately did more than the park designations for Yellowstone and Yosemite combined to protect our precious national forests from destruction. Along the way Lake Tahoe somehow found time to invent the ski industry, spark the sexual revolution, and win countless Academy Awards. With a little help from Reno, Tahoe even built the foundations of the mighty Nevada gaming industry long before Las Vegas came along to steal the show.

At a purely personal level, understanding the full depth and complexity of the lake's life story certainly took me some time—about thirty years, to be precise. In 1981 I set out west from Williams College in Massachusetts to begin working on my PhD at Stanford. Offered a part-time job at Lake Tahoe along the way, I figured I'd stop off just long enough to earn a little extra cash before moving on to graduate school. Instead I found myself employed part-time for the next ten years as a Tahoe snow shoveler, Tahoe ditchdigger, Tahoe dishwasher, Tahoe toilet cleaner, Tahoe night watchman, and even a Tahoe garbageman—anything and every-thing to avoid the mind-numbing, soul-crushing fate I referred to as "low-altitude sickness" (more commonly known as the grad school grind). For ten years after that—sandwiched in between sleepy classes down amid the palms—I returned to Lake Tahoe time and again, eventually wrangling more glamorous employment as a Tahoe folksinger, Tahoe ski instructor, Tahoe rock-climbing instruc-tor, and occasional guest lecturer on Lake Tahoe's literary history. Once I even joined a Tahoe-based Everest expedition to avoid writ-ing my dissertation.

In retrospect I see that I should have sensed what Tahoe was try-ing to teach me from the very beginning. My first summer in the Sierra, I found myself sleeping in a cabin built by John Steinbeck. From my window I could look out toward the far shore where Mark Twain first floated toward freedom on a homemade raft he'd hewn from Tahoe timber. A stone's throw away was another rickety little Tahoe cabin, once occupied by British philosopher Bertrand Russell during the darkest days of the Second World War. Seventy years old, bankrupt, and blacklisted from every university in the country, Russell sat stark naked at his typewriter all one summer, tapping out the manuscript of a book modestly entitled *Meaning and Truth*. This book and Steinbeck's work eventually launched them both toward Nobel Prizes.

Like a young trout lunging toward some fabulous fishing lure, I was hooked before I knew what hit me. The shadowy ghosts of Lake Tahoe's hidden history possessed me. It no longer mattered that I'd only planned on just passing through, a gypsy scholar on my way out west. Instead, much like the Donner Party, a big part of me never made it past the granite gates of the Tahoe Sierra. In the end, even my dissertation turned blue, focused as it was on John Muir—another Tahoe-area author whose life and legacy permanently altered the nature of America.

Of course I was hardly the first to succumb to Lake Tahoe's inky allure. "Three months of camp life on Lake Tahoe," Mark Twain once quipped, "would restore an Egyptian mummy to his pristine vigor, and give him an appetite like an alligator. I do not mean the oldest and driest mummies, of course," Twain added wryly, "but the fresher ones." As it turns out, the very "oldest and driest mummies" in all of North America have, in fact, been found right here in Tahoe territory. But even measured in purely literary terms, Twain's little joke points toward another phenomenon hidden deep beneath the surface of what might be called the Tahoe Blues: Time and again, exhausted and deeply discouraged, an internationally famous author has arrived on the shores of Lake Tahoe at a crisis point in his or her career, threatening to give up the writing life forever. Yet after just "three months of camp life on Lake Tahoe," that same prematurely mummified author returns to work reinvigorated and essentially reborn, filled with renewed inspiration—ready, willing, and able to change the world.

Admittedly, no one thinks of Tahoe as a literary capital, not even me. Yet the list of celebrated authors who have spent significant time in Tahoe territory includes two Nobel Prize winners (Steinbeck and Russell), America's best-known humorist (Twain), and the founder of the American conservation movement (Muir). They are among the more than one dozen authors whose steps we will retrace in search of lost Tahoe Time. Granted, they all lived in different eras, wrote in different genres, and fought very different battles. But what they all have in common, deep beneath the surface, is an unquenchable taste for stinging social commentary: the kind of writing that moves mountains.

Clearly we can learn much about the nature of American literature by viewing it through the watery blue lens of Lake Tahoe.

But we can also learn much about ourselves. What are the origins of inspiration, the deep wellsprings of insight, of imagination, of healing, of courage, of renewal? What is the relationship, the living link, between each of these lost American generations and our own? For at the very bottom of Tahoe's history, woven through every fact and fantasy, and etched into the watery landscape of the lake, is one rock-solid truth: that Tahoe transforms the lives of those it truly touches, just as Tahoe itself has been transformed—repeatedly, violently, deeply—through at least ten thousand years of Tahoe Time.

It's a long story: Measure out Tahoe's ten thousand years of continuous human habitation against the lake's own 1,645-foot maximum depth, and just the first twenty-seven feet of surface water will suffice to cover the entire span of the lake's modern history, since the arrival of Euro-American explorers here in 1844. Plunge down another sixty feet beyond that, to the very limit of what seems visible from the surface, and you'll already have exceeded the entire span of American history since the arrival of Columbus. All the rest—more than twenty times as deep, locked in perpetual darkness, all the way down to the bone-crushing depth of one-third of a mile—corresponds to what anthropologists refer to as "prehistory." But it is not prehistory to those whose ancestors have lived by these shores for at least three hundred human generations. Nor is that prehistory lost to the lake itself, given that every single particle of debris which falls into Tahoe remains locked beneath its surface essentially forever. Human corpses included.

Measured out on a map, the Tahoe watershed extends from the central summit crest of the California Sierra east through the Truckee River Canyon near Reno, and then north and east for a few more sagebrush-studded desert miles to Pyramid Lake—where the snowmelt waters of Lake Tahoe bleed invisibly into the desert sky. In this circular sense Tahoe may well be among the purest, most self-contained watersheds on Earth: a microcosm; a mandala—so different from those run-of-the-mill lakes and rivers that give themselves, in the end, only to the ocean. Tahoe gives itself only to the sky.

Perhaps, I wake up dreaming, there is a spirit lake somewhere deep inside us as reflective as Tahoe itself—a place where all our deeds, good and bad, flow and collect and merge together; a place that mirrors our own being back to the sky. Storm-tossed at times, sleepy blue at others, with invisible currents and upwellings we scarce understand, through long abuse its clarity can be diminished, not so much from one great cataclysmic toxic spill as from the daily imperceptible erosion of all that surrounds us, especially all the human-created gunk and goo we coat our outer lives with, all that unnecessary and ultimately disposable stuff of suffering and grasping and clinging and desire. Except that in this great basin of the heart nothing is wasted, not even sorrow, not even excess. Instead it all ends up flowing into this sky water lake we call our lives. Tahoe *Tao*.

For newcomers, this circular, self-enclosed nature of Tahoe's hydrology is not easily grasped. I can't count the number of times I've heard tourists stammer, "You mean all this water *doesn't ever* flow to the Pacific?" They're not alone. Right up to the 1850s, generations of mapmakers remained stubbornly convinced that there must be *some kind* of river connecting the Great Basin deserts to the Pacific. Even after California first became part of the United States, otherwise sane and sensible cartographers continued to picture a fantastic (and entirely fictional) river flowing from Lake Tahoe directly west to the sea, all on the basis of no evidence whatsoever. John Frémont, the first white explorer to "discover" Lake Tahoe, etched these errors into the maps he used to carve out the official boundaries of the new State of California—accidentally sawing the lake in half: two-thirds in California, and one-third in Nevada. Oops.

"But why *doesn't* Tahoe flow to the Pacific?" bewildered visitors still ask. You might as well ask, "How did Tahoe get to be so deep?" For as it turns out, these two answers are one and the same. Here's a little thought-experiment to help you understand why. For simplicity's sake, I call it "Tahoe in a Tub."

First, lie back in an imaginary bathtub and let the water soothe you. Now imagine that the porcelain depression in which you are immersed was formed by a kind of sudden slumping or slipping downward from the topmost surface of the tub itself, an oblong hollow "valley" enclosed on all four sides: the lengthier sides of the tub, where your arms are resting, are much like the two parallel arms of the Sierra Nevada, which split (briefly) to form the immensely steep and deep mountain valley. Later a series of volcanic eruptions caulked and sealed the outlets of this mountain valley on all four sides, trapping an immense body of water within a deep, steep-sided granite basin more than a mile above sea level.

Buff and polish the edges with some glaciers, then place an "overflow drain" about halfway down from the rim, and there you have it: Tahoe in a Tub—a highly oversimplified but still vaguely accurate working model of the entire Lake Tahoe Basin, including the Truckee River Canyon, which drains the lake's overflow from just above 6,000 vertical feet above sea level onto the flat dry floor of the Nevada desert some 1,500 feet below, not unlike a bathtub overflowing onto the floor.

And then what? Well, then nothing: once spilled onto the desert floor the water simply puddles up and evaporates, leaving little behind but a ghostly white chalky residue that has, over the eons, helped to form the famous tufa "pyramids" of the eponymous Pyramid Lake.

How much water does your Tahoe Tub hold? Hold your breath. As the largest U.S. lake by volume west of the Mississippi, Tahoe contains a mind-boggling 39 *trillion* gallons of water—a number so large that our poor little human minds bloat and stagger like cosmic bladders straining to take it all in. Famously, that's enough water to flood all of California under a lake more than two feet deep; or enough to drown all of America, from sea to shining sea, in a one-inch puddle. It's also enough water, measured in human terms, to provide every single man, woman, and child in the United States with 550 gallons of pure Sierra snowmelt *per day* for the next five years. Enough to fill 312 trillion little plastic pint bottles of Evian or Perrier—every drop of it just as pure as the stuff you pay for, but bottled up in a huge drowned Yosemite Valley deep and steep enough to swallow the entire Empire State Building, with room enough left over on top to float the *Queen Mary*. Burp.

Granted, many other lakes and man-made reservoirs look far larger on a map. Shyly, perhaps even slyly, Tahoe hides its inmost depths. Given a pop quiz, how many Americans would guess that our largest single body of water west of the Mississippi is Lake Tahoe, not the Great Salt Lake? Yet Tahoe contains more liquid than all ten of the largest man-made U.S. reservoirs combined, including Lake Mead and Lake Powell. Sure, the Great Salt Lake is wider, and Oregon's Crater Lake is deeper; but these are mere puddles compared to Tahoe in terms of sheer volume. Measured in terms of *average* depth, Tahoe ranks among the top ten deepest lakes on Earth. Factor in altitude, and (depending on how you weight your calculations) Tahoe is widely considered to be the second-largest high-mountain lake on Earth, right behind South America's Lake Titicaca.

Perhaps it's all just a clever, protective disguise. Out here in the Wild West, as the saying goes, "Whiskey is for drinkin' and water is for fightin'." While Tahoe, to date, remains virtually untouched, several lakes of comparable size and stature have long since been sucked bone dry. Consider, for example, the tragic fate of Tahoe's broad-shouldered brother, once known as Tulare Lake—a huge sheet of shallow water located at the heart of California's Central Valley with a shoreline so extensive during flood season that it easily ranked as the largest body of freshwater (measured by surface area) west of the Great Lakes. It was home to one of the earth's richest concentrations of migratory waterfowl: the feathered flocks visiting Tulare Lake's shallow shores once rivaled the flamingos that still blanket the surface of Africa's Lake Tanganyika. To feed them, Tulare Lake harbored one of North America's richest fisheries, easily supporting a thriving population of Native Americans as well with its bounty. Yet by the early 1900s Tulare Lake had been drained and plowed under, its intake rivers impounded for irrigation, and its rich swampy bottomlands "reclaimed" for industrial agriculture. These days you won't find Tulare Lake on any maps *at all*—although occasional flooding does, as in the 1980s, soak a couple hundred square miles of farmers' crops. That's what makes the murder of a lake the perfect crime: dead lakes, like dead men, tell no tales.

Still not convinced of the danger to Lake Tahoe? Consider the tragic fate of the mighty Colorado River, so dammed, drained, and diverted that not one drop of its red-stained water ever makes it to the Pacific Ocean—or even across the border into Mexico in drought years. Likewise the great Salton Sea in Southern California, first formed when the Colorado River overflowed its banks, has shrunk through evaporation and impoundment to the size of a stinking puddle, leaving the farms and former luxury resorts scattered around its margins high and dry. How did Lake Tahoe escape the same fate?

Or has it? During the nineteenth century Tahoe's once inexhaustible forests were clear-cut from lakeshore to ridgeline so completely that local timber companies were finally forced to pack up and move elsewhere; Tahoe's famous fisheries, after shipping tens of thousands of pounds of trout annually to San Francisco and New York (in railcars packed to the gills with Tahoe ice), collapsed so completely that whole species went virtually extinct, including the world's largest trout, the Lahontan. Nor has the pace of change lessened in recent decades. Crime, gridlock, and smog have become persistent plagues around the edge of the lake. Each year since accurate measurements were first taken, back in 1967, Tahoe's legendary sky-water has become cloudier, murkier, muckier, and greener—choked with increasing loads of dissolved and suspended sediments, artificial nutrients, and the endless legions of free-floating microorganisms which feed off them. Over the past forty years visibility in Lake Tahoe has dropped by almost half—falling by as much as three feet in a single season when

Tahoe's periodic floods and mudslides sloshed massive amounts of debris into the lake. As for the future, burrowing bark beetles and catastrophic wildfires now threaten the overly dense, markedly less diverse second-growth forests that ring the lake—and global warming could bring drought on a scale as yet undreamed of. The news is not all grim. As any scientist will tell you, there are dozens of fronts in the ongoing battle to Keep Tahoe Blue, ranging from blocking local nutrient seepage to assessing the impact of airborne pollutants carried across the Pacific from China. Yet due to increasing loads of organic nitrogen and phosphorous, there is still an ever-growing danger that Tahoe Green will replace Tahoe Blue. This same combination of local and global pollution has also rendered Tahoe's forests increasingly vulnerable to acid rain, drought, and disease. These grave threats cannot be easily dismissed as environmentalist propaganda: dozens of enormous lakes worldwide, including Lake Geneva and the Dead Sea, have suffered disastrous declines; others have died or dried up entirely—most notably Central Asia's once blue and fertile Ural Sea.

In a desperate last-ditch effort to defend Tahoe's legendary waters from what scientists call *eutrophication*—the process whereby algal blooms can starve even the largest lakes of oxygen and literally choke them to death—one of the world's largest and most successful regional water treatment systems has been constructed, pumping virtually every drop of human sewage produced within the Lake Tahoe Basin up over the mountains' rim to be treated and released as irrigation water in the deserts of nearby Nevada. No shit. Even so, Tahoe's overall water quality, by most measures, continues to decline. Worse yet, since scientists estimate that it takes approximately seven hundred years for Tahoe's waters to fully cycle through, whatever muck our generation pours into the lake today will remain there for at least the next seven centuries. What happens in Tahoe stays in Tahoe.

Fortunately that same longevity gives Lake Tahoe a profound capacity for self-healing, while the layered muds which line the bottom of its concave granite cranium seem as folded and convoluted as our own gray matter, but with a memory infinitely longer, deeper, and more detailed than anything we can comprehend. Celebrated as the seething "Main Street of the West" from the California Gold Rush to the Nevada Silver Boom, Tahoe staggered into the twentieth century raped and all but abandoned by its private owners; today, according to the California Tahoe Conservancy, that trend has been reversed, with over 80 percent of reforested land within the basin now returned to some form of public ownership and control, and the rapidly diminishing clarity of the lake showing recent signs of leveling off. From a scientific perspective, Tahoe may be the most intensively studied body of water on Earth. From a human perspective, its history proves beyond a shadow of a doubt that the world's great lakes are not automatically doomed to destruction.

Meanwhile the shores of Lake Tahoe are among the most contested, conflicted, expensive, and controversial landscapes in all of America—wrestled over by a welter of interlocking governmental agencies, feuding corporations, private landowners, and activists with visionary global agendas, all fighting desperately for control of the American future. Somehow, amid all the shouting, Tahoe has managed to remain among the world's most popular (and beautiful) mountain destination resorts, attracting millions of tourists annually and spawning a bewildering array of world-class ski resorts, casinos, strip malls, high-rise hotels, golf courses, amusement parks, wedding chapels, and billionaires' waterfront mansions—each with its own stake in the heart of the lake.

New battles are beginning to be waged. In the wake of the 2007 Angora Fire, which torched hundreds of homes, Tahoe exploded across television screens worldwide with images of smoldering cabins and flaming forests. Today in an era of looming climate change, planetary pollution, invasive species, catastrophic wildfires, and even renewed nuclear brinksmanship, the fragile ecological health of Lake Tahoe will continue to serve as a sky-blue canary in a planetary coal mine.

Those who doubt the wisdom of such warnings should simply step out of their cars at the rest area on Interstate 80 as it crosses

Donner Summit—not far from where members of the Donner Party met their fate in 1846. Take a deep breath. Suck in some of that sweet pine-scented, exhaust-tinged mountain air. Look around you. The tide of changes these lands have unleashed defies description. Just a few feet from the edge of the highway, ancient petroglyph images cut into stone loom up right next to the still-visible remains of pioneer wagon-train wheel ruts, steps away from where the world's first transcontinental railroad tracks were laid by gangs of Chinese workers, and parallel to the world's first transcontinental highway (the old Lincoln Highway), now lost amid the roar of the interstate freeway—with invisible tentacles of fiber-optic cables and natural gas pipelines hissing just beneath the surface like subterranean snakes.

Nowhere in all of America is the pulse of human history as palpable and powerful as it is right here. If the old gods, as these petroglyphs may imply, really did play dice with the universe, then surely Lake Tahoe was the place they picked to go gambling.

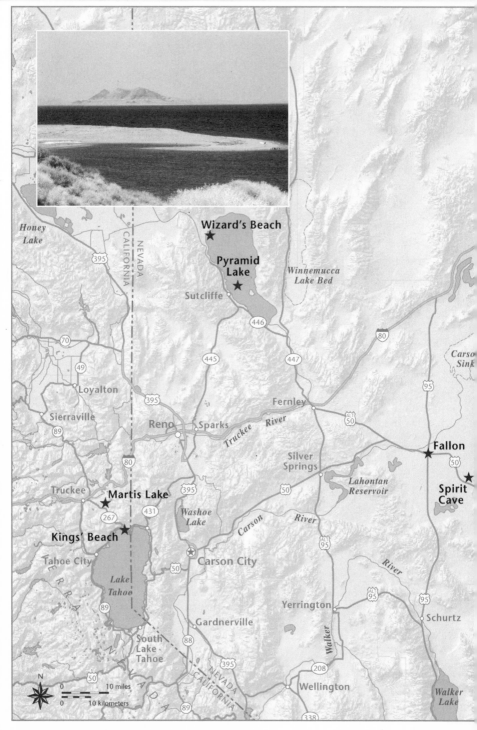

Spirit Cave is near Fallon, Nevada, east of Lake Tahoe. Pyramid Lake, where Wizard's Beach Man was found, is pictured above

two

SPIRIT CAVE MAN

Curse of the Ice Age Mummy

Even Hollywood fright films can't match the nearly ten-thousand-year-old tale of Tahoe's own true-life Spirit Cave Mummy—or the scientific prophesies of doom which his resurrection unleashed. After all, the Egyptian mummies Hollywood favors are at best some three thousand years old. But the Spirit Cave Mummy is at least three times as old as King Tut, dating from an era when most of Europe still shivered beneath massive ice sheets, at a time when even Babylon and the very earliest Sumerian civilizations of the Fertile Crescent were but a distant dream.

Like most horror stories, this one begins innocently enough. In 1940 a partially mummified human corpse known as Spirit Cave Man was unearthed in a shallow cave located less than seventy air miles east of Lake Tahoe, near Fallon, Nevada. In the 1970s another partially intact skeleton, this one known as Wizard's Beach Man, was also recovered—this time well within the range of Tahoe's own geographic watershed, at Pyramid Lake. Together they represent some of the oldest human remains yet found anywhere in North America. American history begins here.

In the case of Spirit Cave Man, only the skull and a portion of the right torso remained intact, but these were so well preserved that large pieces of skin and even strands of shoulder-length dark hair were found still clinging to the scalp. Sydney and Georgia Wheeler, the husband-and-wife archaeological team who made the discovery, were reportedly tipped off by local guano miners to the presence of ancient Indian artifacts hidden in the dozens of caves nearby. Together they launched a systematic investigation. Entering Spirit Cave Man's cave for the first time, they were initially disappointed. Perhaps trophy hunters had gotten there first. Just beyond the main cave, however, they discovered a smaller, hidden room which was apparently undisturbed. There it was, buried literally underneath another human skeleton of almost equal antiquity, that the Wheelers unearthed the partially mummified remains of Spirit Cave Man—along with a grand total of sixty-three astonishingly well-preserved artifacts, ranging from the finely woven tule mats and intricately stitched rabbit-skin robes in which Spirit Cave Man's remains had been wrapped to the moccasins which accompanied him on his final journey.

Based on minute examination of the skeleton, scientists now estimate that Spirit Cave Man died in his mid-forties to early fifties, having suffered from a wide variety of ailments including a broken right hand, a partially healed hole punched into his skull, arthritis, a fractured disk, and serious dental abscesses in both his upper and lower jaws. Remarkably, even the fossilized vestiges of Spirit Cave Man's last supper were intact inside his intestines, revealing the wide variety of very small fish bones and seeds he had ingested during his final days on Earth. The fish were so small that woven nets or weirs must have been used to trap them.

Given the mummy's extraordinary state of near-perfect preservation and the wide array of intricately made artifacts surrounding his body, archaeologists at first estimated the remains to be no more than two thousand years old—considerably less than those Egyptian mummies Hollywood is so fond of filming. For the next fifty-four years, Spirit Cave Man's remains languished ignominiously in a specially constructed wooden box inside the newly opened Nevada State Museum in nearby Carson City.

Then, in 1994, portions of his remains were retested using improved radiocarbon dating methods and mass spectrometry—this time focusing on specific amino acids painstakingly recovered from his hair follicles, as well as similar organic materials recovered from the woven mats and rabbit-skin robes in which his body had been wrapped. As *The New York Times* soon reported in an article titled "Oldest Mummy 'Found' on Museum Shelf" in April of 1996, "The Spirit Cave man's age was determined by Ervin Taylor, an anthropology professor at the University of California at Riverside, who was working on a new method of testing ancient hair using a technique known as accelerator mass spectrometry, which allows scientists to count individual carbon atoms."

Astonishingly, these new tests revealed that Spirit Cave Man had died approximately ninety-four hundred years ago, near the end of the last Ice Age. At the time of testing, these were the very oldest human remains yet discovered anywhere in North America. Twelve years later, Spirit Cave Man's mummy is still ranked among the oldest human remains recovered on the continent, in addition to being the most reliably dated.

In effect, this makes Spirit Cave Man the First American—not to mention the first known inhabitant of the original Tahoe nation. "It's a big surprise," admitted Robson Bonnichsen at the time, director of the Center for the Study of the First Americans and a professor of anthropology at Oregon State University. "All of a sudden," added David Hurst Thomas of the American Museum of Natural History, "something that's not that interesting when it's two thousand years old is earth-shattering when it's nine thousand years old."

But who were Spirit Cave Man's people? What kind of civilization had they built? And what was their relationship, if any, to the contemporary Paiute, Shoshone, and Washoe tribes who still inhabit the wider Tahoe region some ten thousand years later?

These are sensitive, potentially explosive questions. To make matters worse, early (and unreliable) forensic reconstructions based on various cranial measurements seemed to imply that there was no physical resemblance between Spirit Cave Man and the contemporary Indian tribes of Nevada. Indeed, some anthropologists argued openly—at times even aggressively—that Spirit Cave Man bears a stronger resemblance to the so-called "Caucasoid" inhabitants of Europe.

Choosing the label "Caucasoid" was especially unfortunate—not to mention premature. To be blunt, such language sounds too much like an echo of the now utterly discredited "Aryan" theories first propounded by British archaeologists working in India at the turn of the twentieth century—and later made a centerpiece of Nazi ideology. Implying that the First Americans were Europeans, the story exploded in the national media, sometimes with ugly overtones.

Local news reports also fanned the flames of controversy. As the *Reno Gazette-Journal* trumpeted at the time, "Spirit Cave Man's remains are now the focus of worldwide excitement and nationwide controversy. The man does not resemble American Indians, anthropologists say, and he may represent a population already established in North America when the ancestors of the Indians arrived." In retrospect, such statements seem hasty at best and radically one-sided at worst—even though the words "may represent" were carefully inserted into reports like this one to provide some scientific wiggle room. Doubtless the scientists making such statements were sincere: but this does not excuse their apparent ignorance of the disturbing legacy of their own profession, as documented in detail by, among others, paleontologist Stephen Jay Gould in his book *The Mismeasure of Man*. In the final analysis, Spirit Cave Man became the latest in a long line of mummies to be "mismeasured."

To his credit, the local *Reno Gazette-Journal* reporter assigned to the story, Frank X. Mullen, soon followed up these reports with a more careful series of in-depth interviews with the forensic scientists themselves—many of whom turned out to be far more cautious in their speculations about Spirit Cave Man's ethnicity than the early reports indicated. This time Mullen was also careful to interview local Native American leaders—many of whom had already initiated suits under federal law governing the repatriation of Native American remains, to assure that Spirit Cave Man would be returned to his Native people.

Down to this day, the legal battle has continued unabated—making Spirit Cave Man perhaps the oldest American ever to find himself tied up in court. As one tribal leader explained bluntly, "We don't want to see our grandfather buried in a file cabinet." And who among us can blame them? From a Native American perspective, white anthropologists and commercial trophy hunters have often behaved with little more dignity than ghoulish grave robbers. Such grievances reach all the way back to the earliest days of American history. As any careful reader of William Bradford's *Pilgrim's Progress* can attest, the very first thing the Pilgrim Fathers did after setting foot on Plymouth Rock was plunder Indian gravesites. Later founding fathers, like Thomas Jefferson, excavated Indian burial sites for public display in both Washington and Europe. In retrospect the double standard is painful: imagine the uproar that might have ensued had American Indians dug up Jefferson's corpse. Today's local tribal leaders see the removal of Spirit Cave Man's bones in much the same light—and with much the same mix of pride, outrage, and anger.

At the heart of their suit is a sweeping federal law passed in 1990 requiring the prompt return—"repatriation"—of all identifiable Indian remains to local Indian tribes for proper reburial. Known as the Native American Graves Protection and Repatriation Act (NAGPRA), the law has facilitated the return of literally thousands of remains from museums and archives nationwide—including the bones of Ishi, perhaps the most famous of all California Indians, whose brain was recently discovered floating in a vat of formaldehyde in some deep recess of the Smithsonian Institution. However, nothing in the original NAGPRA language ever anticipated the discovery of a ten-thousand-year-old mummy—or the archaeological and anthropological battles that might be triggered as a result.

The question at issue is simple: which, if any, present-day Native American tribes can convincingly claim this mummy as a distant member of their own present-day civilization? For daring to make such claims, Indian leaders were all too quickly branded as ignorant, superstitious obstructionists bent on blocking the progress of Western science as a whole. In one fifteen-minute Halloween-night documentary titled "Angry Spirits," for example, Sacramento's KCRA opened with what, at first glance, seemed like uncontroversial footage: the lead anthropologist in the Spirit Cave Man case, Amy Dansie, explaining that the discovery was "unprecedented." "We haven't had a find of this magnitude in my lifetime," Dr. Dansie added. "These textiles," she explained, gesturing to the woven mats and fabrics with which Spirit Cave Man was interred, "represent an extremely sophisticated ability to weave fabric by hand at a time when we didn't realize that people were doing that before."

So far, so good. But then Dr. Dansie went on to claim bluntly— and without apparent need for qualification or self-doubt—that measurements of the skulls of Spirit Cave Man and others buried near him "do not appear similar to any living Native American in North America. They have receding cheekbones, narrow faces, long faces. Some Indians have some of those traits, but as a group those are Caucasoid traits." Based in large part on her repeated and unequivocal use of the word "Caucasoid," the U.S. Bureau of Land Management (BLM) quietly moved to block any efforts whatsoever by the local Fallon Paiute Shoshone Tribe to recover Spirit Cave Man's remains under NAGPRA. The ensuing court battles have now lasted more than a decade.

Looking back, what makes Dr. Dansie's early televised statements about Spirit Cave Man's alleged European or Caucasoid traits so alarming is that she said nothing whatsoever about the far more obvious and overwhelming *similarities* between the ancient artifacts and people and modern ones. Nothing, for example, about the strikingly similar (and in many cases literally identical) weaves of fabrics and mats and baskets and robes still prized by Native American tribes living within Nevada today; nothing about the equally striking similarities in burial practices and food gathering patterns, not to mention the other "genetic" physical features, such as the structure of the mummy's teeth and hair—all of which match modern Paiute practices and physical features. Indeed it would be difficult to think of *any* culture *anywhere* on Earth which can demonstrate such a consistent and widespread set of continuous cultural practices across such vast spans of time.

In their most recent court briefs, dated January 31, 2006, the Fallon Paiute Shoshone Tribe summarized the mass of scientific evidence assembled by the BLM's own panel of experts as follows:

> Overall the hair and dental analyses by Goodman, Martin, Turner and others establish a significant genetic relationship between the Spirit Cave remains and contemporary Native Americans generally and the Nevada Paiute particularly... The dietary information and pollen present in the fecal material indicate both desert shrub and marsh environments were present in the area [much as they are today]...the burial practices utilized for the oldest Spirit Cave remains...have "several similarities" with ethnographic Northern Paiute burial practices...and...fit comfortably within a Great Basin burial pattern that persisted into ethnographic times, and which distinguished the people of the Great Basin from surrounding culture areas....The twining techniques used in the Spirit Cave materials were used by people in the western Great Basin from the time of the Spirit Cave burials into ethnographic times, and the key element in the textiles (Z-twist cordage wefts) remained the same throughout. Nevada Museum scientists and other scholars have noted that twined mats such as those found with the Spirit Cave remains "were used extensively in the western Great Basin dating from rather recent times to as far back as 9460 B.P.," and "twined twisted fur robes were common throughout Great Basin prehistory into the historic era, usually rabbit fur."

Resting their case, the tribe argues that "In short, for every available cultural indicator from Spirit Cave—including burial practices, textiles, diet, and subsistence strategy—there is a significant relationship to similar practices among Native peoples who were indigenous to the Great Basin or nearby areas at the time of contact."

The courts agreed. In his most recent ruling from the bench, dated September 21, 2006, U.S. District Judge Larry R. Hicks began somewhat ominously by framing the case solely in terms of religion versus science, much as KCRA had done in their televised "Angry Spirits" report more than a decade earlier:

> The heart of this matter concerns the right to possess the remains of an extremely ancient habitant of Northern Nevada. On the one side, BLM seeks possession of the remains to allow for further study by scientists around the world. On the other side, the Fallon Paiute-Shoshone Tribe ("Tribe") seeks possession of the remains to allow for reburial. The Tribe believes that because the remains have been disturbed the spirit of their ancestor is required to wander the world in a state of unrest.

Yet to his credit Judge Hicks immediately shifts the grounds of his ruling back toward more scientific and procedural grounds, regardless of their religious and/or cultural implications. In language bluntly critical of the government, he sides strongly and unequivocally with the Fallon Paiute Shoshone Tribe's position, concluding sharply that:

> In this matter, there is no cogent explanation why BLM chose to deny the repatriation request. There is no weighing of the competing evidence, nor is there an explanation why the Tribe's evidence is not sufficient or the [BLM's own] Review Committee's findings are not persuasive. While the court can understand how the difficult procedural morass that this proceeding became could make it difficult for BLM...

this failure cannot be excused. The [BLM's own expert] Committee reviewed all the materials before it, including the BLM's submissions, and concluded that the remains were affiliated and should be repatriated to the Tribe. The Committee then forwarded all this information to BLM for its consideration....It is therefore ORDERED that the Tribe's Motion for Summary Judgment (#31) is GRANTED.....The matter is remanded to BLM for further proceedings consistent with this ORDER.

Pending review, it now looks increasingly certain that Spirit Cave Man's reburial is, so to speak, just a matter of time.

Admittedly, Spirit Cave Man's remains do not fall within the physical watershed of Lake Tahoe proper—just nearby. Such is not the case, however, with the celebrated set of human remains recovered during the late 1970s on the shores of Pyramid Lake—literally bathed in the waters of Lake Tahoe via the Truckee River as it empties into Pyramid Lake. As the *Mammoth Lake Trumpet* reported later, "An early Holocene skeleton, known as the Wizard's Beach man, was found in 1978 when a prolonged drought had lowered the level of Pyramid Lake northeast of Reno...about 100 miles from Spirit Cave." Once again new radiocarbon dating techniques were applied to the remains; to the astonishment of anthropologists worldwide, they were found to be roughly ninety-two hundred years old—making Wizard's Beach Man a near-contemporary of the Spirit Cave mummy.

But that's where any resemblance between these two men ends. Clearly, Wizard's Beach Man was far taller, stronger, and altogether healthier than the battered and disease-ridden Spirit Cave Man, "having a diet that included more fish and meat than stone-ground seeds," as one scientist concluded. Unlike Spirit Cave Man's mummy, nothing but a partial skeleton of Wizard Beach Man remains—all the rest, including any clothing, or even stomach contents having been washed away over the intervening millennia by the wave action of Pyramid Lake itself. Hence scientists have been forced to infer the contents of Wizard Beach Man's diet almost solely from the intricate patterns of wear and tear on his teeth, finding "the wear was gradual and lost dentin had been replaced, unlike teeth found in all later seed-eating people." In short, Wizard's Beach Man seems to have grown exceptionally tall and strong on a steady diet of fish supplemented by protein drawn from stone-ground seeds.

"He was a big guy," one anthropologist enthused. "Obviously lots of protein in his diet." At five feet, six inches tall, he was described by another anthropologist as having large, dense bones. His cause of death, unlike Spirit Cave Man's, is as yet undertermined by scientists. What they can infer is that he and his people must have harvested a rich array of fish and plant products directly from the waters of Pyramid Lake. Significantly, more than nine thousand years later, when the first white explorers were greeted by the Paiutes of Pyramid Lake, they too remarked on the size and strength of the men and women who dwelled there—and praised the sheer delicious abundance of the enormous trout (so large they called them "salmon trout") which Native people harvested, using woven nets and weirs installed in the Truckee River Canyon just upstream from Pyramid Lake.

What about the landscape itself, you might wonder. What kind of world did Wizard's Beach Man inhabit? "During the late Ice Age, there were camels living near what is now Pyramid Lake in northeastern Nevada," responds Professor Donald K. Grayson, who also served as an expert witness in the Spirit Cave Man case. These days, of course, "The camels, glaciers, lakes, and low-elevation trees are…gone." In their place stands the "typical" Wild West landscape of sagebrush, pinyon pine, and saguaro cacti we see today. But what came in between? The rise of this celebrated Sagebrush Sea, as Grayson concludes bluntly, is "a remarkably recent state of affairs."

How recent? Even the last few centuries—roughly since the arrival of Europeans—seem to have sent whole forests marching up and down the corrugated slopes of the Great Basin ranges—ebbing and flowing like great green tides. In short, the so-called timeless landscape of the "Old" West isn't either timeless or old after all. Instead it's a quite recent product of equally recent shifts in climate patterns, here in Tahoe territory and beyond.

Much like the forests themselves, Grayson reports, human settlements also ebbed and flowed wildly up and down the slopes of the Basin and Range region. In the early 1980s, for example, archaeologists in Nevada surprised the world by discovering clear and irrefutable evidence of permanent human settlements located well above 10,000 feet, some of which had been inhabited in the not-too-distant past. Today the climate at such altitudes is far too harsh to support year-round subsistence settlements. Lower down, dozens of other technically and artistically advanced cultures have flourished and died, chief among them the now-extinct "Fremont" culture— named in honor of the first white explorer ever to set eyes on Lake Tahoe. What, then, if anything, can finally be inferred about the ecological history of Lake Tahoe itself during this same 10,000-year time period since Spirit Cave Man's death? Here again we are in for surprises. Unlike Lake Lahontan, Tahoe never dried up entirely (it is far too deep and too high to do so). Yet recent studies do clearly indicate that during prolonged periods of drought, Tahoe's water levels shrank drastically—sometimes by dozens or perhaps even hundreds of feet—allowing huge forests to spring up along its freshly exposed shores. According to Tahoe limnologist P. R. Caterino, who conducted a series of remarkable underwater surveys of Sierra lakes using SCUBA gear (thereby becoming Cousteau's real-life successor, some might say):

> The surface elevations of the lakes of the Sierra Nevada have stood considerably lower than the present for extended periods of time. The magnitude of drops in the levels of these lakes is supported by existing paleo-environmental evidence; by a series of radiocarbon dates on trees drowned by the rising waters, by submerged archaeological features in the lake, and by historical documentation of lower lake levels....In lakes ranging from Tenaya Lake, Yosemite National Park, in the

southern Sierra Nevada to Lake Tahoe, Donner Lake, and Independence Lake in the northern range, there has been compelling evidence of sustained lower lake levels.

How could mummified trees hundreds of years old possibly have survived for up to six thousand years underwater? Because, as we have seen, bacteria and other microscopic life-forms do not grow easily in the waters of Sierra lakes. At Tahoe, not only do dead bodies fail to rise, but dead trees fail to decay—even when submerged for many thousands of years. In this sense the drowned underwater stumps of the Sierra Nevada are nothing short of a mummified forest.

Like the mummified remains of Spirit Cave Man himself, or the bones of Wizard's Beach Man for that matter, the sheer antiquity of these submerged forests boggles the mind. As Caterino himself concludes, "Through SCUBA surveys, stumps that have been dated range from 4,800 B.P. [before the present] to 6,300 B.P. in Lake Tahoe to 600–700 B.P. in other lakes of the Sierra Nevada. Remarkably, many of these ancient trees have the same coloration and bark cover as they did when they were first drowned." To my ears it all begins to sound like something drawn from a science fiction novel—with SCUBA divers soaring like underwater eagles amid the drowned forests of the distant past; or underwater time travel, Tahoe-style.

Who could have imagined that lake levels in an immense body of water the size and depth of Lake Tahoe could possibly have fluctuated so wildly? This is not mere idle speculation. Based on paleobotanic data gathered from a wide range of sources, the precise durations of the droughts during which those forests grew have long since been pinned down. Approximately one thousand years after Spirit Cave Man's death the climate of the Sierra grew rapidly drier, thereby dealing a final death blow to his ancient Lake Lahontan. Subsequent waves of prolonged droughts came amid bursts of wetter weather, all separated by centuries. So the trees tell us—and even their pollens whisper.

Today, lulled into a false sense of security, we blithely assume that we have faced "the worst nature has to offer" already. But have we? Was this the stern warning which Spirit Cave Man and Wizard's Beach Man trekked across ten thousand years to deliver to us? As Caterino himself wisely acknowledges, "Modern scientific observations…are augmented by a rich and ancient Washoe oral tradition that provides unconventional commentary on landscape changes observed by generations of Washoes. Ancient observations on the rise and fall of lakes in the Tahoe Basin have prompted at least two traditional accounts that center around the area, explained through the antics of the 'Weasel Brothers' and the fearsome activities of 'Waterbabies'"—stories we'll explore in depth in a later chapter.

Clearly these ancient Washoe stories are meant to serve as warnings—but they also serve as poignant reminders of the Paiute and Washoe people's own survival across countless centuries of droughts, floods, plagues, and famines. As for any trace of human presence along the shores of Lake Tahoe itself, we have evidence aplenty. Just five miles from Tahoe's north shore, for example, is a prehistoric cave used for shelter more or less continuously since roughly 8000 B.C. Located just east of the Tahoe town of Truckee, this low overhanging cave juts from the lip of a forested volcanic outcropping high above a sagebrush flat known today as Martis Valley. As David Beesley, professor emeritus of history at Sierra College, concludes in his ecological history of the Sierra, *Crow's Range*, "Many Ancient people from the Tahoe Reach, Martis, and Kings Beach archeological complexes used this area seasonally from about 8000 B.C. to around A.D. 1000. The valley and adjoining areas were used until early historic times by the Washoe people. That means that this valley has been in continuous use for all of the Sierra's human history."

Admittedly, no human skeletal remains, to say nothing of full-fledged mummies, have yet been recovered from the immediate vicinity of Lake Tahoe. Why? For once the explanation is relatively simple: outside the desert rain shadows of Nevada, Tahoe's far wetter climate hastens rapid decay. Even so, an astonishing assemblage of human artifacts has been recovered from the immediate environs of the lake, including everything from spear tips to arrowheads to grinding stones. Among anthropologists and collectors Tahoe has long been noted as one of the richest archaeological sites in all the West.

Taking their cue from Tahoe's topography, archaeologists have labeled this wide assemblage of tools the Martis Complex and the Kings Beach Complex—both names representing tribal groups widely considered to be the ancestors of the modern-day Washoes. Of course we don't know for sure: the people who made these tools may simply have migrated elsewhere, or found themselves pushed out by the Washoes themselves—or driven out by catastrophic climate change.

What we do know a great deal about is their weaponry: both the Martis and the later Kings Beach cultures left behind ample toolkits, including the doomsday weapons of their own Stone Age arsenals, such as atlatls—powerful spear-throwing devices used with great effect for hunting everything from elk to bear. Apparently the bow and arrow didn't arrive in the Tahoe region until some eight hundred years later, just in advance of the Spanish in Alta California. It's enough to make you wonder if our own culture won't be noted, ten thousand years from now, chiefly for our own doomsday devices, nuclear weapons among them.

Then there are those ancient granite-topped "kitchen counters" to consider: as historian Margie Powell writes in her book *Donner Summit: A Brief History,* "Many Martis campsites, including a number on Donner Summit, can be located by finding their grinding rocks. Mortar holes and metate slicks associated with seed and nut grinding are often found on the same rocks as the petroglyphs. The meals made from these nuts and seeds were either baked into a tortilla-like bread or cooked into a gruel." Centuries later, when the first Europeans arrived, the Washoe people were still using these same techniques to grind pine nuts and leach acorns carried over the crest of the Sierra from California each summer. In this regard, it's worth noting that all early Northern European peoples, including my own ancestors, the Celts, used ground acorns as their staple food until the advent of settled agriculture after the Roman invasions.

Based on just such harvesting technologies, twentieth-century anthropologists have tended to label both the Martis Complex Indians and the contemporary Washoe and Paiute people as "hunter-gatherers." Since this label often carries negative connotations in our own culture, Tahoe National Forest archaeologist Hank Meals carefully explains, "'Hunters and gatherers' were very intelligent and highly adaptable people who knew far more about the environment, including the use of plants, and the behavior of animals, than people in the modern world will ever know." In fact, on a calorie-for-calorie basis, many so-called "primitive" hunter-gatherer societies spent less time than we do now physically earning the means to feed and clothe and house their families—with ample time left over for stories, myths, romance, rituals, travel, trade, and, above all, art.

As longtime author, editor, publisher, and Native American rights activist Malcolm Margolin points out, "Native people tended to do everything with a sense of 'art,' even when making baskets for cooking or arrows for hunting. In general, they did not have a separate area of their life that was 'art' and therefore totally different from other areas, just as they did not segment only a part of their life as pertaining to spiritual realms." That certainly seems to include the people who made the petroglyphs and grinding stones here. A local petroglyph expert, Bill Drake, concludes, "When most people think of petroglyphs they think of the Southwest. Not many people realize that Northern California has numerous petroglyph sites, many believed to be several thousand years old." Technically, the style of these Tahoe-area glyphs is called Central Sierran, "featuring designs that are pecked—not painted—into the surface of the granite like a permanent stone tattoo."

Though the location of most of these rock art "galleries" remains a closely guarded secret (to discourage vandalism), one especially notable collection of ancient petroglyphs sits mere inches from Highway 40, just above historic Rainbow Bridge at Donner Pass.

Faded to near invisibility through many hundreds (perhaps thousands) of winters, these Donner Pass petroglyphs display a breathtaking diversity of designs: spirals, snakelike curves, concentric circles, and even stylized representations of deer and elk are all easily recognizable, along with rattlesnakes, huge stylized grizzly bear paw prints, and even the image of a dancing man—or is he a god?—sporting what is almost certainly an enormous erect penis (a common fertility symbol worldwide). Remarkably, some of these symbols can be found spread out across thousands of miles of Great Basin desert. Far from being isolated or obscure, this place was a crossroads, it seems, for many cultures. Still is.

Like most petroglyph sites in the Sierra, the location of this one is truly breathtaking: stand within the semicircular amphitheater of graven images and a dizzying picture-postcard panorama of the entire northern Tahoe Sierra region emerges at your feet. Granted, the blue expanse of Lake Tahoe itself is not quite visible from this vantage; but the sagebrush flats of nearby Martis Valley are. So too are the hazy blue playas of the Eastern Nevada deserts where Wizard's Beach Man and Spirit Cave Man once roamed, almost ten thousand years ago. Look hard enough into the morning sun and you might see them waving.

To be honest, no one has much of a clue what these petroglyph patterns mean, or even how to make sense of the images they present. Do their patterns somehow fit together? Were they intended purely as spiritual totems, invoking the powers of gods, animals, or ancestors? Or do they represent the larger cultural myths and stories which once linked every stream and stone to sky and to the land? Could they even be considered an early form of writing? As LaVan Martineau argues in *The Rocks Begin to Speak: Understanding Indian Rock Writing*, "Indian rock writing is a language—a very precise language—to be read and understood by those who follow." If so, the literature of Lake Tahoe begins right here on these granite pages.

As for what the future may hold, I'd like to return one last time to the tale of Spirit Cave Man's ongoing legal battles—not on scientific grounds this time, but on spiritual grounds (literally). For if those Hollywood fright film writers ever do decide to concoct a film about the Curse of the Tahoe Mummy, they couldn't do much better than to trace the history of Fallon, Nevada, ever since the year 1940, when Spirit Cave Man's mummy was first unearthed—his spirit thereby condemned to wander the earth unhoused and unsatisfied (or so the Paiutes believe to this day). As I imagine it, the film would open with the construction of Fallon Naval Air Station in 1942, in the wake of the attack on Pearl Harbor, bringing with it frantic fears of the Yellow Peril and an Asian invasion of the West Coast. That scene would be followed in my imagination next by the detonation of the world's first atomic bombs just to the south of Fallon in the Nevada Test Range after 1945; and then my film would culminate in 1963 with the underground detonation of a 12-kiloton nuclear device just twelve hundred feet beneath the surface of Spirit Cave Man's cave itself. What that detonation created, in fact, is a new and far more ominous underground cavern more or less directly beneath Spirit Man's cave, filled to the brim with enough radio nucleotides and heavy metal toxins to poison the region for the next ten thousand years, should they escape. Who needs a ten-thousand-year-old mummy's curse when you have nuclear weapons and their ten-thousand-year half-life to contend with?

Hence it should come as no surprise to learn that a deadly cancer cluster was recently detected in Fallon, involving the deaths of more than a dozen children and teenagers and following close on the heels of rumors concerning the secret use of depleted uranium munitions at the famous Top Gun bombing range nearby, not to mention a resurgence of mercury poisoning from nearby gold mines recently reopened. Throw in the increasingly ironclad predictions of deadly droughts triggered by man-made climate change, and I, for one, am fully in favor of consigning the Spirit Cave Man's mummy to the earth again immediately—if not out of respect for his own culture's survival, then in mortal fear for our own.

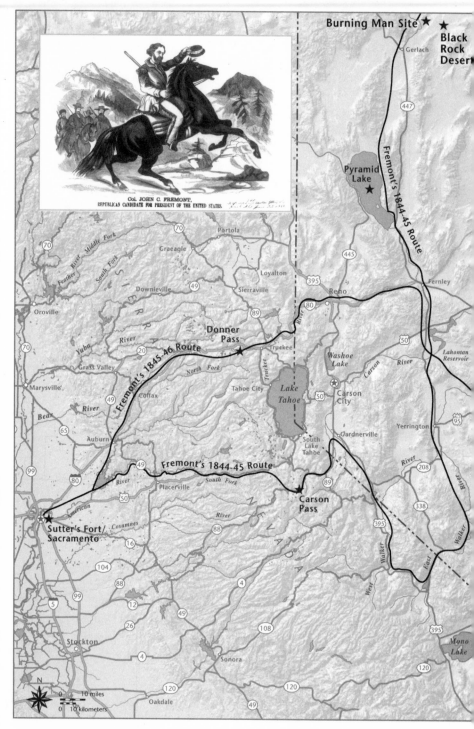

Burning Man Site ★ ★ Black Rock Desert

Gerlach

Fremont's 1844-45 Route

Pyramid Lake ★

Portola

Graeagle

Loyalton

Sierraville

Reno

Fernley

Downieville

Oroville

Donner Pass ★

Truckee

Washoe Lake

Carson River

Lahontan Reservoir

Grass Valley

Fremont's 1845-46 Route

North Fork

Tahoe City

Lake Tahoe

Carson City

Marysville

Colfax

Placerville

South Lake Tahoe

Gardnerville

Yerrington

Bear River

Auburn

Fremont's 1844-45 Route

Carson Pass ★

Sutter's Fort/ Sacramento ★

American River

Cosumnes

River

River

Walker River

East Walker

West Walker

Stockton

Sonora

Mono Lake

Oakdale

N

0   10 miles
0   10 kilometers

Col. JOHN C. FREMONT,
REPUBLICAN CANDIDATE FOR PRESIDENT OF THE UNITED STATES.

John C. Frémont, Republican candidate for president of the United States, Baker & Godwin, 1856. Courtesy of the Library of Congress, Prints & Photographs Division, LC-DIG-pga-03112

three

JOHN FRÉMONT

The Man Who "Discovered" Lake Tahoe

Driving down South Lake Tahoe Boulevard today you'll find, hidden amid a clutter of fast food joints and strip malls, a cartoonish mural depicting the explorer John Charles Frémont, "The Man Who Discovered Lake Tahoe." Squinting up at the painted concrete, how many Tahoe tourists realize that Frémont was also the Republican Party's first-ever candidate for president? Or that he issued an Emancipation Proclamation (in Missouri) long before Lincoln? Or that he was America's first true mountaineer—not to mention our first real whitewater rafter? No, to see all that you'd have to look deep beneath the surface of American history itself—and chip off some of the whitewash on the Lake Tahoe History Museum's mural.

Part hero, part huckster, Frémont could have been remembered in the same breath as Abraham Lincoln and Ulysses S. Grant. Instead his once-stellar reputation as America's "Pathfinder" collapsed amid allegations of corruption, incompetence, and even cannibalism, leaving him little more than a footnote

33

in American history. Yet therein hides the key to many a lost Tahoe legend: for just as Frémont's failures crash-landed his own career, they also drew a sharp political fault line straight across the heart of Lake Tahoe itself—and reshaped the nation in the wake of the Civil War.

Here are the facts: on February 14, 1844 (Valentine's Day), a brash and fiercely handsome American lieutenant named John C. Frémont made the following brief entry in his expedition journal: "Ascended the highest peak to the right," he scribbled, "from which we had a beautiful view of a mountain lake at our feet, about fifteen miles in length, so entirely surrounded by mountains that we could not discover an outlet." With that single sentence the English-language literature of Lake Tahoe begins.

But much of Western American history begins there as well. For the next two decades Frémont remained America's most beloved explorer—easily eclipsing the fame of Lewis and Clark or his own pioneering partner Kit Carson. Then with fearsome suddenness his reputation imploded, leaving the aging hero forgotten, discredited, and bankrupt. His greatest error? Freeing the slaves too early, and then running for president against a soon-to-be martyred Abraham Lincoln.

The scope and complexity of Frémont's career eclipse anything that can be compressed into a short chapter about Lake Tahoe. Long before he first sighted the lake from a summit in the Sierra, for example, Frémont had already earned international fame as America's first true mountaineer—planting the stars and stripes on the 13,000-foot Frémont Peak, in Wyoming, an event hailed around the world. It was on the return leg of that same expedition that he arguably became America's first true whitewater raftsman as well—descending the North Platte River Falls in an India rubber raft of his own design. Today there are dozens of similar peaks, passes, and places scattered across the American West which still bear his name (and hundreds more which were first named by him). It was John Frémont, for example, who first described the entrance to San Francisco Bay as the "Golden Gate."

What first launched the handsome young Frémont's rapid climb to fame, however, was his scandalous marriage to the young, beautiful, and highly gifted daughter of America's most powerful Western politician, Missouri's Thomas Hart Benton. The illegitimate son of a ne'er-do-well Frenchman and a headstrong Southern belle, Frémont clearly lacked the social status to even begin dating debutantes. Yet within mere months of Frémont's meeting Benton's sixteen-year-old daughter, Jessie, the two lovers had already eloped. Reconciled to his "bastard" son-in-law's ambitions, Senator Benton eventually used his considerable political clout to land his protégé a place on U.S. military expeditions. It was during the course of one such expedition in 1844, in fact, that young Lieutenant Frémont accidentally "discovered" Lake Tahoe.

Of course Native Americans had known of the lake's existence for at least ten thousand years. Indeed without their help and guidance Frémont and his men would never have survived to tell their tale. Weeks earlier, flagrantly disregarding direct orders from his own immediate superiors in the Army, Frémont had mysteriously turned southward from the Oregon Territories across the forbidding black rock deserts of Northern Nevada—exactly where the annual Burning Man festival is held today. Finding nothing to hunt on that high desert playa, Frémont and his men finally stumbled, exhausted and hungry, onto the shores of Pyramid Lake: none other than the ancestral home of Wizard's Beach Man!—and then the home of the Pyramid Lake Paiutes, at the time under the leadership of a clan chief Frémont quickly dubbed "Captain Truckee."

All of this was flagrantly illegal under international law. Frémont's excuse for entering Mexico's Alta California, he claimed, was that he was searching for the legendary Bonaventura River—a mythical waterway long rumored to link the central regions of the American West to the Pacific Ocean (much as the Columbia River does further north). In fact upon sighting the hitherto "undiscovered" Pyramid Lake from afar, Frémont briefly assumed that he had indeed found the source of the mythical Bonaventura. Quickly disabused of this notion—Pyramid Lake has no outlet!—the young explorer nevertheless waxed poetic in his journals over the desert lake's famous towering tufa-stone formations, the tallest of which he blithely compared to the Egyptian pyramids: "[The pyramid] rose," he wrote, "according to our estimate, 600 feet above the water; and from the point we viewed it, presented a pretty exact outline of the great pyramid of Cheops." With all his usual flair for the melodramatic, Frémont then painted the eponymous "Pyramid Lake" in florid nineteenth-century Romantic prose: "It broke upon our eyes," he said of Pyramid Lake, "like the ocean. The neighboring peaks rose high above us, and we ascended one of them to obtain a better view. The waves were curling in the breeze, and their dark-green color showed it to be a body of deep water. For a long time we sat there enjoying the view, for we had become very grateful. It was set like a gem in the mountains, which, from our position, seemed to enclose it almost entirely."

In short, having failed to discover the mythical Bonaventura River, Frémont simply invented a whole new mythic landscape to take its place. Or to be more precise, he and his wife, Jessie, reinvented this new landscape—the "West of the Imagination" as it has since been described. Here's how: immediately upon his return from each expedition, Frémont would hand over his raw notes to his faithful (and highly talented) wife, who would rapidly edit the manuscript for release to an adoring worldwide audience. Hence if John Charles Frémont is justly remembered as the first white man to discover Lake Tahoe, Jessie Benton Frémont was the first to describe it. As historian Rebecca Solnit reminds us in her book *River of Shadows*:

> The West had been imagined and publicized by Jessie Benton Frémont more than anyone else. Daughter of the great expansionist senator from Missouri, Thomas Hart Benton, she had caused one scandal by cutting off her hair to pass as a boy and another by showing up for a family wedding in a man's military uniform. Realizing that manhood wasn't available for her, she eloped at age seventeen with the adventurer John

Charles Frémont of the U.S. Topographical Corps. Thanks to his father-in-law's political influence, he went off and had the trailblazing western adventures she yearned for, and she rewrote his journals into reports whose literary merits captured the national imagination and made him a hero. The pivotal first-person tales of a man encountering the West were ghostwritten by a young bride in the East.

Meanwhile Senator Benton provided the young couple with his own rhetorically charged version of Manifest Destiny—with Jessie Benton serving as Frémont's full-time muse, political consultant, and media handler.

But now back to the unvarnished facts: as Frémont (or rather Jessie) reports, the thriving Indian village he had encountered at Pyramid Lake seemed surprisingly friendly. They called them-selves *Kuyuidokado*, or "Fish Eaters"—and soon laid out a splendid feast of enormous Pyramid Lake trout (the world's largest) to greet the famished explorers. These were, Frémont claimed, literally the finest-tasting fish on earth, whether served baked, grilled, or stewed. Tragically today, after more than a century of overfishing and water thievery, the Pyramid Lake trout are teetering on the brink of extinction.

Fed and rested, Frémont hoped to persuade the Paiutes to guide his expedition across the mountains into Mexican California. To his chagrin, the young Paiutes "only looked at each other and laughed" when confronted with the absurd idea of crossing the Sierra Nevada in midwinter. So in frustration Frémont and his men pressed even further south along the base of the Sierra toward what would later be known, in honor of Frémont's sidekick, as the Carson River. There they met another tribe of Native Americans, who called themselves "Washoe"—and whose ancestral territory included the place we now call Lake Tahoe.

Wading hip-deep through the snowdrifts, Frémont and his men were astonished to see the Washoes "skimming along like birds" on snowshoes. According to Frémont's report, one of his men went ahead of the main party, "sat down to tie his moccasins, when he heard a low whistle near, and, looking up, saw two Indians half hiding behind a rock about forty yards distant; they would not allow him to approach, but, breaking into a laugh, skimmed off over the snow, seeming to have no idea of the power of fire arms, and thinking themselves perfectly safe when beyond arm's length." Far from being hostile, much like the Paiutes, these Washoe men were both friendly and curious.

Approaching the white explorers on their graceful snowshoes, the Washoes offered handfuls of pine nuts (their staple food) as a gift of friendship. Frémont, in return, gave them a few trinkets from his stores. As Frémont (or rather Jessie Frémont) described it:

> We explained to the Indians that we were endeavoring to find a passage across the mountains into the country of the whites, whom we were going to see; and told them that we wished them to bring us a guide, to whom we would give presents of scarlet cloth, and other articles, which were shown to them. They looked at the reward we offered, and conferred with each other, but pointed to the snow on the mountain, and drew their hands across their necks, and raised them above their heads, to show the depth; and signified that it was impossible for us to get through.

Just like Chief Truckee's Pyramid Lake Paiutes, the Washoes considered any effort to cross the Sierra in winter literally suicidal.

Again and again Frémont blindly insisted on ignoring the Washoes' earnest warnings. Within a week, with the help of a reluctant Washoe guide, Frémont and his men had climbed twenty miles further toward the crest of the Sierra. Here they encountered "timber of extraordinary size"—in addition to yet more snow. At a camp in Faith Valley more Washoes appeared, desperately attempting to warn them back. All they would find if they continued, the Washoes cautioned, was "rock upon rock—rock upon rock—snow upon snow—snow upon snow…even if you get over the snow you will not be able to get down from the mountains." As Frémont described it:

> He made us a sign of precipices, and showed us how the feet of the horses would slip, and throw them off from the narrow trails which led along their sides. Our Chinook, who comprehended even more readily than ourselves, and believed our situation hopeless, covered his head with his blanket, and began to weep and lament. "I wanted to see the whites," said he; "I came away from my own people to see the whites, and I wouldn't care to die among them; but here"—and he looked around into the cold night and gloomy forest, and drawing his blanket over his head, began to lament again.

So from here on out, the forlorn little expedition was on its own, with Frémont and his men (including several Native Americans from tribes east of the Mississippi and one free Negro) left to flounder on desperately through the snow toward Alta California. Or die trying.

Looking back, this decision to press on against all odds literally became the defining moment in Frémont's career—capped by the discovery of Lake Tahoe from the highest crest of the great Sierra Nevada. Mile by mile they stamped out a thin trail through towering snowbanks to make way for their pack animals, who (having no snow shoes to support them) sank up to their bellies in the drifts. To prevent snow blindness the men tied black silk handkerchiefs over their eyes. It literally became a death march. One by one they slaughtered their mules for food. On the night of February 12 they ate the last of their dogs. It was, Frémont noted, "an extraordinary dinner—pea soup, mule, and dog."

Then came the moment of truth—at least for the history of Lake Tahoe. Two days later, on February 14, the expedition's German mapmaker, Preuss, and Lieutenant Frémont climbed together to a nearby summit (probably Red Cloud Peak) to gain a better sense of the route ahead. From the summit they glimpsed the outline of an enormous mountain lake in the distance—the same lake Chief Truckee had clearly described to them as the source of his Pyramid Lake.

Alas, both Preuss and Frémont failed to make the obvious connection—assuming instead that the lake flowed into the Pacific Ocean. Quickly noting the new lake's position, Frémont instead praised the "beautiful view" in his journals and returned to his camp. So much for the glorious "discovery" of Lake Tahoe— which appears as little more than a footnote in Frémont's *Report of the Exploring Expedition to the Rocky Mountains in the Year 1842 and to Oregon and Northern California in the Years 1843-'44*.

Yet for all the brevity of his comments, no one has ever left a more indelible mark on the present-day landscape of Lake Tahoe than John Frémont did that day. To understand why, let's fast-forward all the way to the 1849 California constitutional convention, a mere five years later. The convention was being hosted near Frémont's new Monterey mansion. Taking place in the wake of the Bear Flag Rebellion and the Mexican-American War, the whole lavish affair was being paid for by California's fabulous Gold Rush windfall. The former Lieutenant Frémont had already served as California's first appointed, not elected, governor. Subsequently he became the acknowledged leader of the abolitionist forces struggling to keep California from entering the Union as a slave state.

Integral to this bitter battle over the future of slavery in California was the burning question of where precisely the borders of the new Golden State should be drawn. Ominously, the pro-slavery, pro-South forces had hoped to split the southern half of California into a separate slave state (to be known as Colorado); failing that, they pushed hard for an extension of the eastern borders of the new, unitary state all the way east to the edge of the Rocky Mountains (figuring that such an enormous "super-state" would soon break up into smaller slave states). Either way, California's entry into the Union would have tipped the balance of power in the United States Senate decisively in favor of the

South. To their eternal credit, Frémont and his allies were dead set against it.

After weeks of bitter political maneuvers it seemed certain that the powerful proslavery forces would win. Then miraculously, in a last-ditch desperate midnight maneuver, Frémont and his band of antislavery allies somehow found the votes to redraw the boundaries of California along the eastern edge of the Sierra Nevada—exactly where they lie today. Given the desperate backroom battles being fought at that convention, no one can know for certain exactly how and why California's eastern boundary was finally determined—but here's my theory: pulling out Frémont's own map of California, published to great fanfare in 1848, he and his fellow constitutional conventioneers boldly marked out the new free state's boundaries straight down the eastern slope of the Sierra—fully intending to include the rich natural resources of Lake Tahoe within the borders of their new Golden State.

Alas, what Frémont and his antislavery allies did not realize—what they could not possibly have realized yet—is that an innocent measurement error in Frémont's California map had placed Lake Tahoe further to the west than it actually was. Worse yet, Frémont's map erroneously showed a river flowing directly from Lake Tahoe to the Pacific Ocean by way of San Francisco Bay. Shades of the mythic Bonaventura! More than a decade later, government surveys confirmed what should have been obvious all along: as set forth by the California constitution, only two-thirds of Lake Tahoe actually fell within the boundaries of the new Golden State. And not one drop of Tahoe's precious water flowed west to the Pacific through California.

It was a stupendous error: for had Frémont's measurements been correct, California might long ago have dammed or drained Lake Tahoe to slake its farms' and cities' bottomless thirst. Instead, time and again these entirely accidental, schizophrenic, absurdly fractured political boundaries have stood between Lake Tahoe and mass water diversions in either direction.

As far as I know, I am the first historian ever to offer such an explanation. But if so, I am certainly far from the first to note Frémont's little mapping error. As the eminent UC Berkeley professor John LeConte lamented as early as 1883, in an article entitled "Physical Studies of Lake Tahoe," "On Frémont's map the lake is laid down tolerably correctly as to latitude, *but it is misplaced about one-fourth of a degree in longitude;* thus throwing it on the western slope of the Sierra Nevada, and making the head branches of the American River its outlets." [emphasis added]

That, in a nutshell, is why Lake Tahoe still finds itself controlled by two competing states, Nevada and California—a two-headed political hydra which shapes every aspect of the region's political economy. Later, in 1864, when the boundaries of the new Silver State of Nevada were fixed and settled along the same lines, the untold riches of the great Nevada Silver Bonanza lay just beyond California's control as well. In other words, had the boundaries of California been fixed just a few miles farther east, the richest silver mines in all of human history might have fallen within the borders of the new state of California too—not to mention all the watery resources of America's largest mountain lake.

The flood of ironies doesn't end there either. For the Native American tribes of the Lake Tahoe region, the cost of Frémont's blunders would be paid in blood, not silver. For despite his lifelong political support for the abolition of Negro slavery, Frémont himself controlled hundreds of de facto Indian slaves in California. Incomprehensible as it seems to us now, the first man ever to run for president of the United States on an abolitionist platform nevertheless relied on Indian slave labor to run his Mariposa Ranch. Indeed, the first act of the newly formed California State Legislature after ratification of the new constitution had been the passage of the so-called "Indian Protection Act," effectively legalizing Indian slavery in California under much the same lines first laid down by its previous Spanish and Mexican colonial rulers.

The story of Frémont's direct participation in this vast system of Indian slavery seems especially poignant given the central role that his legendary crossing of the Sierra in 1844 played in abolitionist rhetoric. During the 1856 election the newly formed Republican Party's campaign slogan was "Free Speech, Free Press, Free Soil, Free Men, Frémont, and Victory!" To which Frémont's proslavery opponents shot back with angry cries of "Freesoilers, Frémonters, Free Niggers, and Freebooters." One of America's most popular nineteenth-century poets, the fiery abolitionist John Greenleaf Whittier, even penned a campaign poem immortalizing Frémont's conquest of the Tahoe Sierra. In Whittier's windy rhetoric, what Frémont *really* discovered up there at "A Pass in the Sierra" was not just a mountain lake or even a path to California but literally a whole new path to human freedom: a way for all Americans "To break from Slavery's desert land / A path to freedom's plain." Indeed, Whittier framed Frémont's illegal backdoor entry into California (by way of Lake Tahoe) as perhaps the greatest turning point in all human history. From there forward, plastered across the front of many a Frémont campaign poster, you'll find engraved images of his legendary Sierra crossing. "Rise up, Frémont," Whittier sings, "The hour must have its Man!"

> They set their faces to the blast,
> They trod the eternal snow,
> And faint, worn, bleeding, hailed at last
> The promised land below.

If all this campaign rhetoric seems a bit overblown by modern standards, recall that prominent African American abolitionist leaders, including the great black orator and author Frederick Douglass, rallied passionately to Frémont's side—and remained his steadfast supporters even when Frémont ran *against* Abraham Lincoln four years later, in 1864.

Alas, the shadow of brutal Indian massacres also stains Frémont's legacy in California. During the Bear Flag Rebellion, as his political opponents noted, Frémont and his compatriot Kit Carson bragged openly of their brutal destruction of whole

Native American villages. In Frémont's own words, "I resolved to anticipate the Indians and strike them a blow." It was pure bloodlust. Without warning or provocation Frémont and his men rode roughshod through a series of Maidu villages near the Sacramento River, slaughtering men, women, and children by the dozens. Even one of Frémont's most admiring modern biographers, Ferol Egan, minces no words in his *Fremont: Explorer for a Restless Nation* in describing the horror:

> Barbaric and cruel beyond belief, this was a bloodbath
> without any semblance of sanity, and both whites and the
> Delawares [Frémont's eastern Indian guides] joined in the
> killing with a strange and sick excitement. They had been
> ordered to prevent the slaughter of Americans by these
> Indians [though no Americans had been threatened]. Well,
> by all that was demonic, they had taught these Indians, these
> peaceful people, a lesson they'd never forget....to Frémont
> and all the rest, the California Indians were not the same as
> the Plains Indians. They were a lesser people, a people they
> called "Diggers," and a people they could not trust. But these
> Indians knew fear, and by God, they had given them their
> share of it.

Add to the stench of blood the stink of corruption. Scant years later, with dispossessed Native Americans already working as slaves on his Mariposa Ranch, Frémont entered into lucrative government contracts to supply beef to Indians forced onto one of America's first-ever Indian reservations, near present-day Fresno. Mysteriously, most of that meat was never delivered. Instead Frémont and his partners lined their pockets and let the Indians starve—thereby initiating a tradition of graft and embezzlement that has plagued America's Indian reservations right down to the present day. Meanwhile the dozens of Indian treaties Frémont had helped initiate—including one named the Frémont Treaty—were annulled and ignored by the U.S. Congress, which never even bothered to vote on them at all.

Appalling as such revelations may be, it cannot be denied that Frémont embodies, in one bizarre lifetime, all the contradictions and conflicts of the pioneer era. Once among the most famous of all living Americans, he is now arguably among the most fiercely forgotten. Even those places named in his honor seem to have lost track of his legacy. Working as a college professor south of San Francisco, I have many students who hail from nearby Fremont, California—but few know much if anything about the man for whom their city was christened. My own pioneer family traces its roots back to Fremont County, Colorado—not far from where Frémont nearly lost his life searching for a railroad route through the Rockies—but I knew nothing of his legacy when I was growing up there. One hundred miles further north, I nearly lost my own life while skiing solo near Colorado's Fremont Pass (not to be confused with California's Fremont Pass, which I often cross between Tahoe and L.A.). As a teenager, I spent many happy weeks in Wyoming's Wind River Range south of Yellowstone, climbing everything in sight—including Fremont Peak. Years later I worked briefly on Fremont Street in downtown San Francisco; I even took a "Fremont-bound" BART train beneath the bay to get there. But never until recently did I begin to fathom the deep connections between these places and The Man Who Discovered Lake Tahoe.

Finally, there's the famous Fremont Street in Las Vegas to (re) consider, where the glittering façade of Fremont Casino stands draped in a perpetual neon glow. As one Nevada guidebook breathlessly explains, "Fremont Street, home to some of the city's oldest casinos…has been pedestrianized and covered with a ceiling of millions of light bulbs. Every half an hour, all of the casinos turn off their neon advertising, and the ceiling comes alive with a stunning sound and light show." With twelve million LEDs and a 550,000-watt sound system, and "the world's largest gold nugget" on glittering display, Frémont would have loved it. In its own gaudy way, Frémont's monument outshines Lincoln's.

Ironically, there is nothing at Lake Tahoe named in Frémont's honor—just that cartoonish mural splashed across the cinderblock wall of the little Lake Tahoe History Museum. Instead you'll just have to catch a glimpse of Frémont's ghost etched across the map of Lake Tahoe itself, where the jagged Stateline border becomes the greatest of all monuments to Frémont's Folly. As biographer Ferol Egan concedes bitterly, "The ultimate curse of being a national hero is that once the fires of acclaim go out, only the ashes of criticism remain." Or the outlines of an error.

Given the magnitude of Frémont's failures, perhaps it is better left so. For all his early successes, time and again Frémont ended up a loser—first losing the presidency to Buchanan and then later to Lincoln, who fired him as a military commander after Frémont's premature emancipation order freeing the Missouri slaves. As a business tycoon he was an even greater failure: first losing his fabulous California Gold Rush empire to crooks and claim jumpers; and then losing his Golden Gate mansion to the U.S. Army (which seized it to build Fort Mason during the Civil War); and later losing what little remained of his Gold Rush fortune in a last, failed bid to build an alternative transcontinental railroad in 1873. Yet for all his many follies, Frémont's influence over the Western landscape remains unmatched. Even late in life, his health broken and his fame forgotten, he was named governor of Arizona Territory (where, true to form, he initiated some of the first great water diversion schemes in the American West)—only to resign, as usual, amid scandal and disgrace.

So even if Frémont's fame has not endured, his mistakes sure have. As David Thompson rightly concludes in *In Nevada*, "It is the pattern of a gambler, not so much professional as innate." His greatest jackpot? Crossing the Tahoe Sierra in the dead of winter in 1844. And if his luck later turned sour—his wealth stolen, his schemes shipwrecked, his reputation shattered—so what? Win, lose, or draw, his unending series of wildcat wagers permanently altered the nature of America as we know it now—including the map of Lake Tahoe. Come to think of it, there are indeed four magnificent monuments dedicated to Frémont's memory right here by the shores of Lake Tahoe today: those glittering, glass-encased high-rise South Shore Stateline casinos, gaudy temples of a trickster god.

Studio portrait of Sarah Winnemucca Hopkins in beaded dress and moccasins, 1883, photographed by Elmer Chickering of Boston, Massachussetts, to publicize her lectures in that city. *Courtesy of Wikipedia*

four

SARAH WINNEMUCCA

The Burning Woman

How did the Pyramid Lake Paiutes react to the unexpected arrival of John Frémont and his men in their ancestral homeland in that fateful winter of 1843–44, some nine thousand years after Wizard Beach Man's demise? Ordinarily to answer such a question we would have to rely entirely on the written reports of the white pioneers themselves—supplemented, perhaps, by Native American oral histories handed down for generations, and then translated (often inaccurately) into English by non-Indian authors. But for once we have a far better source: the first full-length book written in English by a Native American author, penned by a Pyramid Lake Paiute woman named Thocmetone, better known to the English-speaking world as Sarah Winnemucca.

"I was a very small child," she begins, "when the first white people came into our country. They came like a lion, yes, like a roaring lion, and have continued so ever since, and I have never forgotten their first coming." Set against the bitter background of her tribe's struggle for survival, the 1883 publication of Sarah Winnemucca's

Life Among the Piutes: Their Wrongs and Claims remains a landmark event in the history of Native American literature by any measure. First presented as a series of stirring lectures for the benefit of standing-room-only audiences from San Francisco to Boston, Winnemucca's book retains all of the rhetorical flash and flourish of her platform performances.

Seeking to challenge the deeply ingrained cultural prejudices of her all-white audience, Winnemucca's book places special emphasis on the story of the lifelong friendship of her maternal grandfather, Chief Truckee, with his "white brothers"—especially John C. Frémont himself. Recalling the exact moment of Frémont's arrival at Pyramid Lake in 1843, she reports:

> My people were scattered at that time over nearly all the territory now known as Nevada. My grandfather was chief of the entire Piute nation, and was camped near Humboldt Lake, with a small portion of his tribe, when a party traveling eastward from California was seen coming. When told that they had hair on their faces, and were white, he jumped up and clasped his hands together, and cried aloud,—"My white brothers,—my long-looked for white brothers have come at last!"

Although the old chief's offers of friendship were finally betrayed, according to his granddaughter Sarah Winnemucca old Truckee never once wavered in his lifelong resolve to treat these white explorers and settlers as "lost brothers"—even in the face of mounting evidence of pioneer atrocities, including the cannibalism practiced two winters hence by the notorious Donner Party.

Winnemucca exaggerates her grandfather's status as "chief of the entire Piute nation" to please a white audience ("chiefhood" and "nationhood" being largely white inventions commonly superimposed on Native cultures, which existed primarily in smaller, far more independent familial clusters and clans). Yet by painting her grandfather's exploits as a "Chief," in terms more familiar to her white listeners, Winnemucca also enables them to see pioneer history through Native American eyes—perhaps even to laugh at themselves: to the Pyramid Lake Paiutes, she reports wryly, Frémont and other early white explorers looked "more like owls than anything else. They had hair on their faces, and had white eyes..."

Predictably, the free Negroes who accompanied Frémont and other pioneers struck the Paiutes as being even stranger than the whites: "That following spring," Winnemucca states dryly, "there came great news down the Humboldt River, saying that there were some more of the white brothers coming, and there was something among them that was burning all in a blaze. My grandfather asked what it was like. They told him it looked like a man; it had legs and hands and a head, but the head had quit burning, and it was left quite black...It was two negroes wearing red shirts!" Within a few years, free Negroes (as well as black slaves) within the Lake Tahoe region would become a fairly common sight. At one point, Chief Truckee even deserted a white wagon train he was guiding, disgusted by the brutal whipping of a black man by a white muleteer. Yet black frontiersmen were not always relegated to the ranks of servants. Indeed it was the great African American mountain man Jim Beckwourth—a comrade of Kit Carson—who first opened an alternative trans-Sierra wagon train route just fifty miles north of Lake Tahoe. It is still known today as Beckwourth Pass, and the little California town of Beckwourth sits nestled at its base.

These days the town of Beckwourth is famous for another set of reasons entirely: located en route to Nevada's nearby Black Rock Desert playas, where the annual Burning Man festival is staged, it sees in excess of fifty thousand mostly young, mostly white party-hound pilgrims pass through the region each summer. All of which makes me stop and wonder: do any of those self-styled postmodern primitives realize that Nevada's original "Burning Men" were the black cowboys, explorers, and settlers who first came to Nevada more than a century and a half ago? Or that the ten thousand-plus Burning Man participants are camped on what was once Paiute land?

Like most suburban white kids in the 1960s, I grew up playing endless variations of cowboys and Indians in the backyard of my family's middle-class ranch-style home. This was in Denver—a far cry from the true cowboys and Indians of Colorado's past. In these games, in which I would brandish my toy six-shooter or carry my brother's plastic bow and a quiver full of arrows tipped with suction cups, the Indians always "started it." And the cowboys always won. This particular leap of childhood imagination was not by any means an accident. Like children in any culture, we were simply reenacting the myths of our tribe. Decades of Hollywood films and TV Westerns—many of them shot on location at Lake Tahoe—had passed on countless images of hostile Indians and white-hatted cowboy heroes that were now implanted deep within our boyish brains, fixing them tighter than a suction-cup arrow stuck to the center of a plastic bull's eye.

Today it's easier for me to see how such a childish plot flies in the face of historical fact: more often than not, violence on the frontier was in fact "started by" the pioneers. To counteract these all-pervasive anti-Indian stereotypes, already so firmly fixed in the public's imagination by the 1880s, Winnemucca relentlessly stressed the stubbornly peaceful, generous, openhanded attitude with which her grandfather Chief Truckee greeted white settlers and explorers. Writing explicitly to build political support back in Washington, D.C., for her cause, she strategically omitted incidents which might reflect poorly on the Paiute nation. At times this renders her account one-sided. Yet *Life Among the Piutes* remains a landmark event in American literature—because from Plymouth Rock to Pyramid Lake, many Native American tribes did, in fact, initially greet the earliest explorers ever to enter their ancestral homelands with the same openhanded hospitality which her grandfather Chief Truckee so courageously displayed.

This makes Chief Truckee and his granddaughter Sarah Winnemucca controversial figures in some circles. Whereas some view Winnemucca's grandfather as a hero, others abhor him as a sham, a sellout, and a sucker: a kind of Indian Uncle Tom.

Similarly, whereas some American Indians still praise Sarah Winnemucca for "selfless motives and tremendous energies and high purpose," others insist that her true motives were solely "self-aggrandizement by exalting her father." In the words of Professor Catherine Fowler at the University of Nevada at Reno, "Some recognize her genuine achievements as the founder of an independent school and her continuing influence on those attempting to preserve an Indian voice and to secure better conditions on local reservations. Others see her as a tool of the military, for whom she worked at various periods in her life, and even worse, as a traitor who caused members of her own tribe to be killed and captured in various campaigns." Yet as David Brumble retorts, nowhere in her narrative was there ever once "a moment when she decided that, really, she preferred the white to the Paiute way." In other words, as Brumble argues, "In reading her book we may see implicit in some of her experiences features of a cultural identity crisis, but she seems herself not to have thought about her life in this way." Instead, as Andrew S. McClure contends, the question of her so-called assimilation becomes richly complex, even compelling, "because she often made direct appeals to the romanticized, invented constructions of Indian identity, even as she dismantled these constructions in her work." In plain English, she wasn't a sellout; she was a saleswoman—and a revolutionary warrior in defense of the rights of her tribe.

Predictably, the reactions of Nevada's political leaders toward Winnemucca's legacy have often been similarly conflicted. Until recently no monument or statue cast in Winnemucca's memory could be found anywhere in the entire state. Only within the last decade has she been widely recognized—and duly honored—as among Nevada's earliest, most accomplished, and most courageous authors.

But before cataloging her literary legacy, let's first return to the pivotal events of 1843 and Frémont's arrival at Pyramid Lake. To help explain her grandfather's lifelong stance of friendship toward these strange, pale, owl-eyed outsiders—not to mention those "burning men" who were traveling with them—Winnemucca recounts a miraculous creation story. So miraculous, in fact, that it might easily serve as a postmodern creation myth for the twenty-first century.

Winnemucca's published version of this Paiute myth was custom-tailored to appeal to a white audience. How could it not be? For modern readers, this raises some disturbing questions: was Winnemucca's printed, English-language version of this Paiute myth influenced (consciously or unconsciously) by Christian narratives, such as the story of Cain and Abel? Were other alterations—perhaps even additions—made to the story in order to fit prevailing Victorian notions of proper literary "style"? We know, for example, that Winnemucca's editor, Mary Mann (wife of education reformer Horace Mann), "corrected" Sarah's Indian English to suit prevailing upper-class standards of grammar, punctuation, and spelling. Beyond this, however, Mann vigorously denied that she made any changes, additions, or alterations to Sarah Winnemucca's original manuscript whatsoever.

Regardless, Winnemucca's version of the story remains a classic in every sense of the word—and offers a radically different perspective on John Frémont's arrival within Tahoe territory. "In the beginning of the world," declares Chief Truckee, according to his granddaughter, "there was a happy family in this world":

One girl and one boy were dark and the others were white.

For a time they got along together without quarrelling, but soon they disagreed, and there was trouble. They were cross to one another and fought, and our parents were very much grieved.

They prayed that their children might learn better, but it did not do any good; and afterwards the whole household was made so unhappy that the father and mother saw that they must separate their children; and then our father took the dark boy and girl, and the white boy and girl, and asked them, "Why are you so cruel to each other?"

They hung down their heads, and would not speak. They were ashamed.

He said to them, "Have I not been kind to you all, and given you everything your hearts wished for? You do not have to hunt and kill your own game to live upon. You see, my dear children, I have power to call whatsoever kind of game we want to eat; and I also have the power to separate my dear children, if they are not good to each other."

So he separated his children by a word. He said, "Depart from each other, you cruel children;—go across the mighty ocean and do not seek each other's lives."

So the light girl and boy disappeared by that word, and their parents saw them no more, and they were grieved, although they knew their children were happy.

And by-and-by the dark children grew into a large nation; and we believe it is the one we belong to, and that the nation that sprung from the white children will some time send someone to meet us and heal all the old trouble.

Now, the white people we saw a few days ago must certainly be our white brothers, and I want to welcome them. I want to love them as I love all of you.

But they would not let me; they were afraid.

But they will come again, and I want you one and all to promise that, should I not live to welcome them myself, you will not hurt a hair on their heads, but welcome them as I do.

Here's how Sarah Winnemucca herself viewed the increasingly frequent arrival of pioneer wagon trains from a Paiute perspective: "It was at this time that our white brothers first came amongst us," she reports of one wagon train's arrival. "They could not get over the mountains, so they had to live with us. It was on the Carson River, where the great Carson City stands now." For the benefit of a skeptical white audience, she makes certain that the central point of this little vignette remains crystal clear: "You call my people bloodseeking. My people did not seek to kill them, nor did they steal their horses—no, far from it. During the winter my people helped them. They gave them as much as they had to eat. They did not hold out their hands and say:—'You can't have anything to eat unless you pay me.' No,—no such word was used by us savages at that time."

Here, as always, Winnemucca's use of the word "savages" is a double-edged sword.

Meanwhile, relations between pioneers and Paiutes continued to deteriorate—aided, ironically, by Chief Truckee's protracted absence from Tahoe territory in support of the U.S. conquest of California. Personally recruited by Frémont to act as his scout during his third expedition, Chief Truckee and his men served Frémont loyally throughout the entire Bear Flag Rebellion and the subsequent Mexican-American War—actively helping to bring California under U.S. control.

Left undefended by their strongest warriors, the Pyramid Lake Paiute became easy prey. As Sarah Winnemucca herself explains: "The following spring, before my grandfather returned home, there was a great excitement among my people on account of fearful news coming from different tribes, that the people whom they called their white brothers were killing everybody that came in their way, and all the Indian tribes had gone into the mountains to save their lives....Our mothers told us that the whites were killing everybody and eating them."

For non-Indian readers, it is often difficult to comprehend the sheer depth of terror which such rumors provoked—close, in some senses, to the panic which Orson Welles's notorious *War of the Worlds* broadcasts triggered nationwide in the 1930s. From a Paiute perspective, these pioneers were utterly alien invaders, from another world entirely. At one point Winnemucca's mother became so alarmed by the approach of white intruders that she literally buried her children alive to hide them. "Let us bury our girls, or we shall all be killed and eaten up," her mother cried in desperation. "So they went to work and buried us," Winnemucca continues, "and told us if we heard any noise not to cry out, for if we did they would surely kill us and eat us. So our mothers buried me and my cousin, planted sage bushes over our faces to keep the sun from burning them, and there we were left all day."

Buried alive: could she have found a more poignant description of the future fate of her own Paiute people? "Can anyone imagine my feelings *buried alive*," she wonders aloud, "thinking every minute that I was to be unburied and eaten up by the people that my grandfather loved so much?" As usual, Winnemucca ends her story with a rhetorical flourish: one calculated to appeal to the prejudices, religious or otherwise, of her white audience. "I was once buried alive; but my second burial shall be forever, where no father or mother will come and dig me up. It shall not be with throbbing heart that I shall listen for coming footsteps. I shall be in the sweet rest of peace—I, the chieftain's weary daughter."

Though Winnemucca's prose in such passages strikes many modern readers as melodramatic—much like Frémont's florid reports or John Greenleaf Whittier's poetry—we should remember that Native Americans were just as shocked by news of the Donner Party's descent into cannibalism as white audiences were back East. "Surely they don't eat people?" a young Sarah Winnemucca asks her mother, buried to her neck in the sand. "Yes, they do eat people, because they ate each other up in the mountains last winter," her mother replies emphatically. Once a savage, always a savage, her mother seems to imply.

In addition to these terrifying events, Winnemucca reports on the numerous dark prophesies of disaster preached by the Paiute shaman and other tribal leaders—including one especially grim prophecy dreamed by Chief Truckee himself. Weeping in despair, he once warned his tribe, "I dreamt this same thing three nights,—the very same. I saw the greatest emigration that has yet been through our country. I looked North and South and East and West, and saw nothing but dust, and I heard a great weeping. I saw women crying, and I also saw my men shot down by the white people. They were killing my people with something that made a great noise like thunder and lightning, and I saw the blood streaming from the mouths of my men that lay all around me. I saw it as if it was real." All too soon, it was.

The old Paiute shaman's prophecy, as reported by Winnemucca, was even more accurate: "Our people will not all die at the hands of our white brothers," he counseled. "They will kill a great many with their guns, but they will bring among us a fearful disease that will cause us to die by hundreds." Tragically, this was precisely the Paiutes' fate. Across the West, tens of thousands more Native Americans would die from European epidemic diseases than ever died at the hands of the U.S. Cavalry. Sarah Winnemucca herself died young of tuberculosis—a European disease utterly unknown to her tribe when she was born.

Fleeing before the onset of such evil omens, Chief Winnemucca tried moving his band of followers high into the Tahoe Sierra in search of sanctuary. "Let us keep away from the emigrant roads and stay in the mountains all summer. There are to be a great many pine-nuts this summer and we can lay up great supplies for the coming winter, and if the emigrants don't come too early, we can take a run down and fish for a month, and lay up dried fish. I know we can dry a great many in a month, and young men can go into the valleys on hunting excursions, and kill as many rabbits as they can. In that way we can live in the mountains all summer and all winter too."

Up and down the length of the Sierra, a desperate Indian exodus was taking place. In Tahoe, in Yosemite Valley, and in dozens of other high mountain vales and canyons, formerly secure mountain populations such as the Washoes, the Paiutes, and the Ahwahn-eechees found themselves locked in increasing conflict with Native populations fleeing pioneer intrusions elsewhere. All of which pro-vided a fertile breeding ground for fresh waves of epidemic diseases, not to mention the apocalyptic new Native religions promising the miraculous defeat of the invaders, such as the Ghost Dance cult—another narrative born, like Sarah Winnemucca's *Life Among the Piutes*, within fifty air-miles of Lake Tahoe's shores.

In his award-winning book *Keeping Slug Woman Alive: A Holistic Approach to American Indian Texts*, Greg Sarris points out that Native American narrators have a disturbing tendency to "disappear" from their own books, almost as if they had been kidnapped by white ghost writers. "It is well known," Professor Sarris reminds us, "that John G. Neihardt, editor of *Black Elk Speaks*, the best-known narrated American Indian autobiography, not only rearranged Black Elk's narratives in certain ways but added to them." Indeed, as Sarris points out sharply, "the oldest and most common" of these ghosting games "is what David Brumble calls the 'Absent Editor strategy,' where the editor edits and presents the Indian's narrative 'in such a way as to create the fiction that the narrative is all the Indian's own...that the Indians speak to us without mediation.'" It's the old ventriloquist's trick dressed up in Hollywood Indian war paint: a convincing fake, like puppets on a string.

Recent scandals in which whites have represented themselves as "Indian authors" (only to be unmasked once their works earned national acclaim) have only added to this thicket of confusion. How much of so-called "Native American literature," I often wonder, was actually written by Native Americans themselves? Similarly, many critics have wondered if Sarah Winnemucca's autobiography didn't fall victim to this "as-told-to" syndrome of false authorship—at least in some chapters. We'll never know for certain. Since Winnemucca's original handwritten manuscript has long since been lost, we have nothing to go on now but suspicion, innuendo, and raw intuition.

My own gut sense is that Winnemucca did indeed write the entire book herself, virtually word for word—based in large part on the hundreds of platform lectures she delivered to white audiences across the country over the years. As her most recent biographer, Sally Zanjani, argues, there is "no doubt" that her editor, Mary Mann, "was *working on a manuscript written by Sarah.*" As mentioned earlier, Mary Mann herself fiercely denies putting words into Winnemucca's mouth: "In fighting with her literary deficiencies," insists Mann, who was Sarah's friend and ally as well as her editor, Winnemucca "loses some of the fervid eloquence which her extraordinary colloquial command of the English language enables her to utter, but I am confident that no one would desire that her own original words should be altered."

In truth, Winnemucca's book was far from "the first outbreak of the American Indian in human literature" as her editor once claimed: numerous autobiographical accounts written by Native Americans were published throughout the eighteenth and early nineteenth centuries. Admittedly these works were all much shorter than Winnemucca's book—mere pamphlets by comparison. And all of them were written by male authors. Nevertheless these works can still claim pride of place as the first American Indian literature published in English.

And yet there is something both unique and original about Sarah Winnemucca's *Life Among the Piutes*, which speaks with a voice the likes of which American literature had never heard before. As Greg Sarris concludes in *Keeping Slug Woman Alive*, "Sarah Winnemucca Hopkins and others wrote autobiographies that were more extensive than the eighteenth and early nineteenth century apparently unmediated accounts of conversion to Christianity by Indians such as Samson Occom, William and Mary Apes, and George Copway."

On this basis Winnemucca's book still can claim not just one, but three "firsts" in the long history of Native American literature: it is the first personal narrative to be written by a Native American woman; it is the first Native American book to provide an account of life west of the Mississippi; and it is the first book-length work published by any Native American author in English. All three are lasting achievements. All of which makes Sarah Winnemucca every bit as much a pioneer as John Frémont or the Donner Party. In the words of Professor Arnold Krupat, another leading expert on Native American literature, books such as *Life Among the Piutes* were truly written on "the textual equivalent of the frontier."

Yet for all her eloquence, courage, and originality, Sarah Winnemucca's career as a tribal leader, author, and nationwide

Indian rights activist ended in scandal, despair, and disaster. Much of the blame for that tragedy rests squarely on the shoulders of her last husband, Lewis Hopkins, a former military officer whom Winnemucca had met during her days as an Army scout. After their marriage, Hopkins repeatedly absconded with the charity money Sarah had painstakingly raised to support her visionary new school for Paiute children—discrediting her in the eyes of many white sponsors, and casting further suspicions over her motives among her own tribe.

The failure of her school ultimately became a wider tragedy for American education as a whole. In sharp contrast to the notorious Indian boarding schools founded during that same era, such as Carlisle Indian School back east or the Stewart Indian School in Carson City, Sarah Winnemucca's Paiute school emphasized full respect for tribal traditions, tribal language, and tribal culture—providing an institutional structure in which Indian children could learn both English and their own tribal traditions from fully bilingual tribal teachers (including Sarah Winnemucca herself). These were truly revolutionary concepts, decades ahead of their time, both then and now.

Schools like Carlisle, on the other hand, were based on the oft-quoted need to "kill the Indian" inside every pupil—as Carlisle's founder once famously proclaimed. To facilitate the acquisition of English, it was believed that students should be fiercely punished for speaking so much as one word of their own native tongue. Christianity was compulsory. By contrast, Native religions were demonized and disparaged, slandered as devil worship at worst and impotent superstitions at best. Often such Indian schools were located hundreds, even thousands, of miles from the students' tribal homelands.

Bereft of funding, abandoned by her embezzling, abusive, alcoholic, gambling-addicted husband, and slowly succumbing to the ravages of tuberculosis, Sarah Winnemucca died at the age of only forty-seven of what seems, in retrospect, more like heartbreak than consumption. And yet in the estimation of Sally Zanjani, she remains one of the three best-known Indian women who lived prior to the twentieth century, along with Sacajawea and Pocahontas: recently she has been the subject of multiple television documentaries, museum exhibits, book-length biographies, and critical studies. She is also, like Horace Mann, clearly among the nineteenth century's most visionary educators. In Zanjani's own words, "Her school had failed—yet it left a vision of how Indian children might be taught with kindness and respect for their culture, their traditions, and their language." Today Native American tribes across the nation are working tirelessly to teach their children their ancient languages—literally to keep their tribal heritages alive. In this as in so much else, they owe much to Winnemucca's pioneering nineteenth-century example.

It is no accident, then, that Winnemucca's single most loyal supporter, advocate, benefactor, and publisher was the Boston philanthropist Elizabeth Peabody (Mary Mann's sister), the woman primarily responsible for the success of the kindergarten movement in America. It was Peabody, Zanjani reports, who "tirelessly wrote letters on Sarah's behalf to influential friends and arranged talks for Sarah in the homes of Ralph Waldo Emerson, John Greenleaf Whittier, several congressmen, and other members of Boston's intellectual and social elite." And in the end, it was Peabody alone who stood by Sarah Winnemucca's integrity, genius, and vision, sacrificing much of her own fortune to support Sarah's dream of an Indian school worthy of the name.

As for Winnemucca's literary achievements, her stories and speeches literally speak for themselves.

Oh, for shame! You who are educated by a Christian government in the art of war…Yes you, who call yourselves the great civilization; you who have knelt upon Plymouth Rock, covenanting with God to make this land the home of the free and the brave. Ah, then you rise from your bended knees and seizing the welcoming hands of those who are the owners of this land, which you are not, your carbines rise upon the bleak shore, and your so-called civilization sweeps inland like the ocean wave; but, oh my God! leaving its pathway marked by crimson lines of blood and strewed by the bones of two races, the inheritor and the invader; and I am crying out for justice—yes, pleading from the far-off plains of the West for the dusky mourner.

Despite the fierce grief and anger her words convey, Winnemucca's fire and charisma as a lecturer could still bring potentially hostile white audiences to their feet in cheers, or when confronted with the hypocrisy of their own nation's policies, to tears. At one point, she even joked about getting transatlantic train tickets to Ellis Island for all her Paiute people, so that they might "receive free lands (and a welcoming hand) from the U.S. Government." In this regard, the following report, published by *Alta California* in 1879, captures some of the excitement and fervor Sarah could provoke in her live stage performances, garbed in buckskin and velvet to suit her white audiences' expectations of what a true Indian princess must look like:

You take all the nations of the earth to your bosom but the poor Indian…who has lived for generations on the land which the good God has given to them, and you say must be exterminated. [Thrice repeated, with deep passion, and received with tremendous applause.] The proverb says the big fish eat the little fishes, and we Indians are the little fish and you eat us all up and drive us from home. [Cheers.] Where can we poor Indians go if the government will not help us? If your people will help us, and you have good hearts, and can if you will, I will promise to educate my people and make them law-abiding citizens of the United States [Loud applause.] It can be done—it can be done. My father, Winnemucca, pleads with you that the guilty shall be punished, but that the innocent shall be permitted to live on their own lands in Nevada.…We want you to try us for four years, and if at the end of that time we don't learn, or don't work, or don't become good citizens, then you can do what you please [Cheers].

As such reports foreshadow, Winnemucca's greatest passion (as well as her most enduring achievement) was the struggle to bring her own Paiute people back within the wider watershed of Lake Tahoe—back, in short, from the distant federal reservations in Oregon and Washington State where they had been exiled and virtually imprisoned; back again to their beautiful ancestral desert homeland of Pyramid Lake, where the waters of Lake Tahoe still return to the sky.

How did Sarah Winnemucca acquire such tremendous fluency with the English language in the first place? Where, indeed, did she acquire her English name? Therein hangs yet another cautionary tale—one which conceals the forgotten origins of the Western Indian wars along the banks of Tahoe's Truckee River.

Besides being the granddaughter of the legendary Chief Truckee, the girl first named Thocmetone was also the eldest daughter of another Paiute leader, known as Chief Winnemucca (the same man for whom the present-day city of Winnemucca, Nevada, was later named). In time Thocmetone and her brother Natches came to claim their family's pride of place as tribal leaders. Yet as we have witnessed already, little Thocmetone's life was forever altered by the owl eyes' sudden intrusion into the Pyramid Lake/Lake Tahoe region while she was still a small child. Predictably, due to her grandfather Truckee's lifelong friendship with leading white explorers like John Frémont, she and her sister also became the first Paiute children to learn English—which eventually transformed the little girl Thocmetone into the eloquent woman that literary scholar LaVonne Ruoff has aptly described as "the mightiest word-warrior of her tribe."

Admittedly, Thocmetone's newfound fluency in English was initially intended solely to fit her for a career as a domestic servant. American Indian domestics (some would say slaves) had been part of Western life from the time of the first Spanish missions forward. As one 1875 California newspaper bragged brightly, Indian girls made "the best servants in America."

For a woman of lesser talent, persistence, and courage, the iron fate of such domestic servitude might well have been the end of Thocmetone's life story. Instead it was only the beginning of Sarah Winnemucca's war.

The trigger for Winnemucca's personal transformation came by means of the written word itself. When Chief Truckee returned from serving under Captain Frémont in the Bear Flag Rebellion, he brought with him a testimonial letter written in Frémont's own hand, intended to convince settlers, military commanders, and politicians that they should treat Chief Truckee and his Paiute people as allies, not enemies.

The illiterate Chief Truckee called this handwritten letter his "rag friend." No fool, he fully understood the power of the written word to alter the attitudes of his "white brothers" toward the Paiute people. When he died, the old chief even requested that his "rag friend" be buried with him. Yet he himself was a master of the spoken word, and a great orator in his own language—as the passionate speeches his granddaughter faithfully recorded now boldly testify.

As Sally Zanjani, reports, "Thocmetone remembered how [her grandfather Truckee] took his rag friend out and talked to it. He explained its miraculous powers to his people: 'This can talk to all our white brothers, and our white sisters, and their children... The paper can travel like the wind, and it can go and talk with their fathers and brothers and sisters, and come back to tell what they were doing; and whether they are well or sick." He believed that this talking rag, Zanjani concludes, "was the true source of the white man's power." Perhaps he was right.

Protected by the mysterious power of his rag friend, Chief Truckee led a large contingent of Pyramid Lake Paiutes over the

Sierra and into the Sacramento Valley in 1850 or 1851, when Thocmetone herself was only about seven years old. For the tribe, this journey in and of itself was really nothing new. For centuries the Paiute people had maintained trade routes over the Sierra. Often the young adventurers who made the crossing returned from the rich lands of California with prized treasures—perhaps even with wives from other tribes.

Knowledge of these ancient Paiute trade routes was, in fact, precisely what had enabled Chief Truckee to guide Frémont and others over the Donner Pass route. This time, however, Chief Truckee was determined to lead more than just a trading mission, or even a military expedition, into California. Leaving his son-in-law Winnemucca (Thocmetone's father) in charge of the Pyramid Lake Paiute band, he had already taken a group of thirty Paiute families over the crest of the Sierra to find paying work in California the prior year. Now he was determined to take his own family to California with him as well—including his favorite granddaughter, Thocmetone.

Kicking and screaming, a terrified Thocmetone was forced to leave her father—and her desert homeland at Pyramid Lake—to join her grandfather in this warm green land of owl-eyed, hairy-faced strangers. There Thocmetone and her sister Mary had their first encounters with steamships, brick houses, sugar cakes, and all the wonders and terrors of this deeply unfamiliar white world. For the most part, these little Paiute girls remained terrified of white people—and with good reason.

While Thocmetone and her grandfather were away working in California, one of Chief Truckee's own sons was killed, along with nine other Paiute men, by a pioneer party near the Humboldt Sink. Meanwhile in California, Thocmetone's older sister was repeatedly molested and almost certainly raped by white men—a near-universal fate for Indian women in the all-male gold mining camps of the time. Then came news that the remaining Paiutes at Pyramid Lake had been struck down by a major epidemic (probably cholera). Even the sacred waters of Lake Tahoe, the Paiutes told themselves, had been poisoned. Famine soon followed this new plague.

Throughout it all, Chief Truckee insisted that his "rag friend" would protect his people. Time and again, he stubbornly—often eloquently—refused to authorize retaliatory raids on white settlers. For the moment, at least, the Pyramid Lake Paiute band remained on friendly terms with the growing influx of white settlers.

Recalling her grandfather's words years later, Thocmetone rendered them into English with great power: "Some of you may live a long time yet," Truckee told his people, "and don't let your hearts work against your white fathers; if you do, you will not get along. You see they are already here in our land; here they are all along the river, and we must let our brothers live with us. We cannot tell them to go away. I know your good hearts. I know you won't say 'Kill them.' Surely you all know they are human. Their lives are just as dear to them as ours are to us."

Eventually Chief Truckee's best efforts to hold back the tide of terror failed. Meanwhile, through Truckee's own intervention, the Paiutes acquired two new potent weapons of war: horses and the English language. Within ten years, the little Native girl named Thocmetone would prove herself a master of both.

Chief Truckee and his people had probably first learned to ride horses during their service under Frémont in the Bear Flag Rebellion and the Mexican-American War. Prairie tribes further east had acquired horses centuries earlier—forever altering their cultures. On a continental basis, the Paiutes were latecomers to this horseback revolution. Yet Paiute warriors soon acquired legendary skills of horsemanship equal to those of any people on the planet. In the words of one white observer, "It was as easy for a Paiute to ride a horse as for him to breathe. He did not have to learn how. He already knew."

As elsewhere on the continent, the Paiutes' newfound mastery of horses quickly shifted the old balance of power between tribes. Significantly for our own story, the centuries-old conflict between the Paiutes and their horseless mountain neighbors, the Washoes, seems to have tilted decisively in the Paiutes' favor. And those same superb skills of horsemanship also meant that Paiute warriors were now in a stronger position than the Washoes to resist the first onslaught of white settlers.

Despite the strenuous objections of the aging leaders such as Chief Truckee, open warfare soon broke out. So too did an on-again, off-again alliance between white settlers and the "peaceful" Washoes against the increasingly "warlike" Paiutes. Hence the first major battle in the dawning new era of Western Indian wars would be fought—and lost—by U.S. militias against a mounted army of Paiute warriors along the banks of the Truckee River in 1860 (mere months before the Civil War began): an Indian war which would not end, in essence, until some thirty years later, at the notorious massacre at Wounded Knee.

In her own day, Sarah Winnemucca herself was justly celebrated for her skill on horseback. Indeed, during the Bannock Indian War in Oregon those skills literally saved her life—as well as the lives of many of her tribe. But horses were not Sarah Winnemucca's only weapon. Unwittingly, by insisting that she learn English, Chief Truckee had thrust his granddaughter Thocmetone into the very center of a tribal struggle for survival itself.

Sent to work as a house servant in the home of a prominent (but Puritanical) Nevada politician named Major William Ormsby, the Indian girl now known as Sarah was tutored in the basics of English reading, writing, and culture. Years later, perhaps to please white philanthropists, Sarah would claim that she spent three years in a convent school in San Jose. Although she probably was sent to a San Jose convent school to honor the deathbed request of her grandfather Chief Truckee, that school has no record whatsoever of her attendance. Instead, according to her biographer Zanjani, most of Sarah's English literacy seems to have been acquired solely by working as a house servant for Nevada's politically powerful Ormsby family.

While she worked in the Ormsbys' home, the first warning of the impending war came in 1857, when a pair of white men were found murdered in the snows above Lake Tahoe. Washoe arrowheads were allegedly found in the bodies of both men—at least according to Ormsby's Paiute allies, who had been sent to the scene of the crime by Ormsby himself. Whether the Washoes were falsely accused remains uncertain; what is certain is that Sarah's own brother Natches was soon made leader of a Paiute war posse sent to kill or capture the alleged Washoe murderers. Within days two young Washoes accused of the crime were killed, shot in the back as they attempted to flee a white lynch mob in the nearby town of Genoa. From that point forward, relations between the Paiutes and the Washoes broke down completely. According to Sarah Winnemucca, the mother of one of the dead Washoes placed a bitter curse on the Paiutes in revenge: "You may all live to see a day when you will suffer at the hands of your white brothers."

Cursed or not, the Pyramid Lake Paiutes found Major Ormsby himself leading a poorly organized white militia force deep into their territory three years later, in 1860—this time planning to punish the Paiutes, not the Washoes, for the alleged murder of two white settlers. For their part, the Paiutes accused the two murdered men of having kidnapped—and sexually abused—two innocent Indian girls. Ambushed and outmaneuvered by a mounted Paiute war party, Major Ormsby and at least seventy of his men were killed in what came to be known as the Battle of Pyramid Lake—the bloodiest U.S. military defeat at the hands of Indian warriors prior to Custer's defeat at the Battle of Little Big Horn.

Herein lies another of those human mysteries which Lake Tahoe seems to spawn like cutthroat trout: how does Ormsby, the same man whose family educated Sarah Winnemucca, the man who showed her grandfather such kindness, end up leading a fatal, foolhardy military expedition aimed at the very heart of her Paiute homeland? Was this the Washoe curse against the Paiutes at work after all?

Predictably, the Paiutes' initial military victory at Pyramid Lake was short-lived: waves of military reinforcements soon arrived from California, outnumbering the scattered and impoverished Paiute forces. Within a year, old Chief Truckee himself was dead of grief and old age—and his people henceforth confined to reservations, first at Pyramid Lake and then far from their homeland on a new reservation in southern Oregon—and finally all the way north to Washington State. As Sarah herself later wrote, all the bitter prophesies of her cousin Numaga had come true:

> You would make war upon the whites. I ask you to pause and reflect. The white men are like the stars over your heads. You have wrongs, great wrongs, that rise up like those mountains before you; but can you, from the mountain tops, reach and blot out those stars? Your enemies are like the sands in the bed of your rivers; when taken away they only give place for more to come and settle there. Could you defeat the whites in Nevada, from over the mountains of California would come to help them an army of white men that would cover your country like a blanket. What hope is there for the Pah-Ute? From where is to come your guns, your powder, your lead, your dried meats to live upon, and hay to feed your ponies while you carry on this war? Your enemies have all these things, more than they can use. They will come like the sand in a whirlwind and drive you from your homes. You will be forced among the barren rocks of the north, where your ponies will die; where you will see the women and old men starve, and listen to the cries of your children for food. I love my people; let them live; and when their spirits shall be called to the Great Camp in the southern sky, let their bones rest where their fathers were buried.

For the vast majority of Sarah Winnemucca's Paiute kinsmen, these ongoing wars and migrations brought misery without measure. Sarah's life was no exception. Summarizing Winnemucca's personal hardships, her editor Mary Mann remarked, "After her mother and sister died of starvation and two brothers died in unprovoked attacks by whites, she vowed to devote her life to helping her people and to bringing peace between Indians and whites. While working intermittently as a translator and army scout, she wrote pleas on behalf of the Numa [the original native name for the Paiute people] which were published in newspapers in the East. She visited generals and senators and barraged them with letters. Hundreds had died of typhus, tuberculosis, and smallpox."

Yet Mary Mann's bleak assessment is, if anything, far too gentle for the genocidal massacres which the Battle of Pyramid Lake unleashed. In 1865, the *Gold Hill News* of Nevada put the matter bluntly, urging "a final solution of the great Indian problem: by exterminating the whole race, or driving them forever beyond our frontier."

Face to face with the naked terror of this American "final solution," the woman who as a frightened girl had been dragged off to California and later sold into a life of servitude in the Ormsby household somehow found her own voice as a writer, reshaping the English language to serve her own purposes, thereby serving as both weapon and shield for her people. In so doing, Winnemucca drew on reserves of physical, mental, and moral strength that few American authors could match.

Writing was not her only weapon. Like Frémont, Stephens, and the Donners, Winnemucca could be a tireless and courageous wilderness traveler: "In 1878, during the Bannock War," her editor Mary Mann reports proudly, "she rode 223 miles in two days in order to save her father and other Numa." She could also be a tireless campaigner: "In 1880," Mann continues, "she traveled to Washington, D.C., to convince the Secretary of the Interior to help the Numa."

Yet for all her eloquence, for all her heroism, as Mann herself concedes bitterly, "She failed, and her people were forced to move 300 miles to another reservation through waist-deep snow"—the Paiute equivalent of the Cherokee Trail of Tears. It was an ordeal which Sarah recorded in painful, precise detail in *Life Among the Piutes*. Mercifully, her book's warm reception in Washington finally allowed the Paiutes to return to their ancestral homelands at Pyramid Lake, where the waters of Lake Tahoe still flow today.

For all her accomplishments, for all her failures, for all her frustrations, the establishment of the Pyramid Lake Reservation under permanent Paiute control must be seen as her most enduring achievement: in the face of impossible odds, the words she uttered brought her people back to the ancient homeland they had loved and inhabited for at least nine thousand years.

Today it is those waters themselves—or what remains of them— that best tell her tale. Once the world's largest trout, the *hupa-agai*, or Lahontan cutthroat trout, were the keystone species in both Lake Tahoe and Pyramid Lake. The verified world record for a single Lahontan trout was forty-one pounds. Anecdotal and photographic evidence indicates that some grew even larger. But by the 1930s, due to factory fishing and the introduction of competing species, Tahoe's Lahontan trout population was extinct. By the 1940s, Pyramid Lake's Lahontans had died out as well. Fortunately a few fingerlings survived in isolated lakes high in the mountains, where they had once been planted by game wardens—the basis of today's ongoing efforts by the Pyramid Lake Paiute Tribe to restore Lahontan trout populations in both Lake Tahoe and Pyramid Lake. Talk about the big ones that got away.

But something far larger was lost with the Lahontan trout. Forgotten today, the same water diversions that once lowered Pyramid Lake by over one hundred feet doomed another huge, shallow lake nearby to destruction. Fed by the Truckee River, this now-vanished lake was once the most distant terminus of Tahoe's waters, nurturing vast flocks of migrating ducks, geese, and even sea-going pelicans, not to mention enormous populations of Lahontan trout, all contained within a rich seasonal wetland ecosystem not unlike that of California's vanished Tulare Lake. Today what remains is a hardbaked alkaline desert playa. The name of this vanished Eden? What else could it be named but Lake Winnemucca?

As a plaque in the Pyramid Lake hatchery museum states bluntly, "Lake Winnemucca was granted the status of a National Wildlife Refuge in 1936. Actually, by this time it was nearly dry…

and in 1962 its status as a Wildlife Refuge was revoked." Today the outlines of lost Lake Winnemucca are still clearly visible on satellite photos of Nevada, a ghostly white oval in the shape of an open mouth.

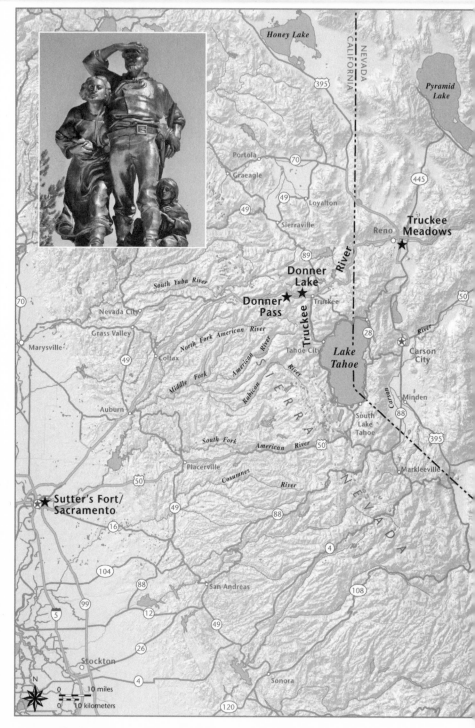

The Donner Party monument outside the Emigrant Trail Museum. Photograph by Scott Lankford

five

LUIS *and* SALVATOR

The Donner Party Murders

The legend of the Donner Party's perilous descent into canni-balism and chaos in the winter of 1846-47 must be the best-known incident in all of California history—next to the mythic origins of the Gold Rush itself. Yet probe beneath the surface of both events in search of the raw truth and you'll soon discover that both the Gold Rush and the Donner Party disaster were linked by the best-kept secret in all of California history: the shameful legacy of Indian slavery before, during, and after California's entry into the Union as a so-called free state in 1849. This makes the true, unvarnished story of the Donner Party disaster seem more like an unsolved murder mystery than a heroic tale of pioneer courage, for-titude, and survival.

Rather than focus on the tragic fate of the Donner Party them-selves, let's focus instead on the far more tragic (yet hidden) fate of the Donner Party's least-known victims: two of John Sutter's Indian slaves, known to history only as Luis and Salvator. Together they repeatedly risked their lives to lead a small group of Donner

Party survivors through the Sierra snows toward safety—only to be shot in the back and cannibalized by members of the same group of pioneers they had been sent there to rescue. And then erased from history completely.

It was a shocking betrayal—made all the more shocking by the silence of generations of Donner Party historians, most of whom fail to acknowledge or discuss these cold-blooded murders in more than a few brief sentences. As contemporary journalist-historian Frank Mullen notes (briefly) in his otherwise deliciously detailed and meticulously researched *The Donner Party Chronicles: A Day-by-Day Account of a Doomed Wagon Train*, "The crime is double murder but no court will ever hear the case. In 1847, Indians are casually killed in punishment for theft or just for sport." Period.

Apparently few modern historians, including Mullen himself, want to "hear the case" either. Instead, like dozens of other Donner Party aficionados before and since, Mullen simply notes the bloody facts of the twin murders and moves on.

Who were Luis and Salvator? Where did they come from? What were their tribes? How did they and other California Indians come to be enslaved, first by the Spanish, then by the Mexicans, and ultimately by the notorious Swiss-French immigrant slave master John Sutter? And how is it possible that tens of thousands of other California Indians remained legally enslaved long after California had entered the Union as a "free" state in 1849?

Stand outside the Emigrant Trail Museum, located inside Donner Memorial State Park, adjacent to the shores of Donner Lake (Tahoe's beautiful little brother) and you can watch scores of tourists gazing upward in awe at a huge thirty-foot-tall bronze statue of the Donner Party doggedly staring westward, ever westward into the teeth of an invisible storm. Legend has it that the statue's massive pedestal was constructed to match the exact depth of the nearly thirty-foot snows in which the Donner Party found themselves entombed during that fateful winter of 1846-47. At its base is engraved the famous motto "Virile to risk and find; kindly withal and a ready help; facing the brunt of fate; indomitable,—unafraid."

Enter the museum and amid the wax-museum models and living-history dioramas you'll find literally dozens of books, films, and documentaries on sale in the ample gift shop, all of them implying, none too subtly, that the Donner Party's story uniquely embodies the heroic nature of America as a whole.

As perhaps it does—though in darker dimensions than any of these authors intended to reveal. Scanning the shelves, a quick bibliography of Donner Party literature emerges. It begins with the diaries and memoirs of Donner Party survivors Patrick Breen and Eliza P. Donner. Over thirty years later, in 1879, the legendary frontier Tahoe/Truckee editor C. F. McGlashan stitched their stories together to publish his own retrospective *History of the Donner Party: A Tragedy of the Sierra*—the one book which, more than any other, triggered the first great wave of Donner Party obsession nationwide. Now fast-forward past a dozen other titles to Bernard DeVoto's *Year of Decision, 1846*, published in 1943, almost exactly a century after the Donner disaster took place. Still considered "one of the ten most influential American history books ever published," DeVoto's work set the standard for dozens of subsequent Donner Party histories yet to come.

Down at the far end of the bookshelf, you can end your brief tour of the Donner Party archives amid a blur of contemporary titles ranging from novelist James Houston's richly imagined *Snow Mountain Passage* to University of Nevada, Reno, Professor Donald Hardesty's path-breaking scientific study, *The Archaeology of the Donner Party*, which garnered nationwide media attention when first published in 2005.

Undoubtedly such books have contributed much to our knowledge of the Donner Party's fate. But why were the fates of Luis and Salvator so consistently omitted from the pages of so many of them—especially given our culture's seeming obsession with murder and cannibalism?

One of the few authors to breach this wall of silence is San Francisco cultural historian Rebecca Solnit, whose 1997 book *Savage Dreams: A Journey into the Landscape Wars of the American West* rejects the whole heroic bronze-statue version of the Donner Party's saga out of hand, naming it a false "paean that has nearly nothing to do with what made these travelers' history." So begins Solnit's grim but enlightening reassessment of American Manifest Destiny as viewed through the lens of the Donner disaster.

As Solnit soon makes clear, the basic facts can easily be summarized in just a few sentences: Setting out from Council Bluffs, Iowa, in May of 1846, a loosely affiliated group of wagon train pioneers only nominally under the leadership of the Donner family suffered through a long series of self-inflicted setbacks, including an ill-advised shortcut across the Great Salt Lake Desert and two murders before they had even arrived, weeks behind schedule, at the crest of the Tahoe Sierra. A fierce series of Sierra blizzards then pinned them down for the next five months in crude makeshift camps near what is now Donner Lake. Starvation and cannibalism took a grim toll—until rescue parties from Sutter's Fort finally led the survivors over the Sierra to safety near present-day Sacramento.

These, then, are the bare-bones facts; but as generations of authors have (re)discovered, the human dramas these events revealed remain both compelling and complex. As DeVoto explained in *The Year of Decision*, the climax of the Donner Party ordeal came just as a splinter group of starving pioneers nicknamed the Forlorn Hope was attempting unsuccessfully to battle their way across the snowbound pass—only to begin cannibalizing each other's corpses when they failed to reach their goal. Here's how DeVoto describes the bloody scene: "Most of them were moaning or screaming in the dark...But not Uncle Billy. He reminded his daughters of their mother and brothers and sisters at the lake, told them they must get through to Sutter's for their sake, bade them eat his body, and died." It was Christmas Eve. On Christmas morning, amid a growing pile of frozen corpses, some of which served as makeshift tent poles, the desperate survivors finally succeeded in starting a fire. "So they cut strips from the legs and arms of Patrick Dolan and roasted them."

Here's the key: that little word "so" in the final sentence seems "so" inevitable that by the time you reach it—on page 400 of DeVoto's tome—the unspeakable act of cannibalism seems more like religious martyrdom. Note, for example, how the implicitly Christlike character of Uncle Billy offers up a willing sacrifice of his own flesh to save his children (on Christmas Eve, no less).

Granted, DeVoto takes great pains to balance his heroic account with what he calls the "degeneration of human personality under stresses that had hardened others into nobility," dissecting in clinical detail the whole disastrous chain of decisions which led the Donner Party toward their grim fate. In essence, DeVoto's Donner Party is not comprised of American heroes but instead of ordinary human beings struggling under extraordinary circumstances to survive—sometimes with courage, sometimes with cowardice, and sometimes by means of cannibalism or murder. Such is the human condition, DeVoto seems to imply.

Hence, unlike most Donner Party historians before or since, DeVoto discusses the murders of Luis and Salvator in some detail and even takes time in subsequent pages to mention other Native Americans who offered crucial help to the survivors along the way. DeVoto also consistently employs the old nineteenth-century racist term "Diggers" to describe the Indians—a word whose resemblance to the word "niggers" is not accidental. Describing the rescue of the Forlorn Hope group by Miwok Indians, for example, DeVoto intones, "It was on January 12 that they found strange footprints in the mud…and came at dusk to the brush huts of a tiny Indian village. Lowly Diggers lived there, but the squaws wept at sight of these living dead.…touched by the sight of the suffering to the residual pity at the heart of life."

This grants the Miwok at least some spark of humanity. Yet why are those doing all the rescuing, the crying, the caring, the feeding, and even the literal carrying of the survivors toward safety so consistently described in terms like "lowly"? DeVoto himself fails to explain. Instead he simply continues, "At last a mangy chief gave Eddy a handful of pine nuts, and they made all the difference."

Again, why describe the chief as "mangy"? What exactly are DeVoto's hidden motives in framing his tale this way?

Questions of so-called political correctness aside, why is it always the white pioneer's courage, not the Indian's compassion, which wins our admiration? And what does that say about our own post-modern vision of the nature of America as a whole?

Fact: it was the food provided by the Indians, more than any-thing else, which finally saved the Donner Party survivors from death—granting them just enough strength and hope and super-human courage to continue crawling on toward Sutter's Fort, and safety. Pine nuts, I might add, are an especially rich source of calories. "This handful of pine nuts had brought Eddy back from his 'dream of combats, of famine and death, of cries of despair, of fathomless snows and impassable mountains,'" DeVoto concludes. "He refused to die." Yet without the Miwoks' help he clearly would have. Indeed the Indians literally carry him down. "Supported on their shoulders, Eddy left bloody footprints across six miles of rough ground and came, an hour before sunset, to a little shack on the edge of Johnson's ranch, the first outpost of settlement, at the east-ern wall of the Sacramento Valley."

Only now does the help of rescuers—white, not Indian—finally become crucial to the Donner Party's survival. Soon four separate rescue parties are sent out from Sutter's Fort to bring the remaining survivors the rest of the way down to safety. Suddenly the tone of DeVoto's description shifts, with the race of the rescuers, none of whom appear to be "mangy" or "lowly": at the first white settler's shack they find, "Young Harriet Ritchie came to the door and Eddy asked her for bread. Harriet Ritchie burst into tears." Soon a hastily organized rescue party hurries back to search for other survivors "by following his bloody footprints."

Picking up the narrative where DeVoto leaves off, Rebecca Solnit traces those same bloody footprints back to the abandoned, well-gnawed corpses of Luis and Salvator—but not without tak-ing a long, complex, crucial detour through California Gold Rush history. In order to solve the mystery of Luis and Salvator's murder

for ourselves, we will have to make the same detour (returning to the specific circumstances of their murders only after we
understand the life circumstances which first led them into the
middle of the Sierra winter in the first place). By necessity our
"detour" will reach forward into the future as well: for within mere
months of the Donner Party's epic crossing of the Tahoe Sierra,
the greatest Gold Rush in human history had been unleashed—
with the stark reality of Indian slavery directly at its epicenter.
In short, without an understanding of the pivotal role of Indian
slavery in the history of the California—both before and after
the Donner disaster—the murders of Luis and Salvator remain
incomprehensible.

Most of us learned the familiar legend back in grade school: the
sudden discovery of gold nuggets at Sutter's Mill in 1848, a mere
two years after the Donners' arrival; the doomed efforts of Sutter
himself to keep the discovery a secret; and the flood of gold-fevered
forty-niners from around the globe just one year later—with Sutter
himself left penniless and bitter following his betrayal.

The only trouble here is that John Sutter didn't actually find
that gold—and neither did his two famous foremen, John Marshall
and John Savage (both of whom actually worked as Indian slave
drivers in the construction of John Sutter's new sawmill). Instead,
those doing the digging—the men who *truly* found the gold, in
short—were Sutter's Indian slaves. Worse yet, the discovery of
gold itself occurred on Indian land to which Sutter had as yet no
legal claim, hoping instead to usurp new lands by force for his ever-
expanding inland slave empire.

For centuries Indian slavery had already formed the backbone
of European colonization and conquest across the Americas. In
Alta California, from the earliest Spanish missions forward to the
Mexican land grants, Indian slavery had made oligarchs like John
Sutter and General Mariano Vallejo wealthy beyond their wildest
dreams. "Sutter himself," Solnit reminds us, "had been a man of no
particular distinction. A native of Switzerland, he invented a cap-
taincy in the French army to impress new acquaintances. He talked

the governor of California into letting him begin an operation using natives much as the Spanish did, as slaves for enterprises that resembled southern slave plantations…and kept a group of young girls for his own use."

How, then, did men like Luis and Salvator first come to be enslaved by Sutter? And why did these Indians have Spanish names? According to Joseph King, in an article titled "Luis and Salvador: Unsung Heroes of the Donner Party" published in 1996, Luis was probably a member of the Ochehamne group of Miwok Indians, located just south of present-day Sacramento (not to be confused with Sierra Miwok groups higher in the mountains, or the Coast Miwok groups located closer to the sea). Under the Spanish occupation, virtually all coastal California Indian nations had been forced to serve as converts/slaves to the Spanish padres. Birth records housed in the Mission San Jose indicate that Luis, originally named Eema, probably would have been just nineteen years old in 1847, when he was first ordered by his new master, John Sutter, to go in search of the Donner Party and bring them down to safety.

Luis's companion Salvator, originally named QueYen, was a member of the Cosumne River Miwok group, south of Sacramento. Mission San Jose birth records indicate that he probably would have been twenty-eight years old when he joined Luis to help form the Donner Party's first rescue team. That makes Salvator old enough to have been born under Spanish rule, the Mexican War of Independence having officially ended in 1821. Not until 1832, however, did Mexican government officials officially disband the old Spanish mission system in Alta California and grant Indians full rights of citizenship—on paper at least—under the new Mexican constitution. In reality, alas, Mexican authorities instead quietly expanded the previous Spanish system of Indian peonage (a thinly veiled euphemism for outright slavery).

How else, the Mexican Californios reasoned, were these newly "freed" inhabitants of the old Spanish mission system to sur- vive but as slaves to their new Mexican masters? After all, their

traditional homelands had long since been usurped and ecologi-
cally altered beyond recognition by vast herds of Spanish pigs,
Spanish cattle, Spanish horses, and the equally invasive European
plant species—not to mention those withering European plagues
which the Spanish had unwittingly unleashed upon them. True,
some had fled to the Sierra foothills in search of freedom, where
they begged to be taken in by other tribes still outside the reach
of Mexican military control. Indeed, many foothill tribes had
already begun mounting guerrilla-style resistance to further Mexican incursions by the time John Sutter came along, financing
their efforts chiefly by stealing Spanish horses and selling them
on the black market across the West (much as the Mexicans sold
human slaves through the same black market channels). Indeed,
so threatened were the newly empowered Mexican authorities by
these marauding bands of Indians hidden deep in the Sierra foothills that they willingly granted the otherwise unwelcome Swiss
outsider direct control over a large swath of land in present-day
Sacramento which had formerly been considered hostile Indian
territory, no doubt hoping to use Sutter and his foreign settlers as
human shields of a sort, arrayed against further Native American
incursions along the coast.

Contrary to popular perception, California Indians were far
from docile converts, making many attempts at armed resistance—often with considerable success. Hence Sutter's Fort
was deliberately constructed as a fortified settlement to fend off
attacks from hostile California Indians resisting enslavement.
However, as Edward Castillo, a professor of California Native
American history at Sonoma State University, reminds us, while
the Donners were crossing the Great Basin deserts, Sutter himself
"was reduced to begging the Mexican government to buy his fort
following a mauling at the hands of Miwok Indians near the Calaveras in June of 1846."

By means of his Mexican land grant, in short, Sutter established
himself as an embattled outpost in Mexico's vast continental slave-
trading system (having already imported slaves of his own from

Hawaii). Most contemporary sources continue to claim that Sutter merely "employed" Indians on his lands. In reality, the terms of this "employment" were enslavement, pure and simple—as verified by numerous eyewitness visitors. Indians who disobeyed Sutter were beaten or tortured. Those who attempted to escape to the mountains were hunted down like animals. According to the Virginia-born mountain man James Clyman, who visited Sutter's Fort in 1846, "The Capt. [Sutter] keeps 600 to 800 Indians in a complete state of Slavery and as I had the mortification of seeing them dine I may give a short description. 10 or 15 Troughs 3 or 4 feet long were brought out of the cook room and seated in the Broiling sun. All the Labourers grate [sic] and small ran to the troughs like so many pigs and fed themselves with their hands as long as the troughs contained even a moisture."

Feeding at those same slave troughs, perhaps, would have been two young men known to history as Luis and Salvator—though trained as skilled horsemen and now serving Sutter as "my good vaqueros." Indeed Indian vaqueros such as Luis and Salvator were actually the historic precursors of Hollywood's familiar white-skinned, white-hatted Wild West cowboys, as evidenced by the Spanish-language origins of so much typical American cowboy lingo, from "lariat" to "rodeo." To put it bluntly, the first true American "cowboys" were California Indian slaves. Somehow that fact was omitted in my grade school history textbooks.

Doubtless the scourge of European plagues had long since factored into Luis and Salvator's displacement from their original homeland. As Greg Sarris, a professor at Sonoma State University and longtime chair of the Federated Indians of Graton Rancheria, reminds us, "In 1838 a smallpox epidemic swept through Miwok and Pomo territories, killing over ninety percent of the remaining Miwok and southern Pomo and over eighty percent of the northern Pomo...Many tribes had only a handful of survivors. Many tribes had none." Long before they were enslaved by Sutter, in short, and long before the Donner Party shot them in the back and cannibalized them, Luis and Salvator were likely numbered among the last survivors of their tribes—the majority long since dead of disease, enforced slavery, or starvation.

All this, you might admit, is of course shocking. But wasn't Indian slavery ended as soon as California entered the United States? As Edward Castillo reminds us, the reality of California statehood for Native peoples was far different:

> Despite entering the Union as a free state in 1850, the California legislature rapidly enacted a series of laws legalizing Indian slavery. One of the laws sanctioned an indenture system similar to Mexican peonage in widespread practice throughout California prior to 1850. All levels of state, county and local governments participated in this ugly practice that evolved into a heartless policy of killing Indian parents and kidnapping and indenturing the victims' children. Indian youth could be enslaved by this cruel act to the age of 30 for males and 25 for females. This barbarous law was finally repealed four years after President Lincoln's emancipation proclamation in 1863.

As Castillo notes, among the very first laws passed by the new state legislature, meeting in the state's new capital of San Jose, was the so-called Act for the Government and Protection of Indians, legitimizing and even expanding the longstanding Spanish and Mexican practice of seizing and trading Indian children as slaves. It took some seventeen years for California to revoke its state laws legalizing Indian slavery.

Why, then, didn't Luis and Salvator attempt to escape from Sutter's control, you might wonder. Here again the truth is grim: Indians who resisted enslavement were simply hunted down or murdered, pure and simple. Indeed the official government-sponsored bounty for Indian scalps remained on the books for the next thirty years. As John McDougall, California's second duly elected governor, bluntly declared in his first address to the new California legislature in 1849, "A war of extermination will continue to be waged between the races until the Indian race becomes extinct."

Ironically, only those Indians who could successfully prove themselves the legal "property" of a white man were shielded from extermination—not because of respect for the sanctity of human life, but because of respect for the sanctity of private property. In effect, you could no more shoot a white landowner's Indian than you could legally shoot his dog. For California's few surviving Native Americans, survival left them with but one choice: give me slavery or give me death.

If you're shaking your head while reading all this, muttering, "I never knew that," you're not alone. That's exactly what I said to myself as I began diving ever deeper into Lake Tahoe's hidden history. In school, I'd always been led to believe that Indian slavery was at best a discredited relic of California's Spanish Mission era (assuming I ever even thought much about Indians at all). I certainly never suspected that Indian slavery had been vastly expanded when California finally fell under United States control. As Margie Powell complains in her 2003 *Donner Summit: A Brief History*, "Tribes are little remembered except for the casinos that they are operating in the foothills today." To her credit, Powell's book goes to great lengths to make the widespread enslavement of Native Americans within the Tahoe/Donner region crystal clear. Yet public ignorance of these facts remains near universal. As a corrective, I sometimes think we should replace the current thirty-foot-tall Donner Party monument with equally enormous statues of Luis and Salvator.

We have, in any case, now assembled sufficient background knowledge about the origins and identities of these two Indians to begin inquiring into the specific circumstances of their murder. As for the Donner Party itself, the specific chain of events leading up to their deaths actually had begun several months earlier, when an advance relief party consisting of just two strong men was sent forward from the main body of wagons as it crossed into present-day Eastern Nevada. The stated goal of this first relief party was to reach Sutter's Fort early and then return immediately with additional supplies—which was exactly what happened, although one of the two rescuers, a family man named William McCutcheon, was initially too ill to make the return journey. Instead, the other rescuer, a young bachelor named Charles Stanton, brought with him two young Indian slaves assigned by Sutter to accompany the mule train laden with emergency supplies: Luis and Salvator.

With their aid, Stanton made the reverse crossing in record time and successfully rejoined the Donner Party at the base of the Eastern Sierra near present-day Wadsworth, Nevada, just as their wagons were finally reaching the Truckee River. With abundant water and additional food, it seemed that their trials were now over. Of a journey of some two thousand miles from Missouri to California, they now had less than one hundred miles left to go. In one of their many fatal errors in judgment, they chose to rest several days in the lush meadows before pushing on toward the Sierra wall. By the time they yoked their teams to press on into the Truckee River Canyon, it was already too late. The brief window of opportunity which might well have let them cross the pass quickly was now slammed shut.

Naturally Stanton—along with Luis and Salvator—did all he could to assist in guiding, pushing, and hauling the heavily loaded wagons over the crest of the Sierra. By October 31 the first group of wagons had reached Truckee Lake (soon to be renamed Donner Lake). With Stanton, Luis, and Salvator all lagging behind to help the slowest wagons, those in the lead now had no guides. With snow falling fast now, they tried pushing forward blindly, only to turn back amid the deepening drifts. By the time Stanton, Luis, and Salvator reached them, a decision had already been made to abandon the wagons for one last desperate rush to the top. Taking the lead, Stanton and one of the two Indians pushed ahead all the way to the summit—but by the time they returned to aid the others, the rest of the main party had already collapsed in exhaustion around a makeshift campfire. This delay, like so many in the coming months, would only seal their doom.

During the night the full brunt of a Sierra blizzard overcame them. With all hope of crossing the pass now erased by the deepening drifts, they retreated instead to Donner Lake, where they built a few crude cabins around the edge. Others in the main party lagged even further behind, camped a few miles down-valley at Alder Creek.

Throughout this whole ordeal Luis and Salvator must have faced endless opportunities to escape. Young, strong, and familiar with the route to safety, they could so easily have fled across the mountains. This was, in fact, precisely the choice made by another group of Indian slaves sent by Sutter to support a second relief effort, this one led by Stanton's partner McCutcheon, who had now recovered his strength. Watching their horses literally disappear up to their noses in snowdrifts, this second group of Indians had wisely fled in the night. McCutcheon and James Reed both turned back the following day, utterly defeated.

For whatever their reasons—perhaps the presence of so many women and children in their group?—Luis and Salvator stuck with the Donner Party to the bitter end. After another eight days of uninterrupted snow, Stanton, Luis, Salvator, and fifteen members of the Donner Party made a second bid to reach the summit. Again they failed. A third attempt another week later failed as well—and Stanton (perhaps stupidly) refused to butcher the mules for meat and press on by foot toward Sutter's Fort. So once again Luis and Salvator floundered back, following Stanton through the drifts to the Donner Lake cabins.

Their supplies of beef now exhausted, starvation gradually began to set in. "Stanton trying to make a raise of some [beef] for his Indian & Self," Patrick Breen wrote in his makeshift diary, concluding grimly that they were "Not likely to get much." With Christmas fast approaching, the Forlorn Hope group made one last attempt on snowshoes to cross the pass. Naturally Stanton, Luis, and Salvator were among them. Snowblind and stumbling, Stanton was the first to die—sitting down by a campfire from which he never stood up. By Christmas Eve, the horrific scene described by Bernard DeVoto in the previously quoted passage unfolded. Although DeVoto fails to mention him, a Mexican laborer known only as Antonio was in fact the first to die that night. Then F. W. Graves, Patrick Dolan, and a boy named Lemuel Murphy followed him. Cutting strips of flesh from Dolan's corpse first, the cannibals began their feast. By the time they left the bivouac, the remaining corpses had all been consumed. To this day it remains uncertain whether Luis and Salvator participated in the feast.

Next came the murders: with supplies of human flesh running low, the survivors began eyeing each other hungrily. Alarmed, Luis and Salvator finally attempted to escape—but too late. As contemporary author Ethan Rarick describes it in his book *Desperate Passage: The Donner Party's Perilous Journey West*, "Finding the two men collapsed and near death…[Foster] shot both men in the head, trying to justify the murders by insisting that the men would have died soon anyway, which might be true." As Rarick is at pains to point out, "The deaths of Luis and Salvador were the only time during the ordeal of the Donner Party that anyone was killed to be eaten." This statement is then followed by a longer, even more sympathetic paragraph acknowledging that "the two Indians, about whom not much is known, probably had little choice but to accompany Stanton on his relief mission, but their courage is not lessened by that fact, and it is indisputable that they helped save the Donner Party before they were killed by one of its members." Yet Foster never faced charges for these murders, nor even rebuke, despite the fact that at least four published accounts at the time described them. Ironically, Rarick's own list of "heroes" at the end of his book fails to list the names of Luis and Salvator.

In a fictional recreation of these nightmarish scenes on page one of his award-winning 1973 novel *Rabbit Boss*, California author Thomas Sanchez imagines what this cannibalistic carnage must have looked like to the bewildered Washoe men who lurked near the edges of the Donner Party's camps, horror-stricken at what they witnessed there. Once hailed as a "landmark of our literature" and an "American epic" comparable in skill and scope to *The Grapes of Wrath*, Sanchez's novel has sadly fallen into obscurity. Yet the opening scene still displays the hypnotic power that helped earn its author the prestigious title of *Chevalier des Arts et des Lettres*, awarded by the French Republic. Who, Sanchez asks, are the true savages here? "The Washo watched through the trees as *they* ate themselves....The body sprawled on the snow, split open, one of *them* standing over it with a hatchet hanging limply in his hand, the thickness of blood dripping slowly from the blade to the snow, each drop silently splashing red into the coldness, lightening into pink as it sought to touch all the flakes with its warmth, its color." In this nightmare world, the act of eating a still-beating human heart comes to symbolize everything about this new, powerful, alien culture which the Washoe observer despises. And it shatters his world beyond repair from that moment forward. Returning to his bride at Big Lake (i.e., Tahoe), the young Washoe tribesman tries desperately to shake the memory of what he has seen from his mind—but cannot. Ours is a culture of cannibalism, Sanchez implies, literally eating itself alive along with all that it touches (including the rapidly vanishing culture of the Washoes themselves).

What kind of fate would Luis and Salvator have faced had they escaped from the Donners successfully—only to witness the onslaught of the California Gold Rush just two years later? One notable answer to this question was penned by a UC Berkeley anthropologist named Robert Heizer, who led the first full-scale archaeological studies of the Lake Tahoe region in the 1950s. Years later, under a fellowship from the Stanford Center for Advanced Studies, Professor Heizer authored a book bluntly entitled *The Destruction of California Indians*. First published in 1971, Heizer's exposé presents extensive press clippings, letters, diaries, and court documents to provide a glimpse into the world of California's Indians in the wake of the great California Gold Rush of 1849.

As the title of his book implies, the historical picture Professor Heizer paints is unbearably grim. While some of the tens of thousands of California Indians who died during the Gold Rush period fell to disease and starvation, Heizer emphasizes, "many of these deaths were the result of simple and direct homicide." Once California had officially become American territory, one might reasonably hope that a chorus of voices would be raised in protest of such wholesale murders and outright massacres. But according to Heizer's groundbreaking research this was seldom, if ever, the case. True, "some humanitarian sympathy for the plight of the innocent California Indians was occasionally voiced by an army officer or a newspaper writer, or a citizen." Yet on the whole, Heizer concludes bluntly, "Californian whites acted as though their survival depended upon the total removal of the 'Indian menace.'"

Only when set against this harsh historical background of public hysteria, Heizer argues, "can we understand the public tolerance of the 1850 California legislative act authorizing indenture of Indians—a thinly disguised substitute for slavery—or the common practice of kidnapping Indian children and women, and openly selling them as servants." For it was during these same Gold Rush years, Heizer further explains, that "Indian men were typically hunted down and shot; while Indian women and children were openly bought and sold as slaves." If all this seems far too gruesome to be believed, recall that virtually one hundred percent of Heizer's evidence dates from original documents openly published during the 1850s and 1860s. There was, at the time, nothing either "lost" or "secret" about the destruction of the California Indians. Instead, bragging about murdering Indians was considered sport. In any event non-whites were barred from giving testimony in a court of law; hence all efforts at prosecution or protection were rendered mute.

Since Lake Tahoe itself had no active gold or silver mines— save for a few phantom strikes near Squaw Valley—you might hope that Lake Tahoe's Washoe tribe somehow escaped the worst of these Gold Rush depredations. Think again. As Tahoe historian Ed Scott angrily retorts, "The general misconception that

Lake Tahoe was a no-man's-land in early California-Nevada history" is simply another myth that begs for correction, "because it lay between the two main arteries of mass migration...five routes in all skirted Tahoe and were used by the [Gold Rush] emigrants." Oddly enough, these five routes did not include Donner Pass: spooked by lurid tales of the Donner Party's cannibalism, white pioneers quickly chose new routes even closer to the shores of Lake Tahoe, such as the so-called "Roller Pass" above present-day Squaw Valley (where covered wagons were literally winched, hauled, and dragged over the steepest solid rock sections by ropes laid over wooden rollers).

Ten years later when the Nevada Silver Boom ignited an equal but opposite mass migration in the other direction, Tahoe again found itself trampled by hordes of voracious fortune seekers. "The Great Bonanza Road to Washoe," Ed Scott explains, "carrying a floodtide of animals, men and materials to the Nevada mines, ran along the lake's southern shore. This turnpike constituted the 'main stem' of the West from 1859 to 1868." To say it once more, the "Main Street of the American West" ran right along the south shore of Lake Tahoe—and hence straight through the heart of the ancient Washoe homeland.

Of course not everyone profited: even Sutter himself died penniless, swindled out of his once vast lands and fortunes by none other than his own son. Just as the chief of a tribe near Sutter's Fort had once warned, gold (like slavery) was "very bad medicine": it belonged to a demon "who devoured all who search for it." For the last one hundred centuries, the California Indians had been wise enough to leave that gold untouched.

Lest you falsely conclude that I consider *all* Western pioneers to be villains, consider for a moment the strange case of the Stephens-Townsend-Murphy Party—a pioneer wagon train group which directly preceded the Donners across what is now Donner Pass two years earlier, in the fall of 1844. Like Frémont, the Stephens Party had been found wandering the desert east of Pyramid Lake by an aging Paiute, and then guided by him to Pyramid

Lake, where they were warmly greeted by Chief Truckee's tribe. But in sharp contrast to the Donner Party, who evinced nothing but hostility and hatred toward the local Native Americans two years later, the Stephens Party emerged from their Pyramid Lake layover fully rested and well-fed, pushing on successfully toward California in late October. That makes the Stephens Party—not the Donner Party—the first wagon train ever to cross the so-called Donner Pass.

So why, then, isn't "Donner Pass" called "Stephens Pass"? For that matter, why isn't Lake Tahoe named "Lake Stephens"—given that the rescue group from the Stephens Party also became the first to reach those shores? Good questions—and ones bitterly asked by old man Stephens himself. As the dean of modern California historians, Kevin Starr, laments, "I've always been fascinated by the fact that the Stephens-Townsend-Murphy Party is almost lost from California history. That great dazzling success, the bringing of those wagons across the Sierra east to west in 1844, arriving with two more people than when you started, no deaths, no major dissensions, in fact a very sophisticated rescue... all that was forgotten under the power, the dystopian power of the Donner Party."

In fact it is the Stephens Party—not John Frémont—who truly deserve the credit for being the first pioneers to touch the sacred waters of Lake Tahoe (whereas Frémont had merely glimpsed it from afar). Trapped in early winter snows, much like the Donners, the youngest, strongest members of the Stephens Party broke away from the main wagon train on horseback, hoping to find a faster route to safety on the far side of the Sierra—only to return from Sutter's Fort with a rescue party. Proceeding rapidly to the headwaters of the Truckee River along well-worn Indian trails, this splinter group—including two young women—soon stumbled right onto the shores of Lake Tahoe, thereby becoming the first non-Indians ever to actually touch the shores of the place the Washoes call Daowaga. Skirting the west shore only briefly, they then turned west to cross the crest of the Tahoe Sierra near present-day Rubicon

Springs—later a popular pioneer wagon route, and one still followed today by four-wheel-drive participants in Tahoe's annual Jeep Jamboree. With two women among their group, the question even arises: could it be that the first white man ever to touch Lake Tahoe was actually a white woman? Let's paint that scene on the side of the History Museum in South Lake Tahoe in place of John Frémont, I say.

Earlier in their journey, two women in the Stephens Party had even managed to give birth to healthy children along the arduous two-thousand-mile route from Council Bluffs, Iowa, to California— in sharp contrast to the multiple murders committed by Donner Party members along the same stretch of trail. Later, members of the Stephens Party went on to become some of California's leading citizens—including the founders of Sunnyvale, Cupertino, and Murphys, as well as California's first state-licensed doctor, who heroically laid down his life, along with that of his wife, while treating victims of a cholera epidemic in San Jose in 1850. Subsequently Dr. Townsend's orphaned son was adopted by Moses Schallenberger, another member of the original Stephens Party, who had once been marooned in a cabin at what is now Donner Lake for months on end, left alone to look after the wagons. Ironically, it was inside Schallenberger's rough-hewn cabin that the Donner Party first took refuge. So perhaps Donner Lake should have been named Lake Schallenberger?

Instead the spectacular success of the Stephens Party was forever eclipsed by the bloody savagery of the Donner Party a few years later. Not until 1994 was a brass plaque in their memory installed at the base of a Tahoe mountain recently rechristened Stephens Peak (as reported by the *San Jose Mercury News*, located on Schallenberger Road). Granted, there is at least one monument to Elisha Stephens in San Jose as well: the perpetually gridlocked Stevens Creek Boulevard, home to the Bay Area's highest concentration of automobile dealerships, making it a great place to shop for a new four-wheel-drive Chevy Tahoe. Alas, San Jose's street signs don't even manage to spell poor old Elisha Stephens's name correctly. Such, apparently, is the price of survival in California—where nothing succeeds like excess.

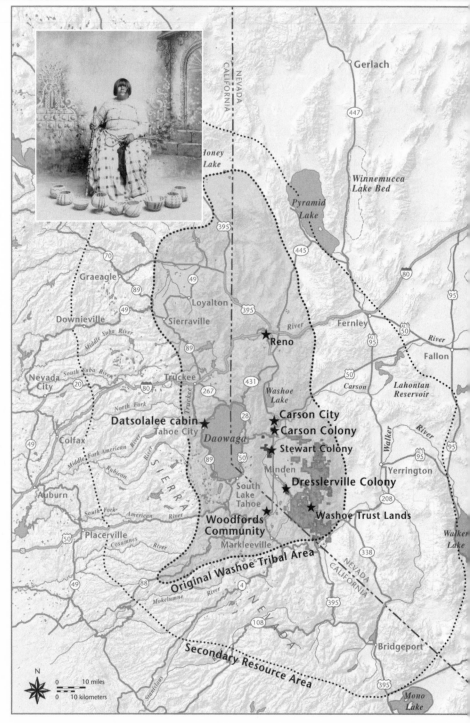

Datsolalee with baskets. Photograph by Abram Cohn, Carson City, Nevada, c. 1899. Courtesy of the Library of Congress, Prints & Photographs Division, LC-USZ62-117637

six

DATSOLALEE

A Washoe Watershed

"What if tomorrow some new people came to America?" asks the plaque in a Washoe Indian exhibit at Lake Tahoe. "What if they took away all our cars, closed our markets and stores, took away our electricity, and made us move naked with no food out of our houses? How many of us would survive and for how long?" Just as that museum plaque implies, something quite similar has befallen Lake Tahoe's Washoe tribe—whose numbers diminished by at least 90 percent during the Gold Rush era. Like Sarah Winnemucca among the Paiutes, no one individual embodies the saga of the Washoe people's survival more gracefully or courageously than Datsolalee, the celebrated basketweaver whose works are still treasured by connoisseurs worldwide, often selling for hundreds of thousands of dollars apiece. Unlike Sarah Winnemucca, however, Datsolalee wove her people's history in willows, not in words.

Women such as Winnemucca and Datsolalee were what Margaret Connell Szasz, a professor of Indian, U.S., and Celtic history at the University of New Mexico, terms "cultural intermediaries" or "culture brokers"—individuals of extraordinary talents and abilities, caught between opposing cultures, who successfully leveraged their knowledge of both in powerfully creative new ways. "Intermediaries became repositories of two or more cultures," Szasz explains; "they changed roles at will, in accordance with circumstances. Of necessity their lives reflected a complexity unknown to those living within the confines of a single culture."

That complexity certainly shapes any discussion of Datsolalee's life during the watershed years of the pioneers' influx into the heart of her Washoe homeland. Like so much of Native American history, however, any honest account of her life must begin with a lengthy catalogue of everything we *do not* know about her. Was she really born in 1829, long before the period of white contact for the Washoe people, as her white sponsors and marketing agents claimed while selling her baskets to wealthy collectors? Or, as seems more likely, was she in fact born decades later, in the 1850s, just as the first great wave of pioneers came flooding through Tahoe territory? Did she receive shamanic inspiration for her unique designs directly from her own dream visions, as she herself is said to have claimed? Or was she instead inspired and influenced in a far more direct and less mysterious way by the popular (and profitable) designs of the Pomo Indian basketweavers, located further west near California's Pacific coast—weavers whose works had already begun to fetch astronomical prices from a growing community of eager white collectors? As an artist, did she feel that her work was adequately rewarded, or was she instead treated as little more than a slave by her promoters?

Then there are the baskets themselves to consider—works of art, hundreds of them. What messages or dreams or emotions or visions, if any, does each basket struggle to contain? What do her designs really "mean"? Or do they mean anything at all? Are the designs and their implications hers alone to decipher, or do they belong to the Washoe people as a whole? Or to all of us together? And what about those evocative titles which her white sponsors attached to each basket they sold? Are such titles representative of Datsolalee's own ideas about these designs, or were they simply fabricated out of thin air to help sell her work to collectors—as one knowledgeable curator in the Nevada State Museum has recently argued?

There are, of course, at least a few facts about Datsolalee's life which we can count on. Regardless of the precise year of her birth, for example, we know that before her marriage at fifteen she would certainly have passed through the Washoes' arduous coming-of-age ceremonies by the shores of Tahoe (culminating with a solo climb of a summit high above Daowaga, the Washoe name for the lake). Because she was raised in a traditional setting, we also know she would have been taught, as all Washoe girls once were, how to gather and weave the wetland willows and ferns so indispensable to the basketmaker's art, gradually mastering the intricate series of stitches and designs which may well reach, at least in memory, as far back as the time of Spirit Cave Man and Wizard's Beach Man.

In traditional Washoe basketry, the function of each basket dictates its design: baskets for cooking acorn mush with hot rocks had to be watertight with an open-mouthed shape; a *keotip* was a pitch-lined water jug; *mayami* were large, open-weave, conical burden baskets for carrying acorns, pine nuts, and other cargo; *modal*, *tababul*, and *singam* were different varieties of winnowing trays, each with a weave and willow rod foundation suitable to separate seeds of a different size or species. The *bickus* was a backboard cradle, made from heavier, rougher, branchlike willow wands, in which a woman, such as Datsolalee herself, might carry her children. Late in life Datsolalee's favorite stitch, regardless of where it was applied, became the tightly spaced "three-rod coil," in which three long willow rods are stacked in a triangular pyramid fashion, allowing each coil to interlock with the next so tightly that the basket becomes virtually watertight and highly durable regardless of its function. As for her most famous and valuable basket designs, such as the gracefully curved *digikup*, these had no basis in traditional Washoe culture whatsoever. Where did her designs really come from? And what do they mean? We will never know.

Then again, what do finicky Western aesthetic distinctions such as "form versus function" mean in the face of the cultural genocide which Washoe women of Datsolalee's generation confronted on a daily basis? Regardless of whether they were ever carried on traditional Washoe woven backboards, for example, both of her children perished from Western-borne diseases unheard of in her grandmother's time. As Datsolalee reached adulthood, the surviving Washoe population had dropped to fewer than a thousand individuals. Their lands usurped, their labor enslaved, and the entire fish-and-forest ecology upon which they once depended under a virtual state of siege, Datsolalee's tribe, much like her family, stood in danger of complete annihilation.

Like most survivors, faced with a stark choice between starvation or servitude, Datsolalee chose servitude, eventually taking work as a household domestic for the Harris Cohn family of Carson City, Nevada, in exchange for basic food and shelter. In this way, as in many others, her life differs little in its basic circumstances from that of Sarah Winnemucca, who as a girl worked as a house-servant in the same town for the Ormsbys. In essence, this distinctively intimate form of Indian slavery was their only viable means of support.

Decades later one of the Cohn children, a boy named Abe, changed the trajectory of Datsolalee's life completely. In the interim Datsolalee herself had remarried, choosing a half-white, half-Washoe man known as Charley Keyser as her second husband. Increasingly unable to bear the burden of heavy housework, she had turned almost in desperation to selling her baskets to survive.

Then lightning struck. One fateful day, as local historian Dixie Westergard writes in her book *Dat-so-la-lee, Washo Indian Basketmaker*, Datsolalee "decided to walk to Carson City and try to sell her work to Harris Cohn's son, Abe, now grown and a successful merchant and businessman." Offering his former maid a few dollars for her handiwork, Cohn was almost immediately able to sell those same baskets to a local collector for twenty-five dollars—a tidy one-thousand-percent profit. Not bad for a day's work, he thought.

Realizing he had a potential gold mine on his hands, Cohn soon offered Datsolalee a modest house with a workroom in which to weave her creations at the back of his family property in Carson City, all in return for the right to sell any baskets she produced there. As usual this was an arrangement perilously close to slavery. For the rest of her life, Cohn kept any and all profits earned from the sale of her basketry. Yet the new arrangement at least provided an aging Datsolalee and her new husband with food, clothing, medicine, and a roof over their heads for life—far more than most Washoes at the time could hope for.

Hence from 1895 until her death three decades later, in 1925, the Washoe elder produced more than three hundred baskets of incomparable intricacy, originality, and beauty—every single one of which the Cohns carefully catalogued, labeled, and sold for ever-more-astronomical prices. A gifted salesman, Cohn may have been the one who changed the weaver's original Washoe name, Dabuda, to the more euphonious-sounding Datsolalee, for the benefit of the tourist trade. Or did Datsolalee herself simply choose her own new nickname? Meanwhile, her legal name, according to official marriage records, was now Louisa Keyser.

In any event, the Cohns' efforts at "branding" Datsolalee and her work did not end with simply giving her a new name. They were also, they gradually realized, selling her life story—presenting her work as a link to the long lost past of the pure Washoe culture as it had existed for so many centuries before white intrusion. Hoping to gain exposure to wealthy collectors, for example, the Cohns took her east by train to do weaving exhibitions; then constructed a small summer cabin for Datsolalee's exclusive use right at the lakeshore in nearby Tahoe City—a cabin preserved to this day on the grounds of the present-day Gatekeeper's Museum. Entering the cabin, curious tourists would donate a few pennies for the privilege of watching Datsolalee at work—a heavyset woman with small, delicate, sensitive hands, weaving new works of art at lightning speed.

By the time of her death in 1925, these works were already fetching thousands of dollars apiece. She had continued to weave throughout the thirty years she worked for the Cohns: it is even rumored that on the day she died, she was working away at the coiled "start" of yet another basket. Refusing to see a Western doctor, she had sought out a traditional Washoe shaman. In this way the girl once known as Dabuda may be said to have died, much as she lived, inside the densely woven circle of traditional Washoe culture.

Today images of Datsolalee remain a popular souvenir item in Tahoe's tourist trinket stores. I've even found Datsolalee staring out at me from gas station postcard racks in Tahoe City. Of course Datsolalee was far from the first, much less the only, great Washoe weaver: many other names deserve to be remembered. Yet for many Tahoe tourists, these faded postcards may be the only reminder of the Washoes' presence in this region they will ever encounter. Hence Datsolalee's baskets, in a very real sense, may be said to contain the entire history of the Washoe people.

I admit that the first time I saw Datsolalee's work for myself, I just didn't get it. If she was trying to tell me something by means of her weaving, I wasn't ready to listen. Not until years later—after I had come to understand the wider story, the Washoe people's history—did I finally return to the various museums where her works are enshrined and find myself both humbled and surprised. For in the final analysis, what astonished me most profoundly about Datsolalee's basketmaking skills were the sagas of her people's suffering and survival woven into every coil.

Recall that as a young girl Datsolalee had become a dream weaver of sorts—the manufacture of "medicine" baskets having long been a cultural practice common to many tribes. At the same time, those willows she wove were gathered directly from the lands and waters of Daowaga itself and nearby Washoe Lake. In a strict sense, then, each basket was both physically and spiritually rooted in a particular place and time in a way which few traditional Western works of art can possibly match.

The complex process of weaving each basket began months before the first stitch was taken. Each spring, Datsolalee and other weavers would begin by gathering a particular species of willow known to the Washoes as *hemu*. No other type of willow would do. Once she had gathered it and separated it into individual branches, she would run a thumbnail under the bark of each new so-called "wand," carefully choosing only the best and most pliant branches, to avoid any imperfections. Today's *hemu*, Washoe weavers lament, is relative sickly and poisoned by agricultural toxins and hence good materials are hard to find. By contrast, the wetlands of Datsolalee's day remained relatively undamaged—"she had better stuff to work with than we do," an accomplished contemporary Washoe weaver once told me.

Once sufficient *hemu* had been gathered, she would split each wand into three equal parts, using mouth, teeth, and hands and cleaning out the inner core to reveal the flexible inner woody layer. Finally, after laboriously scraping and shaping each wand into a smooth, perfectly rounded little rod, she would roll them into coils or stacks or bundles to be stored for the coming season, placed carefully in the cooling shade to prevent their characteristic white sheen from fading. Then she would use the willow in her baskets, as well as redbud and black fern root soaked in mud to bring out their deep hidden hues, singing to herself as she wove her patterns day in, day out, all the year long.

Once at the Tahoe Forest Stewardship Day at Meeks Bay—an annual event cosponsored by the Washoe Tribe of Nevada and California—a Washoe language teacher named Mabel Rakow let me hold some of her family's baskets, handed down to her through several generations. The lightness and solidity of these baskets stunned me. "These baskets have to be soaked in lake water each year," she explained proudly, "to keep them young."

Gradually, under Datsolalee's hands, these same traditional designs began mysteriously shape-shifting, no two the same. Often she claimed to be able to "see" a design in dreams long before the first coil was ever laid. In effect, she had to foresee them in her mind's eye to weave them at all. For each new pattern had to be fitted and adjusted in advance to flow ever so evenly across the smooth face of the basket itself, with that perfect symmetry and unvarying texture which has long helped to make Datsolalee's work world-famous.

That meant each basket took weeks, sometimes months, of patient, painstaking effort. Each one also required thousands of individual stitches. According to Westergard, "The usual count in a basket was thirty-six stitches to the inch." In effect, that meant that tens of thousands of stitches had to be completed in the rows upon rows that made up each piece. In one especially large basket, Westergard estimates that there are some 56,590 separate stitches.

On the certificate of authenticity that the Cohns attached to every new creation, each basket was also given a unique name. But was this a name bestowed on her basket by Datsolalee herself, or by the Cohns? Here as so often in Native American studies, the answer remains uncertain. Abe Cohn's wife, Amy, seems to have struck up a deep friendship with this woman now best known to us as Datsolalee. Indeed it is to Amy Cohn, far more than to her husband, that we owe what little we actually know (and much that we don't) about Datsolalee's life, art, and inspiration. Assigning names to the baskets might have been a mere marketing gimmick, yet each name is genuinely evocative, leading me to wonder if perhaps Amy Cohn, in her conversations with Datsolalee, really did attempt to capture some of the essence of the artist's own intent in assigning each piece a title. We will never know. Hence names like "Myriads of Stars Shine o'er the Graves of Our Ancestors" might easily be the sole inventions of Amy Cohn, nothing more. But they also might embody some echo of Datsolalee's own artistic dreams and visions.

Regardless of who invented these names, they helped to open up my own eyes wide to other aspects of Datsolalee's willowy wizardry. Strange as it sounds to say it now, I actually began to sense something like joy, trapped like light, within the heart of each new basket, with the living memory of an entire culture woven into its design.

Granted, baskets such as "Myriads of Stars Shine o'er the Graves of Our Ancestors" must certainly contain much of sorrow and suffering as well—even in their titles. But could they not also hold much of joy and memory locked within their coils? At times, it seems almost as if such baskets were purpose-designed to contain either of two sets of conflicting emotions, much as traditional Washoe baskets were designed to hold food and water.

Another famous basket is titled "Hunting Game of Air in Sunshine"—this last a work of pure light and shadow. Completed when Datsolalee was reputed to be ninety-five years old, near death, almost blind, and in deep pain, the basket somehow embodies the ache of absence and the fullness of survival. Given the life history of the woman who wove it, how could it not?

Other baskets may well bear witness to this same hunger of memory, such as the multipatterned converging triangular shapes of "Our Ancestors Were Hunters"; or the incomparable shimmering, swirling patterns in "With Aid of Medicine Men's Magic Arrowpoints Abundance of Game Was Slain." Much like their titles, each of these works is unique. Hence a basket titled "The Fledglings" evokes another mood altogether: here Datsolalee's characteristic interlocking diamond-and-arrowhead patterns are laddered in an ascending pattern of rising flight.

Regardless of their authenticity, the titles—like the baskets themselves—deliberately evoke memories of the time before contact, when the Washoes still practiced their ancient lifeways unimpeded. If we can trust the date ascribed by the Cohns to Datsolalee's own birth, 1829, then she would indeed have been born prior to any known contact between her tribe and white outsiders. Not until 1827 did the legendary American mountain man Jedediah Smith travel from the Great Salt Lake to San Gabriel Mission by way of Tioga Pass—thereby becoming the first white man to have crossed the Sierra. Once Smith was there, the Mexican governor promptly ordered him to turn around and go back by means of the same route he had followed. Instead he headed north with his band of trappers, traveling up the San Joaquin Valley, searching for beavers and a route over the mountains. After some futile attempts on the Kings and American rivers, he finally was able to follow the Stanislaus River over the main crest of the Sierra, not far from present-day Ebbetts Pass. But this was still far south of Washoe territory proper.

One year later, in 1828, British Hudson Bay explorer and trapper Peter Skene Ogden worked his way south from the Snake River into the Humboldt Sink, passed Walker Lake, and followed the Carson River into Southern California, passing directly through Washoe territory in 1829, just as Datsolalee herself was coming into the world. By 1833, when Datsolalee was four years old, Old Joe Walker had led a party of beaver trappers into Central and Western Nevada, massacring dozens of Indians in cold blood at several different sites in unprovoked murders. Then he crossed the Sierra, probably at Tioga Pass, on a military spy expedition into Mexican territory, "discovering" Yosemite and the *Sequoia gigantea* groves en route to Yerba Buena (present-day San Francisco), Santa Clara, and Monterey. Refusing to follow the instructions of Mexican governors who detained him near Los Angeles and insisted he return immediately across the Mojave, Walker instead crossed the mountains via present-day Walker Pass, in the southern Sierra.

In 1844, when Datsolalee would have reached the age of marriage, Frémont made his first winter crossing of the Sierra, the first white man to come within sight of Lake Tahoe, the living heart of Washoe territory. From that point forward the floodgates of America's westward expansion were thrown wide open—with the Washoe tribe directly in its path. By 1849 Datsolalee would have reached her twentieth birthday, just as the new state of California made Indian slavery legal, setting out on a government-sponsored campaign of complete Indian extermination. Notwithstanding their reputation as a relatively peace-loving tribe, the Washoes

fought back bravely against these aggressions, making countless efforts to defend their ancient homeland—just as they had
resisted the incursions of other Indian tribes for centuries. But
faced with overwhelming odds, their efforts—like those of their
Paiute neighbors—were doomed to failure. "In the spring of
1854," reports Tahoe historian E. B. Scott, "the [Washoe] Indians would not allow white men to fish in the lake." When "they
tried to drive me off," reported one Tahoe pioneer by the name of
Asa Hawley, "I was not afraid of Indians, except their treachery. I
consider all Indians to be treacherous and think the government
ought to deal with them with a firm and steady hand." Which is
exactly what happened. Somehow Datsolalee and a handful of
survivors clung to their ancient lands—and their ancient lifeways.
As late as the 1890s, as E. B. Scott reports, "the upper Truckee
River, where whitefish abounded, was still a favorite fishing stream
for the Washoe Indian and white man alike." According to Scott,
Washoes of the 1890s even "continued their age-old practice of
whisking the tops off sunflowers in [Squaw] valley, gathering the
seed and grinding them into flour." That's precisely why the present-day name of Tahoe's most famous ski area is Squaw Valley—a
title which many Washoes still consider offensive. It's hard in this
context to imagine modern skiers flocking to a ski area named
"Chink Meadows" or "Nigger Valley"—or mocking any efforts to
have the name changed.

As the Squaw Valley example helps make clear, however, in
the final analysis it was tourism and timber—not terrorism—that
ultimately robbed the Washoe of the very last shreds of their tribal
lands at Tahoe. From the 1870s forward, Lucky Baldwin and other
legendary Tahoe entrepreneurs had built lavish hotels directly on
top of the few remaining tribal hunting and fishing grounds still
left under marginal Washoe control. From the perspective of these
white investors, this "open land" was simply there for the taking.
From the Washoes' perspective, these same lands were their last
best hope for survival. When Baldwin first acquired legal title to
the Taylor Creek meadows on the south shore of Lake Tahoe in

the 1890s, for example, "An uprising was narrowly averted when friendly tribesmen from the nearby Washoe encampment were forbidden to spear and net trout in streams flowing to the lake." By 1895 a now-heavyset sixty-five-year-old Washoe woman named Datsolalee had begun selling her baskets to a man in Carson City named Abe Cohn.

Baldwin's hotel became synonymous with an era of lavish abundance. For the Washoes, however, that same hotel spelled literal starvation. Bereft of their traditional food sources, by the turn of the twentieth century fewer than three hundred Washoes remained alive—most of them living on a forty-acre piece of nearly worthless desert land just south of Carson City.

How many Washoes inhabited the wider Tahoe region when Datsolalee was first born? Here, as so often, a fierce scholarly debate is still being waged, this one over Indian graves. Depending on which sources you choose to trust, estimates of the Washoe tribe's original size now range from a low of three thousand individuals to a high of thirty thousand. But even if you choose the lowest estimate, that would mean that the population of the Washoe tribe declined *by at least 90 percent* during Datsolalee's lifetime. Choose the higher estimate and the death rates reach 99 percent. Most of California's Indian tribes suffered a similar fate. Indeed dozens of tribes died out altogether—including the tribal band to which Ishi, the "last wild Indian in California" according to Theodora Kroeber, had belonged. And all this happened with frightening speed. "The handiwork of these well-armed death squads," concludes Professor Edward Castillo bitterly, "combined with the widespread random killing of Indians by individual miners, resulted in the death of 100,000 Indians in the first two years of the gold rush. A staggering loss of two thirds of the population. Nothing in American Indian history is even remotely comparable to this massive orgy of theft and mass murder. Stunned survivors now perhaps numbering fewer than 70,000 teetered on the brink of total annihilation."

From this utter low point in their ten-thousand-year history, the Washoe tribe made one last desperate plea for mercy, directly to U.S. President Grover Cleveland. In a chilling and cursory response, Cleveland wrote: "There is no suitable place for a reservation within the bounds of their territory, and, in view of their rapidly diminishing numbers, and the diseases to which they are subjected, none is required."

Bereft of any formal treaties, lacking official tribal status, and denied citizenship, many Washoes (like the Paiutes) nonetheless volunteered to fight in the trenches of World War I. Shortly before the war's end, in 1917, when the Washoe elder now known to the world as Datsolalee would have been eighty-eight years old, a local rancher named Dressler willed the tribe forty acres to serve as a home for the few starving survivors. Still known as Dresslerville, it remains the seat of Washoe tribal government today.

By 1924, when the famous American photographer Edward Curtis passed through the region to record the fading traces of Washoe and Paiute culture in the Tahoe region on film, he carefully photographed Datsolalee sitting amid her many baskets. Now ninety-five, she would be dead the following year.

Today the Washoe tribe does not directly control a single acre of land along the shores of Lake Tahoe—although certain federal and state government agencies have recently granted them at least some limited access based on "leases" (easily revoked) at Meeks Bay. Outside the Tahoe Basin, some former Washoe lands were eventually returned to direct tribal control. In 1934, the Federal Indian Reorganization Act allowed the Washoe to reacquire 755 acres in their sacred Pine Nut Mountains, east of Dresslerville—the source of the pine nuts they had offered to Frémont as a token of friendship ninety years earlier, in 1844. By then, of course, most of the old-growth trees had been chopped down.

Finally, in 1970—nearly twenty years after their original claim, was filed with the newly created federal Indian Claims Commission—the Washoe tribe's claim was settled for a paltry $5 million, averaging approximately $2.24 per acre.

"Was this a fair exchange for this, our ancient territory?" So asks an anonymous speaker on a plaque in a local museum. Consider that Tahoe lakeside real estate now routinely sells for at least one million dollars per acre. Speaking to anthropology professor Warren d'Azevedo in the 1950s, one Washoe elder summarized the whole sordid history of native claims cases in California over the last century this way:

> That Claims Case says they going to give the Washoes a couple of bits an acre for this territory....Well, I tell you what I think about that. If we sell our country this way, we is finished....My idea is this. We don't take any money from the government on this case. When they get around to settling with us, we don't settle. We say, "You ain't got enough. How can you pay enough money for what you took? How can you pay for what is gone...all the silver and gold in them mountains...all the trees that used to cover these here hills and valleys...all that fine long grass used to be along the water...all them different animals used to come around these places? How you going to put back them big trout up at Tahoe? Our old folks could reach right in and catch them with their bare hands. They's gone now. You whites came and fished them all out and shipped them down to Sacramento and all over. When them old Indians come up there like they been doing since the beginning of the world, well the whites took shots at them. There weren't even no place for Indians to camp up there. White people didn't want no Indians around there unless they was working for some white man. It still like that right to this day. You don't see no Indians camping up there. There ain't no place for Indians...just them white tourists."

Granted, you won't usually hear the Washoes' story told quite this way—or find Datsolalee's life story woven quite so deeply into the story of the lake itself. Instead her baskets have become disembodied aesthetic objects—what Professor Greg Sarris has bitterly called "a culture under glass." Often the glass itself is badly distorted.

Yet it's only when set against just such a background of disasters and distortions, I would argue, that the deeper meaning, perhaps even the magic, of Datsolalee's artistry itself can be understood. Much like the other "cultural intermediaries" and "culture brokers" in American history, Datsolalee consciously leveraged her position between the Indian and white worlds to create unique works of art that literally weave her people's lost history back into white history. These are memory baskets. That is their function. History itself is what they contain.

As noted, contemporary Washoe weavers I have spoken with often complain that the reeds and willows they need for weaving have noticeably withered and stiffened as the wetlands of the Tahoe watershed have been rapidly drained, drenched with pesticides, and invaded by non-native species. In this sense every one of her baskets—and theirs—speaks volumes about the health of the wider, wilder world from which it was first woven, not unlike those ten-thousand-year-old woven mats in which Spirit Cave Man's corpse was first interred.

Individual memories unravel. So do individual words. Caught up in a complex dynamic of language, landscape, and culture, the We Mel Ti, the Hung A Lel Ti, and the Pau Wa Lu clans together comprise what we have much later come to think of, at least in English, as "the Washoe tribe." Yet even our English word "Washoe" itself is a deeply misleading misnomer: a mispronounced, mangled label fashioned by local white settlers (and later adopted by white anthropologists) to help categorize (and control?) the complex welter of interlocking microcultures and microclimates which the Washoe people as a whole once inhabited. According to most contemporary Washoe tribal members, the word "Washoe" actually means "one person." Hence "Washoe tribe" must sound, to native speakers, something like "The One-Person People." In their own language, the Washoes call themselves Wa She Shu—roughly translated, "The People from This Place." Or to quote another ancient language, *E Pluribus Unum*.

Similarly, our English word "Tahoe" must sound, from an indigenous perspective, so terribly lonely, even faintly loony in a sad and frightening way: like a shortened, squashed, and tragically misunderstood version of their own word for this great sacred Washoe watershed: Daowaga. Somehow the first two original Washoe syllables, *"Da ow,"* were morphed and mashed into "Tahoe," the name by which we know (or think we know) the Washoe watershed.

But what happens to a place (or to a nation?) when ancient words and histories are hacked up and even amputated in such a mindless way? Today, for example, the Washoe word "Daowaga" is most frequently translated by Washoe speakers themselves as meaning something like "the shores of the lake": the truth is that the Washoe people themselves had no separate word, no separate concept, for the lake itself apart from the lands and lives and legends of the shores which contain and surround it. Within the indigenous Washoe worldview, it was inconceivable, literally *unspeakable*, to think of the lake as something separate, something severed and set apart.

It is only the newcomers, with awkward English terminology and a seemingly infallible "scientific worldview," who keep insisting somewhat insanely on speaking of Daowaga as if it were a limb ripped from a wounded animal: something alone and deeply disconnected; something separate and distinct from the mountains, the forests, the sky, and all the sounds and songs and stories and spirits pouring into and out of and around it. A being inseparable, in short, from the people who first lived here. Indistinguishable, also, from the sustaining forces of water, stone, wind, fire, and soil, and the storylines, songlines, human breath, and bloodlines that Native people and newcomers alike bring to this place; all of which, tangled up together, make up a kind of shared body of knowledge; a shared history; a shared destiny; a shared shadow of destiny and desire. "Whatever happens to Daowaga," the Washoe elders caution, "will eventually happen to us all." This, then, is the message Datsolalee wove into her baskets; the pattern, the wisdom, and the warning they still struggle to contain and convey.

Mark Twain, center, with George Alfred Townsend on his right and David Gray on his left, February 7, 1871. Photographer unknown. Courtesy of the Library of Congress, Prints & Photographs Division, LC-DIG-cwpbh-04761

seven

SAMUEL CLEMENS

Tahoe Twain

Tahoe invented Mark Twain—but nearly killed Sam Clemens. During his three tumultuous years in Tahoe territory, from 1861 to 1864, the unknown young Confederate army deserter originally named Samuel Clemens adopted the pen name which later made him world-famous: Mark Twain. During those same years, Twain also acquired legal title to two separate Lake Tahoe properties, repeatedly promising to move his whole family out from Hannibal, Missouri, to live by the Lake of the Sky. Yet by the end of his time in Tahoe territory, Twain had so completely destroyed his own career that he literally fled the region in fear for his life, all based on a bizarre hoax involving the incendiary (and racist) word "miscegenation."

Simultaneously, the name of the lake previously known as "Bigler" was changed to "Lake Tahoe"—a name Twain claimed to hate with a passion. Why? Hidden beneath the surface of these two seemingly unrelated linguistic moments is a radical shift in Clemens/Twain's own evolution as an author—a transformation reaching all the way back to his boyhood in Missouri, and all the way forward to the publication of *Huckleberry Finn* in 1884 (arguably the greatest of all American novels).

To his legions of loyal fans, the basic outlines of Twain's Tahoe transformation may well seem familiar: flat broke and desperate for a job (any job), in 1862 young Sam Clemens reluctantly took a reporter's position on the fledgling Nevada *Territorial Enterprise*—for the lavish salary of ten bucks per week. This was, he admitted bitterly, a considerable step down from the ten million dollars he claimed to have found (and lost) as a luckless Nevada silver miner just a few short weeks before. Perhaps to assuage his own flaming sense of failure, in early February of 1863 (six months before his second trip to Tahoe) he suddenly began signing his Virginia City columns with the moniker "Mark Twain": a pen name that deliberately hearkened back to his previous successful career as a Mississippi riverboat pilot. Within mere months the name "Mark Twain"—and the whole new comic persona that went with it—were being hailed as far away as San Francisco. Within a decade he had become the most famous writer in America, known the world over. "I am not *an* American," Twain himself once quipped near the end of his life. "I am *the* American."

Today Mark Twain remains perhaps the best-known American author of all time. And the best-known Tahoe author too. So ubiquitous is his white-suited ghost that one Tahoe-area gas station even features a life-sized plaster replica of Twain—mustache bristling, cigar in hand—puffing away in front of their pumps. There's also a wonderful white-haired, white-suited Mark Twain impersonator who performs aboard Tahoe's floating riverboat replica, the *Tahoe Queen*. Several times daily tourists ply the placid waters of Lake Tahoe in this unlikely replica of a Mississippi side-wheeler, as if the crystal waters of Lake Tahoe magically flowed straight into Old Muddy.

As perhaps they do: for two crucial questions about Twain's "Tahoe years" are still fiercely debated by the legions of Twain scholars (including myself) who make a comfortable living discussing his works—mysteries which remain largely unexplained right down to this day: First, what surging psychological forces first triggered his sudden transformation from Sam Clemens to Mark Twain in 1863? Second, what equally mysterious inner forces triggered Twain's bizarre self-destructive spiral just a few short months later, in 1864, very nearly ending his career forever, and just as nearly ending in murder, death, or suicide?

As a self-declared "Tahologist" I will add a third enigma to the mix: what, if anything, do Twain's inner transformations have to do with the fierce Civil War debates raging at Lake Tahoe (and all across America) during those same three years? To put it bluntly, was Mark Twain still a closet Confederate sympathizer during his time at Lake Tahoe? In his youth, was the man who would later become America's greatest antiracist author an unrepentant racist? What secrets do Twain's Tahoe years both conceal and reveal?

Be forewarned: in terms of Twain scholarship, we are entering uncharted waters here. According to one recent issue of *The New Yorker*, there have been more than forty Twain biographies, with at least three in the past five years. Yet somehow the pivotal importance of Twain's evolving stance toward the Civil War—and toward Lake Tahoe along with it—seems to have been overlooked by most of these biographers entirely. Certainly chronology ought to provide one clue: the Civil War years, 1861 to 1864, also mark the *exact* period of Twain's numerous trips to Lake Tahoe.

It's a long story. A dozen years before Twain first set eyes on Lake Tahoe, the California Gold Rush had already decisively influenced his future career as a writer. As soon as news of the strike at Sutter's Mill first arrived in Missouri, more than 5 percent of the entire population of Hannibal immediately sold everything they owned, pulled up stakes, and headed West to seek their fortunes. Many of them crossed the Sierra using one of the four major routes that passed directly through Tahoe territory.

Only fifteen years old in 1849, Sam Clemens was deemed too young to Go West. That particular chapter of his life would come later. But among those who did leave town in 1849 was the former owner and publisher of Hannibal's leading local newspaper. Taking advantage of this man's eagerness to sell, Sam's older brother Orion bought the *Hannibal Western Union* at a fire-sale price, determined to enter the newspaper business himself. Renaming his little rag the *Hannibal Journal*, Orion quickly put his teenaged brother Sam to work as a typesetter. Eventually Sam slipped in a few humorous articles of his own—safely disguised under the first of many pseudonyms. So began a writing career that would span the next six decades.

By 1861 the outbreak of the Civil War had brought Sam's second career, as a prestigious Mississippi riverboat pilot, to a sudden and violent end. The window glass of his side-wheeler's pilothouse shattered by Union gunfire, Clemens reluctantly admitted that his fanciful *Life on the Mississippi* was finished forever. And so it was—except in print.

But where to turn next? Although Orion Clemens had long been a staunch abolitionist, most of Sam Clemens's boyhood friends were still fiercely loyal to the Confederate cause. His family literally torn in twain by the growing national conflict, Sam initially joined the local Confederate militia. Fortunately for the future of American literature, he was no soldier. After a few muddy, discouraging weeks of drilling, marching, and swatting flies, Clemens was ready to do almost anything to escape the oncoming war—including swapping sides in the conflict and throwing in his lot with Orion, a fiercely pro-Union Lincoln sympathizer.

For as fate would have it, Orion's pro-Union newspaper editorials had already landed him a plum political patronage job as secretary to the newly appointed Republican governor of Nevada Territory (all courtesy of the newly elected Republican president, Abraham Lincoln). There was just one catch: Orion had no money. Flush with cash from his riverboat pilot days, Orion's younger brother Sam gamely offered to lend him enough money for a stagecoach ticket to Nevada—as long as Sam Clemens himself could tag along for the ride.

So began the unlikely journey that culminated in Mark Twain's first book, *Roughing It*, published ten years later, in 1871. As we shall soon see, what happened in those pages has everything to do with Lake Tahoe—or rather with Lake Bigler, as the lake had been renamed when Sam and Orion first arrived in nearby Carson City.

By September of 1861, with the Civil War now raging full-force back east, the Clemens brothers had descended from the door of their stagecoach in Western Nevada, two thousand miles from Missouri—and even farther from those bloody new battlefields. Having escaped the war, Sam was now itching to escape from his brother. And having heard that stands of virgin timber surrounded a huge lake high in the mountains not more than ten miles away, Clemens and his new friend John Kinney now set out to find it. Their goal: to stake out a timber claim by the shores of the lake and earn an easy fortune selling lumber. As Clemens himself later recalled in *Roughing It*:

> I had nothing to do and no salary. I was private Secretary to his majesty the Secretary and there was not yet writing enough for two of us....We heard a world of talk about the marvelous beauty of Lake Tahoe, and finally curiosity drove us thither to see it. Three or four members of the Brigade [a group of Clemens's young rowdy Southern-born friends] had been there and located some timber lands on its shores and stored up a quantity of provisions in their camp. We strapped a couple of blankets on our shoulders and took an axe apiece and started—for we intended to take up a wood ranch or so ourselves and become wealthy.

But first he and Kinney had to find this lake. Lacking money for horses or mules, the two would-be explorers soon set out on foot. "We tramped a long time on level ground and then toiled laboriously up a mountain about a thousand miles high and looked over. No lake there," Twain recalled dryly. Next they "toiled up another mountain three or four thousand miles high, apparently, and looked over again. No lake yet."

What follows in *Roughing It* are some of the most moving descriptions of Lake Tahoe ever penned. For despite Twain's worldwide reputation as a humorist, he had an equal—if often less appreciated—ability to paint the textures of a natural landscape in words. Today we associate that power with his nostalgic memoir *Life on the Mississippi*; not to mention certain haunting, fogshrouded, mud-soaked chapters of *Huckleberry Finn*. But that same gift for evocative nature writing received an early airing right here at Lake Tahoe. In Twain's own words:

> The lake burst upon us—a noble sheet of blue water lifted six thousand three hundred feet above the level of the sea, and walled in by a rim of snow-clad mountain peaks that towered aloft full three thousand feet higher still! It was a vast oval, and one would have to use up eighty or a hundred good miles in traveling around it. As it lay there with the shadows of the mountains brilliantly photographed upon its still surface, I thought it must surely be the fairest picture the whole earth affords.

Anticipating generations of Tahoe tourists to come, Twain even praised the lake for its health-giving climate—as well as for what he saw as its as-yet-unspoiled natural beauty. "There is no end of wholesome medicine in such an experience," he wrote. "The air up there in the clouds is very pure and fine, bracing and delicious. And why shouldn't it be?—it is the same the angels breathe."

Most astonishing of all, especially for a mud-soaked former Mississippi riverboat pilot, was the "marvelous transparency" of Lake Tahoe's waters. Stealing an "abandoned" Indian canoe they found alongshore, the two friends spent the next few days exploring the shore—wrapped in a bright haze of pure boyish joy, and feeling as if they were literally flying across the surface of the water:

So singularly clear was the water, that where it was only twenty or thirty feet deep the bottom was so perfectly distinct that the boat seemed floating in the air....Down through the transparency of these great depths, the water not *merely* transparent, but dazzlingly, brilliantly so. All objects seen through it had a bright, strong vividness, not only of outline, but of every minute detail, which they would not have had when seen simply through the same depth of atmosphere. So empty and airy did all spaces seem below us, and so strong was the sense of floating high aloft in mid-nothingness, that we called these boat-excursions "balloon-voyages."

Soon the two friends located a fine stand of tall yellow pine and proceeded to stake their claim, constructing a makeshift fence and shelter in accordance with the minimum requirements for establishing legal title at that time. Then (much like Huck and Jim floating down the Mississippi) they built themselves a raft to sleep on— puffing away at their pipes, swapping stories, and continuing their Tahoe "balloon-voyages" for dreamy autumn days on end.

The lake itself seemed all but deserted: "Three miles away was a saw-mill and some workmen, but there were not fifteen other human beings throughout the wide circumference of the lake," he exulted. Following the outbreak of open warfare at Pyramid Lake between whites and Paiutes in 1860, just one year earlier, had the Washoes taken refuge elsewhere that autumn? In their absence, whoever managed to stake their claim on Lake Tahoe's "deserted shores," it seemed, would soon strike it rich forever—albeit at the Washoe tribe's expense.

To seal their claim, Clemens and Kinney soon filed a legal deed in Carson City under the names of Samuel L. Clemens, William A. Moffett (Sam's sister's fiancé back in Missouri), Thomas Nye (the new Nevada governor's nephew), and John Kinney. According to Margaret Sanborn's *Mark Twain: The Bachelor Years*, the men christened their claim "Sam Clemens Bay."

Today, of course, there is no Sam Clemens Bay on any map of Lake Tahoe. Instead Twain's dreams of riches literally went up in flames—as we'll soon see in detail. Yet for the rest of his life, Clemens used the spectacular landscape of Lake Tahoe as a kind of yardstick for sheer natural beauty of any kind, anywhere on Earth. "It throws Como in the shade," he bragged of Tahoe in letters he mailed home from Europe, unfavorably comparing the most famous lake in the Italian Alps to the crystalline beauties of Lake Tahoe. In his second book, *Innocents Abroad,* Twain even compared Tahoe to the Holy Land. "The celebrated Sea of Galilee is not so large a sea as Lake Tahoe," Twain rhapsodizes. "I measure all lakes by Tahoe," he then exclaims in a footnote, "partly because I am far more familiar with it than with any other, and partly because I have such a high admiration for it and such a world of pleasant recollections of it, that it is very nearly impossible for me to speak of lakes and not mention it." At times he scarcely seems able to pen a plausible description of the Sea of Galilee at all—eclipsed as it is by his sheer nostalgia for Lake Tahoe:

And when we come to speak of beauty, this sea [of Galilee] is no more to be compared to Tahoe than a meridian of longitude is to a rainbow. The dim waters of this pool can not suggest the limpid brilliancy of Tahoe; these low, shaven, yellow hillocks of rocks and sand, so devoid of perspective, can not suggest the grand peaks that compass Tahoe like a wall, and whose ribbed and chasmed fronts are clad with stately pines that seem to grow small and smaller as they climb, till one might fancy them reduced to weeds and shrubs far upward, where they join the everlasting snows. Silence and solitude brood over Tahoe; and silence and solitude brood also over this lake of Genessaret. But the solitude of the one is as cheerful and fascinating as the solitude of the other is dismal and repellant.

After this paean to Tahoe, Twain pours out his heart once again, in an equally heartfelt lament for the lake he once loved (and lost). Easily among the most beautiful lines ever written about Lake Tahoe, Twain's words are well worth savoring—especially since they show Twain himself in a gentler light:

In the early morning, one watches the silent battle of dawn and darkness upon the waters of Tahoe with a placid interest; but when the shadows sulk away and one by one the hidden beauties of the shore unfold themselves in the full splendor of noon; when the still surface is belted like a rainbow with broad bars of blue and green and white, half the distance from circumference to centre; when, in the lazy summer afternoon, he lies in a boat, far out to where the dead blue of the deep water begins, and smokes the pipe of peace and idly winks at the distant crags and patches of snow from under his cap-brim; when the boat drifts shoreward to the white water, and he lolls over the gunwale and gazes by the hour down through the crystal depths and notes the colors of the pebbles and reviews the finny armies gliding in procession a hundred feet below; when at night he sees moon and stars, mountain ridges feathered with pines, jutting white capes, bold promontories, grand sweeps of rugged scenery topped with bald, glimmering peaks, all magnificently pictured in the polished mirror of the lake, in richest, softest detail, the tranquil interest that was born with the morning deepens and deepens, by sure degrees, till it culminates at last in resistless fascination!

Twain's own "holy land," it seems, is Lake Tahoe. Similarly Twain's Tahoe descriptions of life on a raft in *Roughing It* clearly foreshadow his subsequent, far more famous descriptions of life on a raft on the Mississippi River in *Huckleberry Finn*. No, I don't mean to suggest that Twain's 1861 Tahoe balloon-voyages were some kind of conscious dress rehearsal for *Huckleberry Finn*, written more than twenty years later. That would be quite a "stretcher," as Huck himself might say. But I do want to suggest that Twain's Tahoe idylls helped set the emotional tone for the great works to come.

Set their pages down side by side, and Twain's balloon-voyages compare favorably with certain passages from *Huckleberry Finn*. In *Roughing It*, for example, Twain muses, "If there is any life that is happier than the life we led on our timber ranch for the next two or three weeks, it must be a sort of life which I have not read of in books or experienced in person. We did not see a human being but ourselves during the time, or hear any sounds but those that were made by the wind and the waves, the sighing of the pines, and now and then the far-off thunder of an avalanche." By contrast, here's Huck's version of life on a raft: "It's lovely to live on a raft. We had the sky up there, all speckled with stars, and we used to lay on our backs and look up at them, and discuss about whether they was made or only just happened....We said there warn't no home like a raft, after all. Other places do seem so cramped up and smothery, but a raft don't." Viewed in the harsh light of day, of course, the two landscapes could never seem so similar. But in the hazy nostalgia of Mark Twain's memories, maybe Tahoe's waters really did mingle with Old Muddy's after all.

For better or worse, however, both floating odysseys ultimately end with the death of freedom. Huck's friend Jim, an escaped slave, is ultimately returned to his "rightful" owner, while Huck himself can only dream of "lighting out for the territories" someday. For Clemens and Kinney, catastrophe strikes. Returning to their Tahoe timber camp one evening, Sam lights a campfire, turns his back to retrieve a frying pan, and finds that his campfire's sparks have ignited a massive forest fire. In horror the two friends watch stupefied as their entire timber ranch goes up in flames. So quickly does the wildfire spread, in fact, that Sam's friend Johnny has to run directly through the flames to reach the safety of the lake. Soot-faced and smoke-choked, they struggle onto their little homemade raft. Observing the whole conflagration from a safe distance offshore, here's how Clemens remembered the scene in *Roughing It*:

I took a loaf of bread, some slices of bacon, and the coffee-pot ashore, set them down by a tree, lit a fire, and went back to the boat to get the frying-pan. While I was at this, I heard a shout from Johnny, and looking up I saw that my fire was galloping all over the premises! Johnny…had to run through the flames to get to the lake shore, and then we stood helpless and watched the devastation.…Within half an hour all before us was a tossing, blinding tempest of flame!

Now, here's an even stranger point to ponder: in a letter to his mother describing the fire's "devastation," Twain constantly chooses military metaphors to describe the towering flames. Time and again the lake's moods seem to mirror Clemens's own—a "fiery mirror" of fear, loss, shame, and anger. And why not? He'd just burned up his own future dreams of ease and fortune. And Kinney's. Yet in Clemens's own descriptions, these ranks of "standard bearers…wrapped in fire" sound not unlike distant echoes of the bloody Civil War battles from which he had also escaped.

Given a careful rereading of *Huckleberry Finn*, there are numerous other similarities to ponder: both Sam and Huck are out for their first big rafting adventure; both Sam and Huck become temporarily separated from their best friends; both are fleeing from political (and racial) turmoil back home; and both have "lit out for the territories," in Huck's famous phrase. To make good their escape, both Huck and Sam even choose an "abandoned" canoe. All of which leaves us with one last parallel to ponder: the shadow cast by American racism over both the Mississippi River and over Lake Tahoe.

Unraveling this puzzle will require yet another historical detour. This time our quest begins with the invented name "Lake Tahoe" itself; or rather with the name "Lake Bigler," which had been the official name of the lake at the time of Twain's first visit there, in 1861. As California's second elected governor, "Honest" John

Bigler had participated in a winter rescue of pioneers trapped by the lakeshore—for this reason, it is sometimes claimed, the lake was named in his honor. But Bigler's real fame stemmed from his ongoing enthusiastic campaign for the complete eradication of any and all remaining Indian populations within the state of California. For his efforts Frémont's newly discovered "Mountain Lake," already named "Lake Bonpland" by Frémont's Prussian mapmaker, Preuss, was renamed "Lake Bigler" by a grateful California legislature in 1853—a name the lake officially retained, at least according to California, until almost a full century later in 1945.

But that's only half the story. When the total number of surviving California Indians plummeted sharply under Bigler's pogrom, reducing their alleged "threat" by some 90 percent, the notoriously inebriated governor soon needed a new bogey-man to scare up votes. Abandoning his staunch pro-Union stance, Bigler gradually became the leader of the new proslavery, pro-Southern, pro-Confederacy wing of the California Democratic Party—restoring his popularity through a series of fierce anti-Union diatribes.

Recall that fully half of California's voters would cast their ballots *against* Abraham Lincoln in the 1860 presidential election—and thousands more Californians were already leaving the Golden State to join the Confederate volunteers in Texas. It was only a matter of time, they felt, before California would literally split itself in half. The new Confederate president, Jefferson Davis, had even hatched secret plans to seize control of California on behalf of the South. One such plan called for California to secede from the Union (along with Oregon) to form a new "Pacific Republic." With U.S. troops in California already, under the command of a Southern-bred general, Jefferson Davis blithely assumed that he could count on the full cooperation of the U.S. military in his little California coup d'état. Much to his dismay, the Southern-bred general, Albert Sidney Johnston, flatly refused to turn traitor. At least at first. In fact General Johnston later died on the battlefield—defending the South. But he delayed his defection long enough to "save California for the Union."

Many Californians did indeed remain loyal to the Union—including those who fought to change the name of Lake Bigler. At least seventeen thousand Californians volunteered for Union military service immediately—but few of these volunteers hailed from Southern California, which had already voted to become a separate slave state. Only the onset of open hostilities at Fort Sumter had prevented Congress from accepting the statewide resolution creating "two Californias" (one slave, one free).

Regardless of the election's outcome, the California electorate itself remained sharply divided, with true-blue Unionists (mostly concentrated in Northern California) battling for political control of the Golden State against the so-called Copperheads (mostly concentrated in Southern California), who favored the Confederacy, slavery, and secession. Now comes the crucial question: in this, the central political battle of his era, which side was Sam Clemens on?

To answer this question we need to peer even more deeply into this murky world of naming (and renaming). The term "Copperhead," for example, was a common California slang term for Confederate sympathizers (many of whom punched out U.S. copper pennies to wear around their necks as a symbol of their contempt for the Union). Increasingly outraged by the name "Lake Bigler," which they considered a Copperhead endorsement, pro-Union forces proposed half a dozen new alternatives—including Lake Washington, Lake Lincoln, and Lake Frémont. None stuck. Finally a less overtly political name was proposed: Lake Tahoe.

As one fiercely pro-Union newspaper, the aptly named *Sacramento Daily Union*, opined, "A place so picturesque, so destined to become the greatest resort for health, novelty and enjoyment… should not take a name which carries one into the Kitchen Cabinet of the traitor James Buchanan [the pro-South Democratic president who defeated Frémont], or into that species of Copperheadism which breathes nothing but condemnation for the glorious defenders of our Government, and covert sympathy with treason."

Exactly how the pseudo-Indian term "Tahoe" was chosen remains an engaging enigma. According to my own research, at least three *different* versions of this Tahoe-naming story have survived. The first, by R. G. Dean, was set forth in a letter to the *Sacramento Union* in 1870—and it shows just how deeply the Lake Tahoe/Bigler region was embroiled in the passions of Civil War politics:

> The facts in regard to changing the name of the lake are these: Judge Dean, who is now in the Department of Agriculture, Washington, and W. Van Wagner and myself— all strong Union men—were the original proprietors of the old Lake House, situated at the south end of the lake; and when Bigler was venting his Democratic spleen and rebellious ideas; when we found him acting with the anti-Union party of California, and using his best efforts to carry the State out of the Union, we determined to change the name of the lake, to wipe out the name of Bigler, if possible. A variety of names were suggested and discussed, but I insisted on an Indian title....Consequently we sounded every Indian we met for an Indian name of the lake. One of them, more intelligent than the rest, replied, "Taa-oo"—meaning "big water."

In fact the original Washoe name for the lake, Daowaga, only vaguely resembles the invented word "Tahoe."

The other two surviving versions of "how Tahoe got its name" reveal a consistently fierce pro-Union bias as well. In one, the Reverend Thomas Starr King, a superstar pro-Union preacher who had first visited the lake in 1863, is credited with being the first to use the new name "Tahoe" in print, openly equating the lake's own stormy surface with the stormy fate of the Union in battle. In the other, a government mapmaker (and prominent pro-Union Republican) named Henry Knight claims to have singlehandedly erased the name "Lake Bigler" from the federal map, substituting "Lake Tahoe" in its place.

Regardless of who coined the term "Tahoe" first, however, the erasure of "Lake Bigler" from the map was clearly and emphatically intended to signal a pro-Union, anti-Confederate bias. Hence "Save Lake Bigler" became the rallying cry of legions of California Copperheads.

That's where the newly minted name "Mark Twain" comes back into the picture. Which side of the Bigler/Tahoe controversy would Clemens/Twain himself, the most celebrated Tahoe author of his time, support? Take a wild guess. The answer might surprise you.

As Sanborn explains at length in *Mark Twain: The Bachelor Years*, the word "Tahoe" remained "a name Clemens would always object to, claiming that it was Indian for 'grasshopper soup.'" So far this description makes Twain's distaste for the name Tahoe seem something like a joke. In his own mind, no doubt it was. But examine Twain's own words of explanation in closer detail and his anti-Union prejudices soon come peeking out from beneath the sunny comedic surface. Here, for example, is a typical squib Twain wrote for the *Territorial Enterprise* for September 4-5 of 1863:

BIGLER VS. TAHOE: I hope some bird will catch this Grub the next time he calls Lake Bigler by so disgustingly sick and silly a name as "Lake Tahoe." I have removed the offensive word from his letter and substituted the old one, which at least has a Christian English twang about it whether it is pretty or not. Of course Indian names are more fitting than any others for our beautiful lakes and rivers, which knew their race ages ago, perhaps, in the morning of creation, but let us have none so repulsive to the ear as "Tahoe" for the beautiful relic of fairy-land forgotten and left asleep in the snowy Sierras when the little elves fled from their ancient haunts and quitted the earth. They say it means "Fallen Leaf"—well suppose it meant fallen devil or fallen angel, would that render its hideous, discordant syllables more endurable? Not if I know myself. I yearn for the scalp of the soft-shell crab—be he injun or white man—who conceived of that spoony, slobbering, summer-complaint of a name. Why, if I had a grudge against a half-price nigger, I wouldn't be mean enough to call him by such an epithet as that; then, how am I to hear it applied to the enchanted mirror that the viewless spirits of the air make their toilets by, and hold my peace? "Tahoe"—it sounds as weak as soup for a sick infant. "Tahoe" be—forgotten! I just saved my reputation that time. In conclusion, "Grub," I mean to start to Lake Bigler myself, Monday morning, or somebody shall come to grief.

Here Twain's choice of epithets—ranging from "injun" to "half-price nigger"—clearly signal his racist sympathies to a discerning Civil War–era audience finely attuned to such innuendos. Please don't misunderstand my argument here. I'm not declaring Twain to be a lifelong racist. Quite the opposite. Decades later, he famously overcame his own inherited racism in the process of penning *Huckleberry Finn*—perhaps the greatest antiracist novel ever written. But in the wake of *Huckleberry Finn*'s success, it's easy to forget how long it must have taken Twain himself to make that journey toward racial reconciliation—and what a struggle it must have been for him. To put it plainly: Twain was not born an antiracist; he became one. This was indeed part of his great power as an American writer: he truly understood the sensibilities of his rural Southern characters, Huck included, from the inside out—including their deeply inbred and inherited racism. Given his own earlier pro-Confederate service as a Missouri militiaman, it really shouldn't be so surprising to learn that in 1863, with the ultimate success of the Union cause itself still deeply uncertain, and with both California and Nevada deeply divided politically into Copperheads and Union supporters, a young and confused Clemens might easily find himself drawn back toward sympathy with the Southern cause.

Admittedly, it's a complex picture I'm painting—but no more so than those painted by other Twain biographers. Margaret Sanborn argues eloquently that the pernicious racism Twain expressed toward American Indians—including his hatred for the name "Lake Tahoe"—was a consistent feature of his writing throughout his career. In retrospect, Clemens's failure to come to terms with his anti-Indian bias seems all the more dispiriting, given the many other forms of racial (and religious) prejudice he publicly attacked and even lampooned. Even in his earliest Nevada writings, for example, Twain openly parodied the vicious anti-Chinese stereotypes he encountered, defending the Chinese community's intelligence, industry, and thrift. In Twain's opinion, "All the peoples of the earth had representative adventurers in Silver-land," including the so-called "Celestials" (or Chinese).

Alas, Twain extended no such "celestial" welcome to the Washoes, Paiutes, or other Native American groups who had forfeited their land to the Silver Boom—all of whom Twain contemptuously lumped together as "Diggers" regardless of tribe. In sharp contrast to his newfound tolerance for Mormons or Chinese, Sanborn asserts, Twain "was unable to apply this same tolerance toward the Indians beyond the Rocky Mountains, whom he now began seeing for the first time, and who had likewise been shot down, beaten, cursed, despised, misunderstood—and driven, in this case, from a domain that had been theirs for more than twelve thousand years." For Clemens, these so-called Diggers remained the "wretchedest type of mankind" on earth, "inferior to all races of savages on our continent," and "sneaking, treacherous, filthy, and repulsive…prideless beggars." Echoes of these same racist attitudes persist in Twain's portrait of the menacing and monstrous murderer known as Injun Joe in his novel *Tom Sawyer*, published many decades later—and in his joke about Tahoe as "grasshopper soup."

Yet take that same argument one step further and it leads toward a question which even Sanborn fails to consider. To put it bluntly: was Sam Clemens still a closet Copperhead? In fact, by loudly and repeatedly announcing his preference for the name "Lake Bigler" over the name "Lake Tahoe," Twain was unmistakably signaling exactly that message to his readers.

All of which brings us back around to Twain's Tahoe land deals. After the catastrophic forest-fire fiasco with John Kinney, Twain's next extended trip to "Lake Bigler" came at the expense of one Walter Hobart, a twenty-one-year-old former "nobody from nowhere" who had miraculously become an overnight millionaire in the Nevada Silver Boom. By using his already vast silver fortune to gobble up equally vast tracts of Tahoe timber, Hobart's El Dorado Wood and Flume Company was already amassing the fortune in lumber sales that Clemens and Kinney had dreamed of for themselves until the forest fire scorched their plans.

To sing the praises of his growing empire, Hobart soon invited a locally famous author named Mark Twain up for an all-expense-paid stay in his fabulous new lakeside hotel, fully expecting Twain to pump out some favorable publicity. For his part, Twain was more than happy to accept the offer, especially since the trip to Tahoe could now be made by stagecoach in half a day (instead of by hiking laboriously up the mountainside on foot, as he and Kinney had been forced to do just three years earlier).

These same roads brought the first wave of tourists up to Tahoe—including a group of wealthy expatriate Virginians who soon took young Twain under their wings as a fellow southerner. Soaking in all that free Southern Comfort, Twain touted Tahoe for its health-giving waters, for its glorious vistas, and for its incomparable sunsets. Meanwhile he still dreamed of building a little home by the lakeshore and settling his whole Missouri family in it. As he gushed to his mother in a letter dated August 19, 1863, "I found [Hobart's] 'Lake House' crowded with the wealth and fashion of Virginia, and I could not resist the temptation to take a hand in all the fun going. A lot of them had purchased a site for a town on the Lake shore, and they gave me a lot. When you come out, I'll build you a house on it."

Twain's wealthy new friends were, in fact, the legendary "Virginians" of Western film and television fame: rich, aristocratic, Southern slave-plantation owners who had escaped the war to come out west (just as Clemens himself had done a few years earlier). It all sounds innocent enough in Twain's letter—yet today it's easy to forget how loaded such code words as "Bigler" or "Virginian" must have sounded to readers of Twain's own era, when the state of Virginia itself was at war with the Union.

In fact Owen Wister's classic novel *The Virginian*, first published in 1902, is widely considered to be one of America's first Westerns. The plot concerns a group of exiled aristocratic southerners hoping to graft all the ideals of Southern plantation life onto Western ranches amid sagebrush seas. Like Margaret Mitchell's novel *Gone with the Wind* or Hollywood's first big screen hit, *The Birth of a Nation*, such works trade explicitly on an emerging white nostalgia for the antebellum South (minus all the whippings, slave revolts, and working-class white poverty, of course). So, was the Virginians' lavish gift of land to young Mark Twain meant to tempt him back toward the Confederate camp? We'll never know for certain. But such a theory certainly goes a long way toward explaining what happened next.

In December of 1863, Twain abruptly interrupted his third trip to Lake Tahoe—where he'd been touting another lakeside hotel known as the Logan House—in order to meet America's most celebrated comedian, just then arriving in Carson City by stage on the western leg of a nationwide tour. Flamboyant, effeminate, and hard-drinking, Artemis Ward was fast becoming America's first successful stand-up comedian. In the rollicking weeks to follow, Ward would quickly become Twain's most powerful literary mentor—as well as his best drinking buddy. Due to Ward's East Coast connections, on February 7, 1864, Twain's first-ever East Coast byline appeared in the New York *Sunday Mercury* under the title "Doings in Nevada." With truly lightning speed, Twain's nationwide career seemed to be taking off.

Yet within little more than a year of first adopting the pen name "Mark Twain," and less than six months after meeting Artemus Ward, Sam Clemens's literary reputation was once again in shambles, and he literally fled Nevada in mortal fear. What went wrong? What self-destructive demons had seized him? And what role did Lake Tahoe play in Twain's calamitous fall from grace?

Here's what we know for certain: In a column Twain later claimed he had merely published "by accident" in May of 1864, the young humorist half-jokingly alleged that charity money he'd helped raise to aid wounded Union soldiers had secretly been "diverted from its legitimate course, and was to be sent to aid a Miscegenation Society somewhere in the East." Miscegenation, you will recall, refers to interracial marriage—the ultimate outrage in the eyes of the proslavery forces. Twisting the knife, Twain added that his report was "a hoax, but not all a hoax, for efforts are being made to divert those funds from their proper course."

An unmistakable anti-Union slur, Twain's little miscegenation "hoax" backfired badly. Within hours, the offices of the *Territorial Enterprise* were flooded with angry letters to the editor demanding Twain's resignation. Like his disdain for the pro-Union name "Lake Tahoe," Twain's so-called miscegenation hoax was a bright red flag signaling his own unrepentant pro-Confederate sympathies. No one was more outraged than Twain's own family—including his brother Orion (then running for office as a pro-Lincoln Republican in Nevada) and his sister Pamela (whose pro-Union charity back in St. Louis had received the very funds Twain's stupid little hoax now claimed were being diverted). The closet Confederate had finally come out of hiding—in print.

As condemnations poured into the *Territorial Enterprise* office, Twain himself made things worse by biting back at his attackers with his trademark barbs, claiming he was simply defending the honor of the *Territorial Enterprise* from attack. In reality, I would argue that Twain was really defending the sacred honor of the Confederacy itself.

Recklessly, Twain even issued a formal challenge to the editor of a rival newspaper which had attacked him in print: pistols at fifty paces; a duel to the death. Today this sounds like another of Twain's twisted practical jokes, but in Nevada at the time, death by dueling was a common fate. This was no joke. There were real bullets in those guns.

Generations of dedicated Twain biographers have struggled to explain Twain's self-destructive, borderline-insane behavior. Some Twain scholars, Margaret Sanborn included, have simply dodged the question, labeling Twain's actions during this period "erratic" or "impulsive" (and hence apparently inexplicable). Others, such as Andrew Hoffman, argue that Twain's divided psyche made him a borderline schizophrenic—the tears of a clown gone crazy. "A fool, a tyrant, a philosopher, a humorist, an unschooled literary genius, a friend to revolution, a confidant of presidents and industrialists, an insatiable and sophisticated reader of history, a glad-hander, a sham, a self-destructive narcissist: Each of these epithets describes Mark Twain," Hoffman argues. "Their contradictions," he concludes, "create a persona that is at once both larger and smaller than a real person." Hence in Hoffman's view, as in the view of many respected Twain scholars, "We will never know the complete truth about Mark Twain because he changes shape as we study him."

Granted, these are all compelling arguments. But the more obvious answer to the riddle is political—not psychological. Is it really an accident, for example, that the man Twain challenged to a duel was the editor of the *Nevada Union*—a man he had never met in person? In my own view, the whole "miscegenation money" hoax was little more than a desperate insult to the Union cause issued by a confused and increasingly unrepentant Confederate sympathizer.

Further evidence for this claim can be found in the bizarre history of the word "miscegenation"—a term coined just six months earlier as the direct result of an even more outrageous anti-Union hoax. Here's how the whole hoax had unfolded: in the wake of Lincoln's Emancipation Proclamation, his Democratic Party opponents concocted a fake press release promising to make interracial marriage a central plank of the Republican Party. To make the promise sound more believable, they coined the fake but scientific-sounding word *miscegenation* (from the Latin *miscere* to "mix" and *genus* for "kind") to describe what had previously been known chiefly as "race mixing." Similar accusations had, in fact, been successfully leveled at the Republican Party ever since Frémont first ran for president way back in 1856; but now, in the wake of Lincoln's Emancipation Proclamation (and especially in the wake of the great African American leader Frederick Douglass's first official visit to Lincoln's White House), the firestorm ignited by these fake charges was simply enormous. So much so, alas, that the word "miscegenation" has remained a part of the English language ever since. Indeed, miscegenation was officially prohibited by law in many U.S. states, including California, for a full century, until the Supreme Court in 1967 finally found the courage to strike down such blatantly racist statutes once and for all, in the celebrated case of *Loving v. Virginia.*

As journalist and historian Paul Collins points out, as soon as the fake pamphlet *Miscegenation: The Theory of the Blending of the Races, Applied to the American White Man and the Negro* had appeared on Manhattan newsstands on Christmas Day, 1863, "racists went berserk." Soon thereafter, according to historian James Oakes, "The Democrats seized on Douglass's words [in his account of his recent White House visit], churning them back in a pamphlet entitled *Miscegenation Indorsed by the Republican Party,* published at the height of the Presidential election campaign." It was precisely this absurd and incendiary new word, "miscegenation," that Twain had deliberately seized upon in concocting his own so-called hoax. Given the climate of the times—and with his own brother Orion now occasionally serving as the Republican acting governor of Nevada—Twain's words were the literary equivalent of nitroglycerin. Predictably, they blew up right in Twain's own face.

Fortunately for the future of American letters, when the date for Twain's duel to the death finally arrived, he turned out to be both a poor shot and a practical coward. Hands shaking, Twain proved literally unable to "hit the side of a barn" with the fine set of dueling pistols his second had provided. Instead, just as the angry editor of the *Union* arrived, one of Twain's friends swiftly shot the head off a passing bird—and deftly passed it off as Twain's doing. Terrified by this display of (fake) marksmanship, the *Union* editor made his excuses and retreated. Shaking and pale, Twain was declared the victor.

But the story of Twain's self-inflicted suffering is not quite over yet. The bitter self-destructive spiral continued. Faced with a volley of new death threats pouring in from across Nevada, Twain grabbed the next Wells Fargo stage out of town—sneaking off to San Francisco in the dead of night with his best friend, the fellow

Territorial Enterprise humorist Dan DeQuille. Of course Twain's ignominious departure was soon detected—and duly mocked in the press. The very next day, one newspaper in Nevada trumpeted Twain's premature "demise." Soon the rest of the state had bid him good riddance as well.

For now the whole world knew his secret: tail tucked firmly between his legs, Mark Twain had limped out of town like a whipped dog. As the *Gold Hill Evening News* reported in a fake obituary, "Among the few immortal names of the departed—that is, those who departed yesterday morning per California stage—we notice that of Mark Twain. We don't wonder. Mark Twain's beard is full of dirt, and his face is black before the people of Washoe." As usual the choice of the word "black" seems anything but accidental: another case, perhaps, of metaphorical miscegenation?

As the *Evening News* itself explained, "Giving way to the idiosyncratic eccentricities of an erratic mind, Mark has indulged in the game infernal—in short, 'played hell'....He has *vamoosed*, cut stick, absquatulated; and among the pine forests of the Sierras, or amid the purlieus of the city of earthquakes, he will tarry awhile, and the office of the *Enterprise* will become purified, and by the united efforts of Goodman and Dan DeQuille once more merit the sweet smiles of the ladies of Carson." Others, perhaps more prescient, seemed genuinely upset to see Twain go. In the words of the oddly named but sympathetic *Daily Old Piute*, "The world is blank—the universe worth but 57 and 1/2, and we are childless. We shall miss Mark."

Back in San Francisco, Twain's continued erratic behavior only made things worse. Those fabulous silver stocks he'd been banking on selling? They turned out to be nearly worthless. That family land deal back in Missouri he negotiated to pay off his debts? It too collapsed, when his insufferably sanctimonious older brother, Orion, objected to the buyers' plans to use the former Clemens family lands as a vineyard. That plot of land at Tahoe? Worthless too. From the fabulous emotional highs of his "balloon-voyages" on Lake Tahoe, Twain had finally hit bottom, and he knew it. Flat broke and hungry, he briefly found a paying position on a San Francisco newspaper—only to be fired again within just two weeks. In desperation, he turned his back on writing completely, trying his hand one last time at hard-rock mining in Calaveras County.

When that too failed to pan out, he announced himself grimly "resolved" either on marriage to a wealthy widow or "on suicide—perhaps." Same difference. "If I do not get out of debt in 3 months," he wrote in despair to his sister, "pistols or poison for one—exit me." Lest anyone back home miss the hint, he added a pathetic postscript: "There's a text for a sermon on Self-Murder." The ominous ending of the letter he mailed to Missouri from San Francisco was simply: "Proceed."

Once again, Twain's trademark cowardice seems to have saved his life. Staring at the business end of a loaded revolver, he found himself unable to pull the trigger—choosing instead to proceed to the Sandwich Islands, now better known as Hawaii.

You know the rest of the story: How his first hit story, "The Celebrated Jumping Frog of Calaveras County," was published to nationwide acclaim (with Artemus Ward's help). How Twain went on to write *Roughing It*, his first book, incorporating fabulously funny sketches of Western frontier life from Tahoe to Honolulu. How he finally made that trip to Europe and the Holy Land which Artemus Ward had once promised to pay for, but without Ward in tow, bringing back enough raw material to write his second hit book, *Innocents Abroad*. By the 1870s he was back at Lake Tahoe for one final visit, this time as the guest of honor of a wealthy San Francisco surgeon named Dr. Brigham. For by this time, Twain was already being hailed worldwide as America's greatest humorist.

In both of those first two books, Twain had trumpeted the beauties of Lake Tahoe—and yes, he *called* it Lake Tahoe this time, not Lake Bigler. Perhaps that subtle linguistic shift signals the slow erosion of Twain's early racist upbringing, and the gradual evolution of his views on "race mixing" as an older, wiser author. By 1884 his triumphantly antiracist masterpiece *Huckleberry Finn* was finally published, sending Huck and Jim floating forever toward freedom on a raft not unlike the one Clemens and young John Kinney had once shared on their Tahoe "balloon-voyages" way back in 1861. With a little help from Tahoe's healing waters, Clemens's transformation into Twain was now complete.

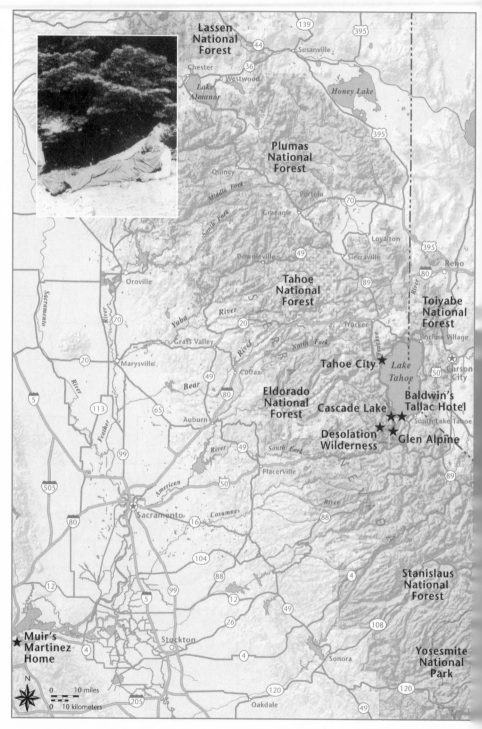

John Muir, c. 1902, photographer unknown. Courtesy of the Library of Congress, Prints & Photographs Division, LC-USZ62-72111

eight

JOHN MUIR

Tahoe National Park

Imagine a poker table high in the Sierra at which five of the most powerful men in America are seated. The prize: the future of Lake Tahoe's forests. As you watch, the rail-thin man to your right studies his cards, fingers his waist-length gray beard, and pushes a huge pile of chips out to the center of the table. His name is John Muir—he is a Scottish immigrant and pioneering Sierra mountaineer who has only recently emerged from a quiet retirement to become the crusading conservationist-founder of the Sierra Club. This time it looks like the old goat is finally going for broke. Pushing his chips out to the center of the table, he wagers everything he has on one last long shot: the creation of a Tahoe National Park.

Across from Muir sits his chief opponent, Lucky Baldwin, a short, mustachioed man who carries himself in a bullish businessman's manner: and no wonder, for he's the president and founder of the Pacific Stock Exchange in San Francisco, one of California's wealthiest men. He's also the proprietor of Lake Tahoe's fabulous new world-class casino and hotel, the Tallac House—not to mention the Santa Anita racetrack, in Southern California, and a huge, as-yet-undeveloped chunk of Los Angeles. They don't call this guy "Lucky" for nothing.

Pushing an even bigger pile of chips onto the table, Lucky Baldwin matches Muir's bet and then doubles it—clearly going for broke himself. His true goal: ironclad private monopoly control over one of Lake Tahoe's last remaining stands of old-growth forest—not for harvesting, but rather as an exclusive pleasuring ground for his wealthy hotel guests (with plenty of no trespassing signs posted all around to keep out the likes of John Muir and other such riffraff).

With Muir's hoard of chips exhausted, the outcome of his wager now depends on what others seated at the table will do next. Fortunately for Muir, just to Lucky Baldwin's right sits a man with even more power, money, and influence than Baldwin can muster: as president of the Southern Pacific Railroad, E. H. Harriman has already fought his way up from the bottom and climbed through the corporate ranks, becoming the clear and undisputed successor to the legendary magnates Leland Stanford and Charles Crocker—indeed, surpassing them by consolidating virtually the entire United States railway system under his personal control. Normally that would make him a natural ally of a man like Baldwin. Instead, he and Muir are fast friends and have long since formed a partnership to break Baldwin's hold on the forests of Lake Tahoe: unlikely as it sounds, the craggy conservationist and the railroad magnate are secretly playing as a team, and for keeps.

So maybe, just maybe, Baldwin won't be so lucky this time after all. As if facing the Muir-Harriman tag team weren't enough, to his left sit a pair of his fiercest local competitors for lakeside tourists. The first is a gnarled-looking old pioneer turned frontier resort owner named Nathan Gilmore. Having accidentally stumbled across a bubbling mineral spring high above Lake Tahoe while herding sheep in 1863 (the same year that Mark Twain first stayed at Hobart's hotel), Gilmore has now become the sole owner and proprietor of the nearby Glen Alpine Springs Resort. Famed for its health-giving mineral waters, Gilmore's resort has lately fallen on hard times—due in no small part to competition from Lucky Baldwin's newer, far more fashionable Tallac Hotel. If Baldwin wins this hand, Gilmore fears, he'll strangle Glen Alpine Springs once and for all. So to stop him, old Gilmore is ready to fight to the death—which is why he has invited his old friend to join the table: a frequent guest at Glen Alpine Springs named John Muir.

Next to old Gilmore sits a mild-mannered, frock-coated Stanford professor named William Price—another old friend of John Muir's. Price's family has recently opened a highly successful boys' camp located midway between Nathan Gilmore's Glen Alpine Springs and Lucky Baldwin's fancy new Tallac House Hotel. He too could be forced out of business if Lucky Baldwin's gambit succeeds. Short on money, but long on connections, Professor Price now has the full faculty firepower of the University of California at Berkeley behind him, as well as that of Stanford University.

Under ordinary circumstances, none of these men would be natural allies. But today Muir, Harriman, Gilmore, and Price stand united in opposition to Lucky Baldwin's monopolistic land-grab schemes—and hence the old mountaineer, the railroad magnate, the hot springs proprietor, and the mild-mannered Stanford professor with a boys' camp to protect pool their resources in one last desperate effort to outbid him. If these four players can just remain united, Muir knows, his dream of a Tahoe National Park will finally be within reach.

Still, there's one more player at the table I haven't yet mentioned: a wild-card wildcat Tahoe timber baron named Duane L. Bliss. Ordinarily Bliss's presence at the table would spell doom for Muir and his conservation cronies. For decades, no one had done more to strip Tahoe of its precious timber than Duane L. Bliss. Yet with his own private timber stands now increasingly exhausted, Bliss has recently seen the light and thrown in his lot with the conservationists. From this point forward, old Bliss has concluded, his family's future fortunes will come from harvesting tourists, not timber.

In fact Bliss has just completed construction of his own luxury hotel at Tahoe City, the fabled Tahoe Tavern. This now puts him in direct competition with Lucky Baldwin's Tallac House—and even makes the old timber baron a surprise ally of Muir's National Park pipe dream. In effect, one of Lake Tahoe's chief destroyers has become one of its most powerful potential saviors.

Of course no such poker game ever really took place. Even so, the players and the stakes they wagered were all too real. For to tell the truth, those six men were gambling with our future as well as with their own.

John Muir has long been celebrated for his visionary leadership in creating Yosemite National Park, but the saga of his failure to establish a Tahoe National Park has somehow been lost to history. Donald Worster's otherwise magisterial biography, *A Passion for Nature: The Life of John Muir*, fails almost entirely to mention Tahoe. Yet it was at Tahoe, not at Yosemite, that the fifty-year-old former mountaineer named Muir first confronted his own deepest fears of failure. It was at Tahoe, not Yosemite, that he finally picked up his pen (and his hiking boots) again after almost a decade's silence, emerging from retirement to become the most celebrated leader of the burgeoning new California forest conservation movement. And it was here at Tahoe—not in Yosemite—that Muir first confronted the appalling devastation that timber and ranching interests had wreaked on his beloved Sierra forests. Above all, it was here at Lake Tahoe that Muir's nitroglycerin mix of outrage, nostalgia, and hope first crystallized on the printed page. And with spectacular results—not just for the future of Lake Tahoe, but for the nature of America as a whole.

Coincidentally, my own first encounter with Muir's writing began at Lake Tahoe—thanks in part to a gift from a former Stanford Sierra Camp staffer named Dave Voss. It was Dave who, after pulling up to the shores of Fallen Leaf Lake, near Lake Tahoe, unlocked the door to that old Steinbeck cabin for me to sleep in; and it was Dave who first introduced me to the intricacies of Steinbeck's old job as a Tahoe-area maintenance man, including such prestigious new duties as snow shoveling, ditch digging, and toilet cleaning: "Scotty, my boy, you're now an official high-pressure hydrosealed blast-cup engineer!" he declared with a wicked smile, shoving a toilet plunger into my hands as if it were a Stanford degree. Which, in a sense, it was: for it was also Dave Voss who introduced me to John Muir's wilderness writings—the future subject of my Stanford dissertation.

So here's what reading John Muir for the first time taught me: that you can start over again. Repeatedly. Season after season, year after year. Even decade after decade. To quote John Muir's own marvelously musical metaphor for self-renewal, "This grand show is eternal. It is always sunrise somewhere; the dew is never all dried at once; a shower is forever falling; vapor is ever rising. Eternal sunrise, eternal sunset, eternal dawn and gloaming, on sea and continents and islands, each in its turn, as the round earth rolls."

It was a lesson he knew from harsh experience, for John Muir also had to start over—not once, but at least five times before age fifty. At which point, upon returning to Lake Tahoe, he started all over again once more. As he once wrote in his journal, "Between any two trees in the forest lies the door to a better life."

Born in 1838 in Dunbar, Scotland, young Muir spent the first ten years of his life memorizing the King James Bible "by heart and sore flesh" in a grim Scottish highlands school where children were literally whipped for forgetting a line of scripture. At age ten he immigrated with his family to a pioneer farm in Wisconsin. There he spent roughly the next ten years of his life helping his family eke out a meager existence on their Wisconsin frontier farm, as lovingly recounted in *The Story of My Boyhood and Youth*, first published in 1913, when Muir was more than seventy years old (and dictated, for the most part, to E. H. Harriman's personal secretary at Harriman's estate).

As a teenage farmhand in Wisconsin, Muir developed a remarkable gift for whittling complex clocks out of hardwood, eventually earning a prize at the Wisconsin state fair—and then a scholarship to the newly founded University of Wisconsin. There he was exposed to the scientific works of Alexander von Humboldt and the Ice Age geologist Louis Agassiz, as well as such celebrated American nature writers as Emerson and Thoreau. When Muir finally did leave Wisconsin it was to escape being drafted as a soldier in the Civil War—fleeing north to Canada for the duration of the conflict and only returning to the United States once the war was safely over. Years later Muir liked to joke that he had simply left the University of Wisconsin to enroll in the "University of the Wilderness"—and so he had.

Nearly blinded in an industrial accident that pierced his left eye, Muir recovered his vision and rededicated himself to the world of nature from that moment forward. After hiking from Wisconsin to Florida—his famous Thousand-Mile Walk to the Gulf—the twenty-nine-year-old would-be explorer nearly died of malaria in an Everglades swamp. Abandoning his romantic plans to follow the footsteps of his scientific hero Humboldt to South America, John Muir instead booked passage to California.

Setting off on foot from San Francisco for Yosemite on his first day ashore, in 1867, Muir spent the next decade of his life (and more) hiking, climbing, exploring, and writing endlessly in his beloved journals about the wonders of the High Sierra, his "Range of Light." It was also during these years that he first set eyes on Lake Tahoe.

Muir's mountaineering exploits during those early Yosemite years have remained legendary right down to this day—and they still form the core of what I call the Muir Myth, which includes fanciful images of Muir surfing massive snow avalanches in Yosemite, clinging for dear life to the cliffs of Mount Ritter, and swaying at the tip of a huge pine tree in the midst of a great Sierra windstorm. Yet for all the lighthearted beauty and adventure such tall tales contain—and Muir spun many a tall tale—it was not until long *after* his early Yosemite years that the old mountaineer finally rededicated himself wholeheartedly to the serious political work of establishing national parks and fighting tirelessly for forest conservation.

Granted, Muir's long hiatus from mountaineering had begun happily enough, with marriage: at the age of forty-two, he prudently decided it was time to hang up his boots, settle down, and raise a family. After wedding the daughter of a wealthy Bay Area fruit farmer in 1880, Muir had soon fathered two baby girls—upon whom he doted. Setting dutifully to work to manage his wife's family fruit farm in Martinez, located between the Sacramento–San Joaquin Delta and the San Francisco Bay, by material standards Muir now had it made in the shade: he owned a fabulous fruit farm, enjoyed the love of a growing young family, and could bask in the fame he'd earned earlier as a popular California nature writer and mountaineer. Today Muir's bucolic Martinez fruit ranch is a national historic site.

But behind the scenes, the daily grind of managing the family farm nearly killed him. For eight long years, California's best-loved nature writer found himself overwhelmed with responsibilities, debts, and indecision. As Muir himself bitterly described it, he soon grew "sick, nervous, and lean as a crow"—too busy with farm work to write much at all, and too "heart sick" to visit his beloved California Sierra each summer. Worse yet, much to the dismay of his loyal readers back east, the flood of nature-loving articles that had once poured from his pen slowed to a mere trickle. The stream of Muir's life seemed to have reached a dead end—or at least gone underground. As for the manifold joys of his legendary Yosemite years, those now seemed but a fading memory.

Then in 1888 Muir's wife, Louie, deeply concerned for her husband's health, finally forced him out of the house for a long-overdue mountain vacation. Soon he found himself traveling in the company of a handful of other naturalists, painters, and literary men, camping and tramping along the shores of Lake Tahoe. More than two decades had elapsed since his first arrival in California, back in 1867. What a difference two decades make.

It could have been a happy ending—with many happy returns. But instead what Muir confronted at Lake Tahoe saddened and appalled him: for by 1888, the inevitable results of the timber bonanza were apparent. Whole forests had been logged from lakeshore to timberline. To Muir, the sheer scale, scope, and speed of the forest destruction were almost inconceivable. Not far from where a young Mark Twain had once staked his original timber claim amid the virgin forests of Lake Bigler in 1861, huge logging operations now swallowed up tens of millions of board feet annually, most of it floated across the lake in the form of huge log rafts towed by powerful steamers, or dragged by teams of twenty oxen, then "flumed" down water-filled gravity shoots or loaded onto hastily constructed railroad lines to be buried forever in the seemingly bottomless pits of Nevada's steaming subterranean silver mines.

Logging in those days was still a brutal business—one Paul Bunyan would have recognized. In fact many a Michigan and Minnesota lumberjack had moved west to Lake Tahoe once the supposedly inexhaustible forests of the Midwestern states had been scalped. Competing against them were teams of Chinese lumberjacks left unemployed after the completion of the railroads (about which we'll hear much more later). Working long before the advent of power chain saws and diesel bulldozers, these hearty Tahoe lumberjacks considered only the choicest part of each titanic tree worth the considerable cost in sweat, muscle, and manpower needed to fell it. In effect, only the prized heart of each tree seemed worth the trouble of dragging to the mill by means of oxen, rail, flume, or steamer. All the rest—the amputated limbs and the stumps, as much as twenty feet high, of countless fallen forest giants—were simply abandoned and left to rot. Indeed, so vast was the destruction that, even a century later, housing developers on Tahoe's north shore had to remove over half a million old-growth tree stumps from a single huge subdivision parcel in Incline Village before they could commence building there. All told, nearly one billion board feet of old-growth timber were stripped from the Tahoe Basin in the forty years between 1860 and 1900.

Following in the wake of these vast logging operations came fiercely destructive wildfires, feeding on the second-growth scrub and the waste wood left behind by the lumberjacks and oxen. In the absence of the semiannual autumn burns the Indians had conducted, the fuel loads grew astronomically higher—and so did the flames. Next came flash floods and mudslides to strip the topsoil from the unprotected mountain slopes, fouling rivers and streams already clogged with sawdust from the mills, and pouring suspended debris into the lake's clear waters. Finally, as if to complete this near-biblical devastation, vast herds of sheep and cattle were now pastured by the tens of thousands within the Tahoe Basin—"hoofed locusts" as Muir himself once bitterly described them, destroying whatever was left of the native plants and grasses still struggling to hold the soil.

Such, then, was the scene which an aging and heartsick Muir now confronted from the window of his rolling railroad carriage as it approached Truckee: save for the hydraulic mining and mercury-based ore refining practiced on the Western slope of the Sierra—which Muir also witnessed—no landscape in all of America had been as systematically raped, abandoned, and destroyed as the Lake Tahoe Basin in the late 1800s: hardly a welcome sight for a famous naturalist on his first summer vacation in almost a decade.

At first the shock simply made Muir silent—a rare condition for the loquacious mountaineer. Upon disembarking at Tahoe City, Muir's normally voluminous daily journal entries shrank to the size of a few broken, spare, brittle sentences: "The road from Truckee is dusty," he lamented; "the ground strewn with fallen burned trunks or tops of trees felled for lumber…" he scribbled weakly. And then his pen fell silent once more.

Under other circumstances, those choked and sobbing journal entries might well have spelled the end of Muir's writing career. Like Jake's journey in Hemingway's "Big Two-Hearted River," this sojourn in a ruined, burned-over landscape made his wounded heart ache and his hands shake. Soon he was sending letters home to his wife suggesting he simply cut the trip short and return home early.

In response, Louie wrote back what is arguably the most important single letter John Muir would ever receive—begging him not to abandon his journey (or his dreams). Mailed to her husband at Lake Tahoe, it reads as follows: "A ranch that needs and takes the sacrifice of a noble life," she argued, "ought to be flung away beyond all reach and power for harm…The Alaska book and the Yosemite book, dear John, must be written, and you need to be your own self, well and strong, to make them worthy of you. There is nothing that has a right to be considered beside this except the welfare of our children."

Brief as it was, that one letter arguably changed the future course of Muir's life completely. Not to mention the future of Lake Tahoe. For instead of simply returning to farm and family, Muir stayed in the mountains—completing his circumnavigation of Lake Tahoe, and then continuing on north by rail all the way to Portland, to Seattle, and on up the Alaskan coastline. Along the way the old alpinist even climbed Mount Rainier—and later helped to survey an Alaskan glacier still known today as Muir Glacier.

En route to Mount Rainier, the startling contrast between the largely untouched forests of Washington and Oregon and the deeply damaged forests of Lake Tahoe awoke him. Here at last was a vivid living reminder of the lost grandeur of the Sierra forests he had known and loved during his Yosemite years. From that moment forward, Muir rededicated himself to the conservation movement already sweeping the nation. Indeed his voice as a writer literally deepened and matured: the early, youthful, ecstatic nature writing which had first made him famous now came with a sting: the forests of the Sierra, Muir argued, must somehow be rescued from further destruction. The wholesale devastation which had been allowed to ruin Lake Tahoe, he vowed, could not and should not ever be allowed to happen again.

To help whip up public sympathy for these Western conservation causes back East, Muir agreed to begin publishing full-length books instead of the magazine articles which had long been his staple. His first full-length book, *The Mountains of California*, appeared in print in 1895, when Muir was fifty-seven years old. Yet it contained not one word about the savagely raped and ravaged landscape of Lake Tahoe. Even in 1895, that battle was yet to begin.

By 1897, the wagers were laid: Muir's last-ditch political maneuvers to create a Tahoe National Park had finally begun.

In the interim he had won many similar battles elsewhere. Most famously, under Muir's leadership Yosemite had been declared America's second national park in 1890 (just two years after his life-changing trip around Lake Tahoe). In 1892, the Sierra Club was formed with Muir as its first president. By 1903, Muir's national reputation was such that he found himself camping with President Teddy Roosevelt—thereby helping to convince the newly anointed Republican president to create a vast new system of national forests stretching from Yosemite all the way north to Lake Tahoe. Hence by 1905, when Muir's second book, *Our National Parks*, was first published, several new national parks had in fact already been created—including Sequoia National Park, not too far west of Lake Tahoe. But the crucial question of Lake Tahoe's own fate remained unsettled.

It was to be a long battle. In effect the poker game continued long after Muir's death in 1913. This arguably makes Muir's lost, half-forgotten battle to save Lake Tahoe his greatest defeat, his true Waterloo—an even more bitter failure, perhaps, than the notorious dam which drowned Hetch Hetchy Valley in Yosemite Park, darkening his spirits during the last years of his life. Yet under different circumstances, San Francisco might just as easily have taken its drinking water from Lake Tahoe instead. And therein hangs the tangled tale of Lake Tahoe's own rebirth and renewal. In fact the reasons for both Muir's failures and his limited successes at Lake Tahoe reach all the way back to Frémont's mapping errors of the 1840s—and forward toward the failed fifty-year-long battle to create a Tahoe National Park.

Back in 1888 Muir and his camping companions had found themselves hiking along the shores of Cascade Lake, a few hundred yards from Tahoe's south shore, where they stayed as honored guests of a wealthy San Francisco surgeon named Dr. Brigham—yes, the same Dr. Brigham who had once entertained Mark Twain (and whose family would someday employ a young John Steinbeck). As fate would have it, Brigham had purchased his Tahoe-area acreage from D. L. Bliss, the notorious Tahoe timber baron.

Since Brigham's personal goal in managing his Tahoe estate was solely recreation, not commerce, he had carefully preserved and protected many of the old-growth pine forests found on his abundant land. Here once again Muir found himself confronted with the stark difference the practice of forest conservation could make. As he hiked through Brigham's Cascade Lake estate, a mere half-mile from Lake Tahoe's own shores, Muir's eyes filled with wonder. And his heart filled with hope. Just as in his Yosemite years, the vivid colors of a Sierra sunrise overwhelmed him: "The sunrise lovely, calm, hushed. Yellow amber light touching the mountains of the western shore, tinting the purple lake yellow." For Muir that sunrise marked a new day in more ways than one.

With Brigham's model of forest stewardship staring him in the face, Muir glimpsed not just the lost past, but the possible future of the entire Lake Tahoe Basin. Given half a chance, Muir now realized, Tahoe's ravaged, burned, cut-over, sheep-trampled landscape could still recover. "The flash and roar of the waves on the shore begins suddenly," Muir confided in his journal, "—a hundred voices stirred by the wind in the forest." But it was Muir's own voice that was stirring now.

The first vague steps toward the creation of a Tahoe National Park had already been taken long before Muir's arrival on the shores of Cascade Lake and Lake Tahoe in 1888—beginning with the creation of California's Lake Bigler Forestry Commission way back in 1885. Although none of the Bigler commission's recommendations were ever implemented, the commissioners did provide a compelling blueprint for the future of forest conservation nationwide—a vision which was, according to environmental historian Douglas Strong, the "first of its kind in the nation." But I'll leave it to professional environmental historians to describe the often-tangled web of reports and legislation which unfolded over the next fifteen years. Instead I want to return to my poker-game analogy in order to highlight the most crucial aspects of the ongoing battle to Save Lake Tahoe—aspects which may long have been overlooked or completely forgotten, even by Tahoe's most dedicated environmental activists.

For as it turned out, the Lake Bigler Forestry Commission of 1885 was in fact just the beginning of a far larger, far longer national effort to protect the nation's forests from destruction. In 1891, as Douglas Strong reveals in *Tahoe: From Timber Barons to Ecologists*, "a little-noticed rider to a public land act [allowed] the president to set aside public lands in forest reserves." From that moment forward, with the stroke of a pen, any president could set aside vast tracts of forestland. Ever since, presidents from Benjamin Harrison and his successor, Grover Cleveland, to Bill Clinton have exercised their presidential prerogative to create new national forest reserves, national monuments, and other restricted areas. Naturally enough, Muir and his allies hoped to persuade the president to do something similar for Lake Tahoe.

Meanwhile Lucky Baldwin hatched his own ambitious plans to acquire additional land in the Glen Alpine region, angering almost everyone he hoped to exclude from his proposed private preserve. In response, the blueprint for a whole new Tahoe National Park gradually emerged, fully formed.

At first Nathan Gilmore simply wanted Congress or the president to declare the land surrounding his own private property at Glen Alpine Springs a federal forest reserve, thereby walling off any efforts by his competitor Lucky Baldwin to squeeze him out, buy him out, or surround him. But how could a little local hotel owner like Nathan Gilmore possibly attempt such a daring feat of political gamesmanship back in Washington? The answer, of course, is that he couldn't. But his old friend John Muir had the kind of clout that could make it happen. As Strong emphasizes, despite his saintly reputation, John Muir had by this time built a web of political connections back in Washington second to none. Indeed Muir had already worked actively in support of a statewide Sierra forest reserve, "and the club wished to see the protection of the Sierra Nevada forests extended north from Yosemite to beyond Tahoe."

So the battle was on: Muir and his old friend Gilmore would team up to save some of the last of the old-growth forests in the entire Lake Tahoe basin. Like a field general commanding his troops, Muir first instructed his Washington lieutenants to launch a sophisticated lobbying campaign in Congress. From the Sierra Club's perspective, it was purely a case in which "everybody is interested in preserving the property for the use of the public on the one side, against a private speculator [Baldwin] on the other." Enclosed along with the Sierra Club's own letters to Washington politicians were petitions signed by dozens of Stanford and Berkeley professors—many of whom were regular guests at Gilmore's Glen Alpine Springs (or who sent their children to Pop Price's boys' camp at nearby Fallen Leaf Lake). Eventually even the governor of Nevada got involved, signing off on a petition to save Glen Alpine's forests for future generations.

Now comes the crux: at first only the handful of forested acres near Glen Alpine Springs had been singled out by Muir and his Sierra Club for federal protection. But within a year, the effort to save Glen Alpine had merged with earlier plans to protect *all* the forests of the entire northern Sierra region—a vast tract of forest more than two hundred miles in length, reaching all the way from Yosemite National Park to Lake Tahoe.

Exactly why and how this "stretching" of the original forest reserve boundaries succeeded is still unclear. I'll suggest two possibilities: first, the Central Pacific Railroad sensed that enormous land-swap profits were there for the taking; and second, backroom political lobbying by the Sierra Club's president, John Muir, and his railroad-magnate ally, Edward Harriman, was even more successful than either man had ever dreamed.

If backroom deals with the likes of powerful industrialists like E. H. Harriman don't fit your preconceived image of John Muir as "Saint John of the Woods," don't worry. Although Muir's methods were sometimes suspect, his motives were still crystal clear. As Muir scholar Richard J. Orsi pointed out years ago in a breakthrough essay, "'Wilderness Saint' and 'Robber Baron,'" backroom political maneuvers launched by the railroad lobby were directly responsible for the creation of virtually every single one of America's early national parks, from Yellowstone in 1872 forward to Yosemite National Park in 1890. In short, Muir's friendship with the railroad baron Edward H. Harriman was arguably the linchpin of his legendary political successes, from the creation of Yosemite National Park forward.

This isn't to say that the railroads weren't acting in their own naked self-interest, as Muir well knew: national parks, the railroad barons realized, could function as world-class tourist magnets and would thereby sell more tickets in the long run than any other form of land use imaginable. Surreptitiously, the railroads even arranged to "swap" lands they owned at Lake Tahoe for more heavily forested, unharvested lands elsewhere. Motives notwithstanding, to put it bluntly, without the direct aid and assistance of the railroad lobby, Muir and his Sierra Club allies could never have gotten anything in Washington done.

So it was that, with Edward Harriman's backing, President William McKinley—soon to be succeeded by Teddy Roosevelt—issued a presidential proclamation setting aside 136,335 acres of forested land to create the new Lake Tahoe Forest Reserve on April 13, 1899. To avoid any last-minute objections, lands already in private hands (such as Nathan Gilmore's Glen Alpine Springs, or Baldwin's Tallac House) were explicitly excluded from these new federal forest reserves.

Of course 136,335 acres were a mere drop in the bucket compared to what Muir and his allies wagered for next. This was the point at which Muir pushed all his chips onto the table. Flush with his success in lobbying for expanded forest reserves, Muir boldly decided to up the ante to include a new Tahoe National Park.

Late in January 1900, Senator William M. Stewart of Nevada introduced a bill in Congress, S. 2320, establishing a large national park in the northern Sierra, embracing not only the entire Tahoe Basin but also much of the western slope of the former Sierra Nevada gold country. Yet at precisely this crucial point, Muir's unholy alliance of railroad and timber barons and resort operators began to unravel. If all of them had now pushed in the same direction, Senator Stewart's legislation might have flown through Congress without a hitch. Instead it stalled in committee—and then the backstabbing started.

First, local hotel owners and other local landowners panicked and withdrew their support, fearing federal control of their own private lands. Next the various quid pro quo land-swap deals secretly worked out by Harriman between the government, the railroads, and the Bliss family—most of which reeked to high heaven of political corruption and cronyism—were exposed to public view. As Douglas Strong laments, "A lengthy and influential article in the *San Francisco Examiner*, run under the headline 'Corporations May Gain Valuable Timber Lands in Exchange for Those They Made Worthless,' objected to the huge land swaps that had essentially made the whole Park scheme possible [including] 'payment of nearly $250,000 in cash or the granting of over 50,000 acres of lieu land to men who have already made millions of dollars within the reservation as proposed.'" Similar objections were voiced to an additional $80,000 tacked onto the Tahoe National Park bill at the last minute by Congress for purchase of "barren, rocky, precipitous land" owned by the Central Pacific Railroad west of the Tahoe watershed.

Today, when prime Tahoe lakefront property sells for literally millions an acre, a $280,000 land-swap deal sounds like a bargain made in heaven, not in hell—especially in exchange for a national park. Alas, San Francisco's objections helped kill the bill forever. Stalled in committee, Senator Stewart's legislation never even came to a vote. As Strong concludes bleakly, "Despite the continued support of [Nevada Senator] Stewart, the Sierra Club, Bliss, and others, the national park bill languished and died." Muir's desperate last-ditch gamble had folded once and for all.

So in the end was this whole Tahoe National Park idea just a tragic, stupid blunder on Muir's part? At times, even Muir himself seems to have thought so. As he wrote privately to forest superintendent Charles S. Newall, he feared the "grossest frauds" by Harriman, Bliss, and the other executives involved: "Not even for a much desired extension of a reservation should such injustice be for a moment considered." Yet in retrospect, Muir may indeed have made one crucial mistake—not by pushing forward too quickly, but by pulling back too fast. No doubt he was proudly planning to insert a brand-new chapter on Tahoe into his forthcoming book, *Our National Parks*.

Of course no such chapter would ever be written, but John Muir and his allies never really gave up the fight: for decades new proposals to create a Tahoe National Park percolated in Washington. In 1910, for example, the Native Sons of the Golden West adopted a resolution favoring the establishment of a John C. Frémont National Park at Lake Tahoe—a proposal the Sierra Club enthusiastically endorsed. Just imagine—poor old John Frémont might finally have gotten his missing monument at Lake Tahoe in the form of a national park named in his honor. Other proposals were reintroduced in 1912, 1913, 1914, and 1918—all without success. According to Strong, the last such proposal to be put forward came in 1935, three decades after Muir's death.

As a bizarre consolation prize, we ended up instead with the magnificent little Muir Woods National Monument north of San Francisco—as fine a cluster of coast redwoods as can be found anywhere on Earth, but certainly a far cry from the millions of acres that might have been protected had a John Muir National Park at Lake Tahoe been created instead.

Even so, the battles Muir and others fought to save Lake Tahoe did produce tangible results—and on a massive scale, for out of the ashes of the Tahoe National Park dream the outlines of our modern National Forest and National Wilderness Area systems first emerged. Indeed by providing a feasible model for forest conservation on a nationwide scale, John Muir's efforts to save Lake Tahoe eventually helped to protect America's forests nationwide.

How did it happen? Recall that as far back as 1899, President McKinley had already placed an initial 136,335 acres aside as a Lake Tahoe Forest Reserve—including all those hotly disputed forest acres surrounding Nathan Gilmore's Glen Alpine Springs. When the Tahoe National Park bill stalled in Congress, Muir and his congressional allies quietly implemented a whole new plan of attack: arguing that a true national "emergency" now existed, Nevada's Senator Stewart demanded that the U.S. Department of

Interior step in independently to proclaim a vastly enlarged Tahoe Forest Reservation dwarfing the original 136,000-acre preserve. Given the scope of the president's newly expanded powers, Stewart argued, *no prior legislative approval whatsoever* would be required to extend the range of forest reserves. Indeed, according to Stewart's interpretation, Congress could do absolutely nothing to *stop* the president from creating such reserves if he so desired.

Now it was simply a matter of convincing the president to exercise these newly envisioned powers. By 1903, Stewart was writing to President Roosevelt directly, urging him to consider the inclusion of "the Lake within the present Forest Reservation." Meanwhile John Muir took his legendary camping trip with President Roosevelt in Yosemite, lobbying the newly appointed chief executive on behalf of his beloved forests. And especially on behalf of Lake Tahoe.

So it came to pass that in 1905 President Theodore Roosevelt declared four vast new forest reserves across all of northern California: Plumas, Trinity, Klamath, and Lassen Peak. In addition, as Strong reports, "Roosevelt proclaimed the long-awaited major extension of the Lake Tahoe Forest Reserve." It was a shocking move—one without precedent in all of American history. All told, Roosevelt's new forest reserves represented the largest single extension of federal lands since the Louisiana Purchase.

Today, under federal and state protection, huge sugar pines, Jeffrey pines, and cedars once again grace the lakeshore, and millions of people from around the world flock to Tahoe to marvel at the splendor of the Sierra's magnificent forests. In Muir's own words, Tahoe remains a "natural park" even thought it never became a national park. This is how he put it in a letter to a friend: "You are no doubt right about the little Tahoe reservation—a scheme full of special personalities, pushed through by a lot of lawyers, etc. but the more we get the better anyhow. It is a natural park."

The century of change that unfolded between 1863 and 1963 saw more upheavals than Muir or anyone else could possibly have imagined. By 1963, Harvey Gross had opened Tahoe's first-ever high-rise hotel (dwarfing anything Lucky Baldwin had ever accomplished).

One year later the landmark Wilderness Act was passed by Congress, resulting in the creation of the Desolation Wilderness Area within full sight of Harvey's, Harrah's, and the other new towering Stateline skyscrapers. Appropriately enough, the new Desolation Wilderness Area surrounded the former township of Glen Alpine Springs, where the battle to save Tahoe's remaining forests had first begun.

Who knows, then, what changes the next century may bring? Today, in the era of man-made climate change and toxic pollution on a truly planetary scale, the future of Lake Tahoe's landscape remains more uncertain than ever. Will Tahoe be declared a national park at last, much as Muir himself envisioned? Or will it instead be dammed, diverted, or sucked dry to create a kind of supercharged National Reservoir? Given the political gridlock that tends to tie up large proposals of this sort in either direction, neither scenario seems likely. But if the history of Lake Tahoe teaches us anything at all, it ought to be that Anything Is Possible. And that passionate individual citizens like John Muir can still move mountains.

In the words of photography writer Nancy Newhall, "The wilderness holds answers to questions man does not yet know how to ask." Certainly Muir and his generation made some pretty wild wagers in their day. When we consider what our own wagers will entail, Muir's most haunting question becomes our own: "What is the human part of the mountain's destiny?":

I often wonder what men will do with the mountains. That is, with their utilizable, destructible garments. Will he cut down all, and make ships and houses with the trees? If so, what will be the final and far upshot? Will human destruction, like those of Nature—fire, flood, and avalanche—work out a higher good, a finer beauty? Will a better civilization come, in accord with obvious nature, and all this wild beauty be set to human poetry? Another outpouring of lava or the coming of the glacial period could scarce wipe out the flowers and flowering shrubs more effectively than do the sheep. And what then is coming—what is the human part of the mountain's destiny?

John Steinbeck, c. 1935. Hulton Archive/Getty Images

nine

JOHN STEINBECK

The Winters of His Discontent

By his own account, John Steinbeck's four-year odyssey at Lake Tahoe began with a girl, a bed, and a knock at the door. While Steinbeck was still a student at Stanford University in 1924, his best friend, Toby, had fallen in love with a young woman up at Lake Tahoe—and soon proposed marriage. Turns out Toby and his intended had both recently been employed for the summer at the Fallen Leaf Lodge, just five miles from the south shore of Lake Tahoe. This was, of course, the same lodge that was founded in 1896 as a boys' camp by William Wightman Price (the Stanford professor who had played a starring role in John Muir's losing battle to create a Tahoe National Park).

Closed down during World War I, the camp reopened as a family-oriented resort just as soon as the war ended. After Professor "Pop" Price passed away in 1920, his widow assumed management of the lodge. She was a strict, matronly woman whose ideals of female propriety had clearly been formed in the Victorian era, long before the new Prohibition-era craze for gin, jazz, and juke joints. Informed that a certain Mr. Toby Street had proposed marriage to one of "her girls" up at the lodge, a suspicious Mrs. Price boarded the next train to Palo Alto to investigate the groom—and to interrogate his friends about the young man's morals. All of this explains how Mrs. William Wightman Price had come knocking— quite unexpectedly—at the door of young John Steinbeck's off-campus cottage near Stanford University, circa 1925. What exactly did Steinbeck know, she demanded, about his so-called friend Mr. Toby Street?

Typical of Steinbeck's friends at the time, Toby Street was a big, brawny, hard-drinking, tough-talking, bar-brawling kind of man— hardly a candidate for Mrs. Price's finishing school. Having lost one eye and two fingers in the war, he had come to Stanford in his thirties as a "federal student," inching toward the goal of a law degree. A decade older than Steinbeck, who was just twenty-three, Street had quickly become one of his closest confidants—someone with whom the young would-be author would share his deepest fears and longings. For in addition to wine, women, and song, these two friends shared a passion for writing—frequently trading manuscripts and talking deep into the night about the craft of fiction. At least until Mrs. Price of Lake Tahoe came knocking at the door. That knock arguably changed Steinbeck's life forever—and soon spelled the end of his Stanford career.

In Steinbeck's own, rather dubious version of these events, Mrs. Price's unexpected arrival interrupted his amorous adventures with his latest girlfriend—thereby causing a chagrined Steinbeck to hide the scantily clad young maiden underneath his bed. Alas, said bed was also the *only* place to sit down within the confines of Steinbeck's tiny cottage. So Mrs. Price sat squarely down on the bed and started firing questions at an astonished Steinbeck—while his girlfriend hid below, stifling giggles.

Like any aspiring fiction writer, Steinbeck quickly concocted a charming little fairytale to highlight the lamblike innocence and strict moral probity of his best friend, Mr. Tobias Street, Esquire. Deeply impressed with Street's outstanding moral character—and with Steinbeck's—Mrs. Price offered him a job at Lake Tahoe on the spot. As if on cue, Steinbeck immediately dropped out of Stanford (forever) to follow his friend Toby up to Lake Tahoe for the summer—and to pursue his own dreams of becoming a full-time writer.

Like Mark Twain's impulsive trip to Nevada with his brother Orion more than sixty years before, Steinbeck's Tahoe odyssey not only altered his own life—it arguably altered the nature of American literature. The sharp political plotlines, lavish natural landscapes, and strong focus on working-class characters that distinguish Steinbeck's best work all crystallized during these early Tahoe years (no doubt shaped by exposure to full-time manual labor, far from the sheltering social bubble of Stanford's palm-lined country-club campus). Similarly, many of the flaws that would mar Steinbeck's mature fiction can be traced to his formative Tahoe years, including a tendency toward heavy-handed moralizing and an adolescent taste for pirates and knights of the Round Table—flaws which made his Nobel Prize in Literature, awarded in 1960, controversial.

Steinbeck's Tahoe transformation did not come easily. Dogged by inexperience, loneliness, and self-doubt, he spent four long, lonely years struggling to finish his first novel and then to find his first publisher—once even begging Toby, in a letter he mailed from the lake, "Do not tell anyone that I am afraid. I do not like to be suspected of being afraid." Yet by the time Steinbeck finally left Lake Tahoe, he had faced those fears, completed his novel, and met his future wife while working in a fish hatchery. All of which makes Tahoe look every bit as much like "Steinbeck Country" as the rugged rural ranchlands of the Salinas Valley, or the windswept *Cannery Row* coast of Monterey Bay.

Between Steinbeck's arrival in 1925 and John Muir's pivotal visit in 1888, much about Lake Tahoe's landscape had changed radically—including transportation: whereas Twain and Muir had traveled to Tahoe on foot, on horseback, by boat, and by rail, Steinbeck arrived by automobile. And although railroads still carried Bay Area tourists to Tahoe in the 1920s (including a

"Snowball Express" for winter sports lovers) the Age of the Automobile at Lake Tahoe had clearly arrived: by 1907, California's first
official "state highway" passed right by the south shore. By 1910
the Golden State boasted more than forty-four thousand automo-
biles—more than all the rest of the nation combined. By 1913, the
south shore's Highway 50 was joined by Highway 40 over Donner
Pass, near the north shore. Connecting both, the spectacular Rim
of the Lake Road also opened in 1913—one year before World
War I broke out. By the 1940s, the last rail lines from Truckee to
Tahoe would be torn up and melted down as scrap to aid in the
World War II effort.

This flood of cars brought many changes to Tahoe's economy.
Rather than finding work as a lumberjack or a sawmill hand, as
Twain and Muir had once done, Steinbeck's first job in the Sierra
was driving Mrs. Price's big sixteen-seater Pierce-Arrow limousine
to town, shuttling mail, guests, and supplies daily from Fallen Leaf
Lodge to the steamer docks at Lake Tahoe. Two small lumber mills
were still in operation in the Fallen Leaf Lake region in 1925, but
these were tiny by comparison to the vast lumbering operations
that once ringed Lake Tahoe itself. Meanwhile the vacation real
estate market for middle-class homes was booming: no longer was
Tahoe the exclusive enclave of the super-rich. By 1925, prime lakefront properties sold for what seemed then the astronomical, but
somehow affordable, sum of five thousand dollars per acre. Yet each
winter Tahoe's roads still shut down completely, and the lake was
nearly deserted. Year-round auto access would not come until after
World War II.

On a more personal level, Steinbeck's arrival at Lake Tahoe
signaled the end of his failed academic career. Measured in ordinary terms, his Stanford years had been a disaster. Painfully shy,
insecure, and lonely, Steinbeck nonetheless sported a trademark
bluster and braggadocio as an undergraduate that had done little
to quell his own inmost fears. As Steinbeck biographer Michelle
Potter admits reluctantly:

Little in Steinbeck's early life seemed to indicate that he would ever win the Pulitzer Prize or Nobel Prize for literature. His parents, teachers, and friends knew he had a modest degree of talent as a writer because they had seen him writing in the margins of his father's used accounting ledgers or heard stories of his dresser drawers full of manuscripts. Few people, however, associated Steinbeck with success. He was tall, awkward, and gangly. He didn't join social groups or clubs. And he constantly worried about his looks. Lacking social grace, Steinbeck came to embrace his role as the class loudmouth or local prankster. After high school, Steinbeck attended Stanford on and off for six years, but never graduated. He attended classes sporadically and relished his status as a bohemian.

The only son of a failed, frustrated, small-town businessman and bureaucrat, John had entered Stanford with the vague but noble goal of becoming a doctor. Six academically disastrous years later, he had still not finished his general education requirements. Instead, by 1925 he had taken enough writing classes to earn the modern equivalent of a creative writing degree. Trouble was, there was no such thing as a creative writing degree at Stanford (or anywhere else in America) at that time. By dropping out of Stanford and moving up to Tahoe with Toby, Steinbeck had apparently decided to enroll in John Muir's "University of the Wilderness" instead.

Throughout his six years at Stanford, Steinbeck had used his vacations to work in factories, farms, ranches, and fields near his family's home in the Salinas Valley. Out of such experiences came much of his best writing—including his first published short story, featured in a campus literary magazine. A roughhewn portrait of the lives of Filipino farmworkers in the Salinas Valley, this first story proved a clear model for later Steinbeck classics such as *Of Mice and Men* and *The Grapes of Wrath*.

Hence Steinbeck's sudden decision to drop out was clearly motivated by his goal of becoming a full-time writer—not by a foreboding of failure. At Tahoe, he figured, he and Toby could work together all day as manual laborers and then work all night on their precious manuscripts. So it was that for the next three summers John and Toby worked together on Mrs. Price's summer maintenance crew—repairing railings, replacing cabin decks, laying shingles, and even building a small office for the lodge. Another project involved blasting and cementing a small catchment basin at the top of a rocky little waterfall near the lodge—the goal being to provide more water for the lodge's tiny hydro-powered generator. Today, scattered remnants of John and Toby's handiwork are still clearly visible underneath the rushing waters of Taylor Creek. As Jackson Benson, the author *The True Adventures of John Steinbeck, Writer*, reports: "They had to move huge granite boulders and in some cases change the shape of the basin itself, and Toby was surprised to find that John, somewhere, had learned all about blasting and how to handle dynamite, even how to set off a charge under water with a fuse." He probably learned these things, Benson speculates, while helping to dredge the Salinas-Castroville slough several years earlier. It was backbreaking work. "The two of them carried, rolled, and pried large rocks into place, drove steel into the ground and into the crevices in the large granite boulders of the basin lip, and mixed and poured concrete to tie everything together."

Somewhere in between pouring concrete, driving limos, pounding nails, and chasing skirts, Steinbeck and Toby both found time to keep writing. Nocturnal distractions at the lodge included listening to the local dance band, or even late-night romantic trysts in the backseat of Mrs. Price's old limousine—at least until Mrs. Price herself came along with her flashlight to shoo the offenders back to their tents. Somehow Steinbeck managed to begin work on his first novel. Robert Sears, one of the other young Stanford students hired to work at the lodge, recalls watching John's silhouette thrown by gas-lantern light against the canvas walls of his tent as he pecked away at his beloved old typewriter.

For his part, Sears clearly looked up to both Steinbeck and Street as manly role models. And Steinbeck clearly relished playing the older, wiser writer to an audience even more innocent than himself. As Sears later recalled:

> John talked to us very seriously about what he was doing. Telling us all about how you write short stories, taking us very seriously, you know, and pontificating to the nth degree. And he read two or three of his unpublished stories to us and told us how wonderful they were....But he was really in his manner an extremely modest man who talked, nevertheless, with a great deal of conviction about what he was doing....I mean the fiction really came through, and I think that was one of the things that impressed us very much. Here was a man who was a real man—I mean, my God, you know, five by five, tremendous physique and tough and had all the macho characteristics, boasting about his conquests in all the whorehouses he knew and so on. And yet, at the same time, he had this great sensitivity and was not afraid to express his emotions openly in stories, and comment on them. It was really quite an experience.

Steinbeck's formal training as a writer had begun as a freshman at Stanford. At first, he tried hard to be a model student. Then illness derailed him. In spring of 1919, during his freshman year, he contracted appendicitis. Falling behind in his studies while in the infirmary, he never truly caught up with his classmates again. But initially, not for lack of effort: years afterward, he still suffered nightmares about studying desperately for exams he was destined to fail.

By his sophomore year, friends rarely found John studying in his room; instead he was over at the dorms playing cards, smoking, joking, and (best of all) swapping stories. From that point forward, Steinbeck stubbornly refused to finish his required classes—enrolling solely in those courses which he personally deemed directly relevant to his future career as a writer. For when it came to the craft of writing, Steinbeck could be almost obsessive—voluntarily repeating both semesters of his freshman English course (one on "Narration" and the other on "Exposition") simply because he felt unsatisfied with his performance the first time through. By the time he moved up to Tahoe, he had taken virtually every writing course Stanford had to offer. On his transcript, you'll find creative writing classes in both poetry and fiction, as well as classes in journalism and advanced composition, and membership in the fledgling Stanford literary club.

Even in English composition, his grades wavered up and down wildly. Predictably, he earned an A in feature writing—where the story counted more than facts. By contrast, he earned a D in news reporting—where accuracy matters even more than imagination.

Surprisingly, despite all his macho posturing, his most influential writing teachers all turned out to be women. For although Steinbeck's behavior toward women could sometimes be chauvinistic (and his female characters often one-dimensional), he awarded his female teachers a lifetime of respect. Chief among them was Dr. Margery Bailey, sponsor of the English Club—and a formidable writer in her own right. Demanding, quick to criticize, and blunt, she could leave Steinbeck's best work bleeding red ink. Yet more than once she also paid him the unforgettable compliment of reading his work out loud to her class. Significantly, given his deep association with Cannery Row, at least one of the English classes he took from Professor Bailey was taught at Stanford's Hopkins Marine Station at Monterey Bay during summer session.

Ever the rebel, Steinbeck would go out of his way to provoke her. According to one campus legend, he once showed up at the English Club dressed in a ragged t-shirt, sporting some kind of scar on his shoulder. When the demure Professor Bailey asked him where the scar had come from, he replied, "A Mexican woman with whom I was copulating bit me."

Steinbeck's other favorite teacher at Stanford was Edith Mirrielees, and she was an even more influential mentor. To his chagrin, she never gave him better than a B in any of her classes. Instead she gave him something much more valuable than any

A: accurate criticism, crucial encouragement, honesty, friendship, mentorship, and guidance.

Years later, Mirrielees Hall on the Stanford campus was named in her honor: but Steinbeck's lifelong admiration arguably remains the better monument. Another student, Dean Storey, recalled that Edith Mirrielees was "one of these odd, prissy, little old-fashioned women who you couldn't imagine John getting along with, and yet he had the greatest admiration for her, and he would take whatever she told him about what he wrote." As biographer Jackson Benson reports:

Steinbeck wrote Carl Wilhelmson that she was "very kind, she hates to hurt feelings. She says that she thinks my stuff ought to be published but she doesn't know where. Don't get the idea that I am swimming against an incoming tide of approbation. I'm not. For every bit of favorable criticism, I get four knocks in the head." Steinbeck became her star pupil—perhaps her all-time star pupil—and yet he never got more than a B from her. At first this irritated him, and he complained that he knew the reason she walked so stiffly— she kept all her A's stuck up her rear—but she spent so much time with him that he at last accepted her grading as a form of encouragement to do better.

Viewed in this light, Professor Mirrielees' timeless advice to young writers still makes for poignant reading:

Writing can never be other than a lonely business. Only by repeated, unaided struggles to shape his yet unwritten material to his own purpose does a beginner grow into a writer. There are a few helps toward general improvement which it is feasible to offer, there are many specific helps in the work of revision, but help in the initial shaping of a story there is none. That is the writer's own affair.

Writing to a friend about Professor Mirrielees' teaching methods back in 1929, Steinbeck himself concluded humbly that "she does one thing for you. She makes you get over what you want to say. Her only really vicious criticism is directed toward turgidity, and that is a good thing."

Inching forward word by word, sentence by sentence, story by story, Steinbeck struggled for years at Tahoe before finishing his first novel. Based loosely on the life of the Welsh-Jamaican pirate Henry Morgan, Steinbeck's *Cup of Gold* looks almost nothing like his later fiction. So why write a Caribbean pirate novel while living at Lake Tahoe?

To start with, young Steinbeck seems to have dreamed of becoming a pirate of sorts himself. Several years before dropping out of Stanford, he even left a note for his roommate claiming that he was "running away to work on a ship bound for China." Much to his embarrassment, no one on the docks in San Francisco seemed interested in his services as a sailor. Instead, Steinbeck had to content himself with backbreaking work at the Spreckels sugar factory near Salinas for the summer—the experiential basis for many of his best novels.

More than pirate ships or even slow boats to China, Steinbeck dreamed of hitting it big as a writer in New York City. In 1925, with Fallen Leaf Lodge shuttered up for the winter, he booked passage on a steamer to New York—by way of Panama. Arriving in New York City with little money and fewer connections (his sister Beth had recently married and moved to New Jersey) Steinbeck found his first job working on the construction crews for Madison Square Garden. It was brutal work, pushing hundred-pound wheelbarrows full of liquid concrete along a skinny wooden ramp, then dumping the contents into the cavernous foundations of the arena, ten long hours a day. At night Steinbeck collapsed into bed, too exhausted to even pick up a pen. When a fellow worker fell from a high scaffold to his death directly in front of Steinbeck's eyes, he quit on the spot.

Through another set of family connections, Steinbeck soon landed his dream job as a writer: working as a cub reporter for the *New York American*. Recalling that D he had earned in news reporting back at Stanford, he was fired within a few weeks. Seems Steinbeck was still better at inventing stories than reporting them. Then disaster struck again: his New York girlfriend dumped him, choosing to marry a boring banker with a car and a steady income. With no prospects for a job, no girlfriend, and no money, Steinbeck rented a tiny room and desperately attempted to find a publisher for his collection of fledgling short stories. According to Steinbeck biographer Catherine Reef, an old Stanford friend encouraged him "to submit his stories to a book publisher. Steinbeck followed this advice. He was overjoyed when an editor at Robert M. McBride and Company, a New York publishing firm, expressed interest in his work. If Steinbeck could write a few more stories, the editor said, his company would publish them as a book."

Filled with hope, Steinbeck worked feverishly to polish his stories, delivering the completed manuscript within just a few more weeks. Yet as Reef grimly explains, "There was just one problem, though. The editor who liked Steinbeck's work had left the company. The new editor would not even look at what he had written. There would be no book, the new editor said." Flying into a rage, a distraught Steinbeck physically threatened the new editor—and then quickly found himself thrown out of the front door, the pages of his rejected manuscript fluttering down the street in the winter wind. In Reef's succinct opinion, "The outburst was an expression more of panic than of anger."

Looking back on these youthful misadventures in Manhattan, Steinbeck later recalled that he'd had a "thin, lonely, hungry time of it there...I was scared thoroughly. I can't forget that scare." Offered work as a merchant seaman on a freighter in exchange for passage back to California, he jumped at the chance to return to Lake Tahoe. As Reef reports, "He arrived in California at the start of summer in 1926 feeling healthy and optimistic once more"—and hungry for another summer at the lake.

The following winter, in lieu of another trip to Manhattan, Steinbeck signed on as a winter caretaker at the Cascade Lake estate of Mrs. Alice Brigham—widow of the prominent San Francisco surgeon who had once played host to Mark Twain and John Muir. Of course no one in the Brigham family suspected that their winter caretaker would someday go on to win a Nobel Prize.

Putting his Manhattan heartaches behind him, Steinbeck hunkered down for eight long, lonely months of winter isolation to work on the manuscript of *Cup of Gold*. It took several more years to complete—so Steinbeck stayed on at Lake Tahoe. Besides working as a winter caretaker, he served as a summer tutor and frequent companion for Alice Brigham's two grandsons, Charles and Harold Ebright—both of whom still live at the lake today. In exchange for his efforts, Steinbeck earned year-round use of the caretaker's cabin, free run of the Brighams' impressive library, and enough pocket money to pay for food and necessities. It seemed an ideal setup for a young writer struggling to finish his first novel.

In the summers he was far from lonely. According to Jackson Benson, "When the family was in residence, [the Brigham estate] employed six or seven servants: a cook, two Filipino house boys, and several Indians to maintain the lawn and grounds and to do the laundry." In this way, Steinbeck came into contact with numerous Washoe Indians. At Fallen Leaf Lodge, Mrs. Price had employed a Washoe woman named Suzie who was fond of retelling the old Washoe legends to visitors. Steinbeck must certainly have known her, and perhaps even listened to her stories from time to time.

By contrast to the Brighams' Washoe and Filipino employees, Steinbeck's status as caretaker seemed that of "an associate member of the family." Interviewed in 2005 for *Tahoe Quarterly* magazine, Charles and Harold Ebright both recalled Steinbeck joining them for family hikes, fishing expeditions, and picnics on the beach. Yet for all the fellowship his caretaker job provided each summer, Steinbeck's reminiscences seem to revolve around the lonely winter season: "I had a job as caretaker on a large estate at Lake Tahoe," he recalled years later. "I was snowed in eight months of the year."

In winter Steinbeck became the Brighams' sole employee, alone at last. There his chief duties were splitting firewood and cutting huge blocks of ice by hand from the frozen surface of Cascade Lake, then hauling them into the Brighams' icehouse to be stored in sawdust for the following summer season.

In addition to these basic icehouse and wood-chopping chores, the one indispensable requirement of Steinbeck's job as a winter caretaker was a tolerance for isolation. As E. B. Scott reports in *The Saga of Lake Tahoe*, "It is said that when a giant pine was uprooted by the wind and crashed through the Brigham home, carrying away two other trees and leveling the house in the process, the budding novelist, who was seated nearby and absorbed in a book, barely looked up."

Yet when the roof of the Brighams' library caved in under the weight of winter snows, Steinbeck waded through drifts in his pajamas after midnight to rescue the books, lovingly brushing the snow off of each one. But not every night was so heroic. Foreshadowing the alcoholism that plagued his later years, young Steinbeck would indulge in long solo drinking binges. In a letter to his friend Kate Beswick he confessed, "I have just finished being drunk for three days, a horrible period wherein I hurled dirty taunts at my spirit, called it a literary magpie…a charlatan and a sneak." Sobered up, he admitted, "I know that *Cup of Gold* is a bad book, but on its shoulders I shall climb to a good book." With admirable resolve he added that "Critics could hurt my feelings, but they couldn't kill this ego. Something there is in me which is stronger than lust and nearly as strong as hunger."

At other times he mocked his lapses in a more lighthearted manner. Having mailed his completed manuscript off to his agent at last in May of 1928, he joked to Beswick that "I have been eight months here with no one about me. And I have been getting out the seven deadliest sins and refurbishing them. Have come to the conclusion that only lust and gluttony are worth a damn."

Winter in Lake Tahoe in the 1920s offered solitude in abundance. As Tim Hauserman reports in a recent edition of *Tahoe*

Quarterly, "Only a few crusty souls dared stay for the snowy winter months." Of course those who lived closer to the railroads in Truckee were not quite so isolated. Besides a booming ice industry—shipping tons of the stuff to Boston and San Francisco in an era long before refrigeration—the town of Truckee sponsored an annual Winter Carnival, complete with towering ice palaces, toboggan runs, and skating rinks.

In addition to the toboggan run, the first ski lift in all of North America had opened for business in Truckee in 1913—a natural outgrowth of the mining and railroad industries, which had used heavy cables to haul bucket-loads up mountainsides for years. Previous to that lift, "Ski Tahoe" meant something closer to skiing *toward* Lake Tahoe from Truckee—thirteen miles up Truckee Canyon with twelve-foot wooden boards strapped to your feet. By the 1920s, Tahoe's first recreational skiers would descend from Donner Pass to Donner Lake in one long schuss, then ride horse-drawn sleighs back to the top for a second run.

Steinbeck's own ski trips were far shorter, and flatter. From his snowbound little Cascade Lake cabin, he made frequent trips on cross-country skis or snowshoes to pick up mail and supplies at Tallac. As Tim Hauserman reports, "Mail was the only communication with the outside world in winter, and whether by ski, snowshoe, or sled, whenever Steinbeck heard the S.S. *Nevada* blowing its whistle, he high-tailed it the two miles to Camp Richardson."

Looking back later on his Tahoe winters, Steinbeck himself frequently refers to the crushing sense of loneliness he felt during those long snowbound seasons. Something far deeper, darker, and colder than mere cabin fever seems to have surfaced within his inmost psyche there. In one pivotal letter mailed to Toby Street during his first long winter in 1926, Steinbeck confessed, "Do you know, one of the things that made me come here was, as you guessed, that I am frightfully afraid of being alone. The fear of the dark is only part of it. I wanted to break that fear in the middle, because I am afraid much of my existence is going to be more or less alone, and I might as well go into training for it. It comes on me at night mostly, in little waves of panic, that constricts something in my stomach. But don't you think it is good to fight these things?"

At other times Steinbeck's fears were of the furry sort: "Last night, some quite large animal came and sniffed under the door," he reported gingerly to Toby. "I presume it was a coyote, though I do not know." The whole incident had frightened him deeply: "The moon had not come up, and when I ran outside there was nothing to be seen. But the main thing was that I was frightened, even though I knew it could be nothing but a coyote."

Fear and loneliness were themes Steinbeck returned to time and again in his personal letters. And in his fiction. Those same themes appear memorably, for example, in Steinbeck's affectionate yet haunting portrait of his friend and mentor, the Monterey Bay ecologist Ed Ricketts, in his classic picaresque novel *Cannery Row*. Much like Ricketts's, Steinbeck's own self-imposed sense of isolation seems to have been as much intellectual as it was physical. In one especially memorable letter he mailed to his friend John Murphy decades later, in 1961, Steinbeck explains that isolation is simply the price of becoming a real writer—a warning still well worth heeding today:

> Nine tenths of a writer's life do not admit of any companion nor friend nor associate. And until one makes peace with loneliness and accepts it as a part of the profession, as celibacy is a part of priesthood, until then there are times of dreadful dread. I am just as terrified of my next book as I was of my first. It doesn't get easier. It gets harder and more heartbreaking and finally, it must be that one must accept the failure which is the end of every writer's life no matter what stir he may have made.

Along with isolation, Steinbeck's other great fear was of failure. Even after decades of success, writing for Steinbeck remained a lonely, bitter struggle. His tenth novel, he claimed, came no easier than his first. Yet finishing that first novel at Lake Tahoe seems to have required an inner struggle of serious, perhaps near-suicidal dimensions—at least judging by the tone of Steinbeck's own agonized letters at the time. In one especially desperate letter to Carlton A. Sheffield, mailed from Lake Tahoe on February 25, 1928, Steinbeck writes, "My failure to work for the last three weeks is not far to find. I finished my novel and let it stand for a while, then read it over. And it was no good. The disappointment of that was bound to have some devastating, though probably momentary effect. You see, I thought it was going to be good. Even to the last page, I thought it was going to be good. And it is not....I have a new novel preparing but preparing very slowly...counting the periods when I walk the streets and try to comb up courage enough to blow out my brains."

Despite such fears—or perhaps because of them—Steinbeck's years at Tahoe ended on a happier note. Upon the completion of his novel, he took a job at the nearby state fish hatchery at Tahoe City (remodeled in 2010 to house a new UC Davis Tahoe Environmental Research Center lab facility). In addition to feeding the fingerlings, Steinbeck was expected to lead guided tours of the hatchery all summer—a task which provided plenty of opportunities for meeting pretty young female tourists (and, as he bragged lustily, experimenting with the fish-gut condoms he had crafted).

After three long winters finishing *Cup of Gold* at Tahoe, Steinbeck now considered his need for isolated winters a thing of the past. And it was during this summer that he met his future wife, Carol Henning, and her sister: tourists on holiday, they visited the Tahoe City hatchery. Although his first date with Carol was a disaster, the marriage that followed (the first of four) lasted thirteen years and produced several children. As Tahoe historian Tim Hauserman explains, "When the captivating Henning sisters from San Francisco came into the hatchery one day for a tour, Steinbeck and Shebley had a double date for the evening. The bachelors were late to pick up the sisters, however, when their car suffered three flat tires on the short trip to the girls' home in McKinney. Things definitely picked up from there: the future Mr. and Mrs. Steinbeck

enjoyed ten wild days together, exploring the best of Tahoe City's
and Truckee's prohibition-era speakeasies."

Yet all the old demons that had once haunted him at the
Brighams' winter mansion would still come a-haunting him here:
Steinbeck biographer Jay Parini even reports that while "terribly
drunk" Steinbeck terrorized an attractive visitor (who had refused
his advances) by suspending her by her ankles out of a second-story
window while she screamed hysterically for help. "One can hardly
overestimate the insanity of this particular act," Parini laments.

When his hatchery boss found the aspiring young author dead
drunk in bed one morning, a bottle of gin in one hand, a pistol in
the other—and blasting holes in the hatchery's ceiling with a lazy
nonchalance—Steinbeck lost his job on the spot. Within days John
and his new fiancée had moved to San Francisco, soon to be married, never to return to Lake Tahoe.

Soon Carol found work as a typist in San Francisco—work
which was the couple's sole source of steady income for many years.
To save money they were married in Steinbeck's parents' home in
Salinas. For the next several years the newlyweds settled down in
a shared flat in San Francisco while Steinbeck started work on his
next novel (another financial failure): To a God Unknown.

It's tempting to conclude, with a knowing nod, that Steinbeck
made a mistake in trying to write a pirate novel while living up at
Lake Tahoe. The blurb for the paperback edition of Cup of Gold
(still in print) captures much of the overly melodramatic flavor of
his potboiler plot: "Henry Morgan ruled the Spanish Main in the
1670s," the dustcover blusters, "ravaging the coasts of Cuba and
America and striking terror wherever he went. His lust and his
greed knew no bounds, and he was utterly consumed by two passions: to possess the mysterious woman known as La Santa Roja,
the Red Saint, and to conquer Panama and wrest the 'cup of gold'
from Spanish hands." So much for subtlety.

Literary critics have long ravaged this first novel, just as its
pirate-hero Morgan once "ravaged the coasts of Cuba." Most,
including myself, consider it pure juvenilia. As one early reviewer

complained in the *New York Herald Tribune* on August 18, 1929, *Cup of Gold* was a "promising stab at a novel of adventure," but "strangely enough, the tale lacks the color and spirit traditional to its genre....Mr. Steinbeck lapses into pedestrian narrative at times." Similarly, the *New York Evening Post* carped that "This 'Novelized life of Henry Morgan, Buccaneer' somehow does not 'come off.' It falls between two stools of style...and they do not harmonize." Subsequent Steinbeck critics have been no kinder. By contrast, Steinbeck's early short stories, composed during this same period, clearly show flashes of the brilliance that would come to characterize his best work—not to mention the Salinas Valley settings which would later come to be known worldwide as Steinbeck Country. "I think I would like to write the story of this whole valley," he wrote to George Albee from Salinas in 1933, "of all the little towns and all the farms and the ranches in the wilder hills. I can see how I would like to do it so that it would be the valley of the world." And so it has become.

By contrast, *Cup of Gold's* cartoonish Caribbean characters and mawkish plot seem to represent Steinbeck's writing at its absolute worst. Indeed, one could argue that in writing that first novel Steinbeck made the most fundamental beginner's mistake of them all: writing about worlds he did not understand, instead of the worlds he knew best. Yet for all its flaws, *Cup of Gold* still found a publisher (and helped pay the bills for a few months). Meanwhile, the struggle of actually finishing that novel in the midst of those long, dark Tahoe winters seems to have taught Steinbeck much about his craft. "I don't know one bit more about spelling and punctuation than I ever did," he admitted wryly in one letter mailed from San Francisco, "but I think I am learning a little bit about writing.... The Morgan atrocity pays enough for me to live quietly and with a good deal of comfort. In that way it was worth selling."

Ironically, salty historical novels about seagoing captains turned out to be among the greatest best-sellers ever penned by Lake Tahoe's shores. They just weren't written by John Steinbeck. I'm referring instead to the celebrated Captain Horatio Hornblower series, written by the British novelist (and longtime Tahoe home-owner) C. S. Forester.

Following the publication of *Cup of Gold*, Steinbeck subsisted for years on his wife's typing and his aging parents' charity. With midlife fast approaching, he was considered by everyone he knew (including Steinbeck himself) to be an abject failure. Yet to his credit, he remained steadfast in his desire to become a true writer.

Finally, in 1935, his Big Break came at last: ten years after he first set eyes on Lake Tahoe, his fifth book, *Tortilla Flat*, was published to unexpected national acclaim. What followed were Steinbeck's greatest years of artistic creativity—culminating in the publication of his Pulitzer Prize–winning novel, *The Grapes of Wrath*, in 1939. Yet much to Steinbeck's sorrow, both his parents passed away shortly before *Tortilla Flat* was published—convinced that their son's life, like their own, would be a failure. As Steinbeck later quipped, "The profession of book writing makes horse racing seem like a solid, stable business."

Success never did come easy for Steinbeck. Even his Nobel Prize in Literature in 1962 was greeted with catcalls by some literary critics, as well as outraged residents of his own hometown of Salinas, California, who considered him a Communist. As Steinbeck's friend the marine ecologist Joel Hedgpeth reminds us, "Publication of *The Grapes of Wrath* in 1939 aroused the wrath of the Associated Farmers and all sorts of conservative folk. Most of the publicity, especially in California, was hostile and unfriendly and Steinbeck's native town disowned him. He was accused of being both a Jew and a Communist." Today Steinbeck's standing in most college English departments remains rather low—but for different reasons: his plots, it is argued, are too wooden; his women too one-dimensional; and his political moralizing too didactic and overwrought, by postmodern standards. In this light, the flaws of his first novel, *Cup of Gold*, remained endemic throughout his career; he never outgrew them. But he did not outgrow the deeper lessons about the nature of being a writer that he learned at Lake Tahoe, either.

In recent years, in fact, Steinbeck's reputation as a novelist has been partially restored, based on what *The New York Times* has aptly labeled "The Greening of American Literature"—the articulation of a vibrant environmental ethic in literature (with Steinbeck in its pantheon). Both physically and philosophically, this "greening" leads us straight back to Steinbeck's youthful roots as a struggling writer at Lake Tahoe. Eventually it led Steinbeck himself back to the Sierra as well. Much like Muir, the aging writer found himself returning to the Sierra late in life, only to confront the stark and surprising contrast between the unspoiled American landscape he remembered from his youth and the increasingly polluted and plundered American landscape of the 1960s.

In Steinbeck's case the journey came in 1963, at the wheel an old pickup camper he nicknamed *Rocinante* (and with his poodle Charley as his loyal companion). In *Travels with Charley*, the aging author recounts—among many other adventures—a sentimental return to the California Sierra. Rather than confront the building boom engulfing Lake Tahoe, Steinbeck stopped instead at a nearby grove of giant sequoias—the world's largest trees, the northernmost stand of which is located just twenty miles due west of the lake, within the Tahoe National Forest. "The vainest, most slap-happy and irreverent of men, in the presence of redwoods, goes under a spell of wonder and respect," Steinbeck opined.

His tone was not always so gentle. In the last book published before his death in 1966, *America and Americans*, penned forty years after that last lonely winter of his discontent at Lake Tahoe, Steinbeck laments:

> Our rivers are poisoned by reckless dumping of sewage and toxic wastes, the air of our cities is filthy and dangerous to breathe from the belching of uncontrolled products from combustion of coal, oil, and gasoline. Our towns are girdled with wreckage and the debris of our toys—our automobiles and our packaged pleasures...All these evils can and must be overcome if America and Americans are to survive; but many

of us still conduct ourselves as our ancestors did, stealing from the future for our clear and present profit.

Characteristically, Steinbeck still tinges his outrage with optimism: "We are no longer content to destroy our beloved country," he concludes bluntly. "We are slow to learn," he argues, "but we learn....And we no longer believe that a man, by owning a piece of America, is free to outrage it." Elsewhere he admits, "It is true that we are weak and sick and ugly and quarrelsome but if that is all we ever were, we would millenniums ago have disappeared from the face of the earth."

In this wider sense, the resilience Steinbeck learned at Lake Tahoe continues to shape his legacy today. As is typical of the authors we've studied, however, there are to date no monuments or museums dedicated to John Steinbeck's presence there. Perhaps none is needed. In 2008 the old state fish hatchery where Steinbeck once worked was converted into a high-tech home for the Tahoe Environmental Research Center's labs—an apt reminder that at least part of Steinbeck's lifelong fascination with marine biology began right here by the shores of America's largest mountain lake. As Steinbeck himself once observed, "We find that after years of struggle we do not take a trip; a trip takes us...Many a trip continues long after movement in time and space have ceased." Not unlike *Cup of Gold*, which begins with a mysterious knock at the door, Steinbeck's Tahoe odyssey began with a knock at his Stanford cottage door, then led on toward horizons unknown.

Bertrand Russell in Argentina, c. 1970. Courtesy of Wikipedia

ten

BERTRAND RUSSELL

The Last Resort

During the summer of 1940, Bertrand Russell's Lake Tahoe retreat offered what he called "an extraordinary contrast between public horror and private delight." Predictably, that "private delight" stemmed from the beauty of Lake Tahoe and its adjacent little brother, Fallen Leaf Lake. But the "public horror"? That assaulted Russell from all sides—and it helped to make Lake Tahoe literally a last resort for the increasingly broke, blacklisted, and beleaguered British philosopher during the darkest days of the Second World War. Yet like Twain, Muir, and Steinbeck before him, Russell used his time at Tahoe to launch an entirely new phase in his long career. Indeed, within ten years of his summer sojourn at the lake, Russell's worldwide prestige had rebounded to such heights that he too would receive a Nobel Prize.

When he first checked in as a guest at Fallen Leaf Lodge, no one but a psychic (or a fool) would have predicted a Nobel Prize for the aging, unemployed professor of philosophy. By 1940, Russell's fifty-year career as England's most notorious public philosopher seemed finished. As he approached the age of seventy, his prestige as a pundit under attack, his bank account barren, and his relevance as an academic philosopher fading into footnotes, he risked being treated as a has-been. Worse yet, American universities from coast to coast had suddenly begun blacklisting Russell, labeling him as a dangerous sexual radical—while across the Atlantic his beloved England seemed to have little, if any, chance of surviving Hitler's military onslaught. For Russell and his young family, these were dark days indeed.

Things had not always looked so bleak. Forty years earlier, at the turn of the twentieth century, a dashing young Lord Russell had been widely hailed as the "Picasso of Modern Philosophy" for his brilliant, often revolutionary pronouncements on everything from logic and language to marriage and morals. His first real contribution to modern philosophy had been a dashing piece of mathematical sorcery still known today as Russell's paradox. Like Einstein's theory of relativity or Heisenberg's uncertainty principle, Russell's paradox became a pillar of the emerging modernist worldview.

In the decades that followed, Russell became a central figure in the Bloomsbury Group, befriending the legendary economist John Maynard Keynes, the philosopher Ludwig Wittgenstein (once his student), and the novelist Virginia Woolf, among many others. As England's most famous pacifist during the First World War, he was briefly imprisoned as a traitor—only adding to his international notoriety as Britain's most iconoclastic and courageous philosopher. Later Russell reinvented himself once more, pouring forth a whole series of books on taboo topics from premarital sex to atheism.

With inflammatory titles such as *Why I Am Not a Christian*, these books ignited a fierce firestorm of debate and scandal on both sides of the Atlantic. Russell thrived on it. Of course by today's standards most of Russell's views are considered mainstream; but in the 1920s and 1930s, decades before the sexual revolution, his pronouncements seemed far ahead of their time. Fanning the flames of controversy, Russell's romantic life was in constant turmoil too: by the time the aging philosopher first reached Lake Tahoe in 1940, his entourage included two young children from a second marriage, plus an infant from his most recent, third marriage, to his children's former governess, now known as the new Lady Russell.

Scandal was, in short, what had brought Russell to Tahoe in the first place; it was not by choice. The prior year, with England once again at war with Germany, he had accepted several lucrative offers from universities in the United States, hoping to shield his young family from the fighting. At first his series of lectures on the philosophy of language at the University of Chicago went smoothly. So did his first season at UCLA. Then, suddenly, he found himself embroiled in bitter battles over academic freedom. "The academic atmosphere [at UCLA] was much less agreeable than in Chicago," Russell concluded bitterly in his *Autobiography*. "If a lecturer said anything that was too liberal, it was discovered that the lecturer in question did his work badly, and he was dismissed." Without cause and without warning, the University of California's famously dictatorial president, Robert Gordon Sproul, quietly refused to renew Russell's contract for a second season. The City College of New York, which was to have been his next destination, likewise revoked his appointment.

By the time the national press got involved, what had begun as a local fight to keep Russell from teaching in New York grew to the scope of a full-fledged nationwide boycott. As Russell himself later recalled, with a wink, "The lawyer for the prosecution pronounced my works 'lecherous, libidinous, lustful, venerous, erotomaniac, aphrodisiac, irreverent, narrow-minded, untruthful, and bereft of moral fiber.'" In an eerie preview of the McCarthy-era blacklists, "Earnest Christian taxpayers had been protesting against having to contribute to the salary of an infidel." Yet given Russell's worldwide fame, the case also became a full-blown cause célèbre—with America's foremost intellectuals lining up to rush to Lord Russell's defense, including the physicist Albert Einstein, the philosopher John Dewey, and Hollywood's Charlie Chaplin.

Locked out, frozen out, and increasingly desperate, England's most famous living philosopher suddenly discovered that he

couldn't get a job. "Owners of halls refused to [rent] them if I was
to lecture," he laments. "No newspaper or magazine would publish
anything that I wrote, and I was suddenly deprived of all means of
earning a living." Despite his aristocratic title, this left Russell literally teetering on the verge of bankruptcy. "As it was legally impossible to get money out of England, this produced a very difficult situa-
tion, especially as I had my three children dependent upon me," he
explained. As one Russell biographer reports succinctly:

> The American right turned, as one, on Russell. Church
> groups, teachers, lecturers, priests, university presidents and
> perfectly ordinary Americans, many of whom had never
> heard Russell lecture or read a word he had written, deluged
> the newspapers with letters of condemnation. There was talk
> of moral degeneracy, repatriation, deviousness, notorious
> foreign atheism, the corruption of pure American youth
> and "barnyard morality." Letter-writers to the newspapers
> reminded one another of Russell's earlier, pernicious views
> and wildly misquoted his words. The Catholic Daughters of
> America declared him an enemy "not of religion or morality,
> but of common decency." The Sons of Xavier and the St.
> Joan Holy Society joined in the chant. A witchhunt broke
> out, with calls for Russell to be "tarred and feathered" and
> driven from the country, while *The Tablet* referred to him
> as a "desiccated, divorced and decadent advocate of sexual
> promiscuity."

So in the end it was persecution and penury, not pleasure, which
first lured Lord Russell to Lake Tahoe—long a favorite haunt of
California professors looking for a cheap place to spend the summer. Ever resourceful, Russell planned to write a book while at
Tahoe that would help bring in some money—not to mention
resurrect his flagging career as an academic philosopher. Coincidentally, the rustic cabin he rented at Fallen Leaf Lodge, just five

miles from Lake Tahoe, was one that John Steinbeck had a hand in maintaining way back in the mid-1920s.

Like generations of visitors before and since, the Russell family soon settled into their rustic quarters—and promptly fell in love with the lake. "We spent the summer in the Sierras, at Fallen Leaf Lake near Lake Tahoe," Russell recalled fondly, "one of the loveliest places that it has ever been my good fortune to know." The cabin they had rented was small: "We had a log cabin in the middle of pine trees, close to the lake," he reported. "Conrad and his nursery governess slept indoors, but there was no room for the rest of us in the house, and we all slept on various porches." Passing their days in a happy haze of hiking, swimming, and boating, "There were endless walks through deserted country to waterfalls, lakes and mountain tops, and one could dive off snow into deep water that was not unduly cold."

Meanwhile Russell plunged headlong into his writing project. His immediate goal, he announced, was simply to turn the lectures he had delivered at the University of Chicago into a book modestly titled *An Inquiry into Meaning and Truth*. But clearly, Russell's larger goal in writing this book was to relaunch his collapsing academic career. For even Russell's defenders had begun to fear that the old lion was past his prime. Fortunately, the book Russell penned at Lake Tahoe is still widely considered a classic and remains in print today, after well over seventy years. Apparently the old lion could still roar.

Ever the naturist, Russell reportedly sat at his writing desk all day dressed *au naturel*. "I had a tiny study which was hardly more than a shed, and there I finished my *Inquiry into Meaning and Truth*," he relates in his memoirs. "Often it was so hot that I did my writing stark naked. But heat suits me," he adds in a sly aside, "and I never found it too hot for work." Perhaps he should have titled his new book *The Naked Truth*.

Far beyond the horizon of Lake Tahoe, the Battle of Britain raged on unabated. "Amid all these delights," Russell confessed, "we waited day by day to know whether England had been invaded, and whether London still existed." One day the mailman even played a cruel practical joke. As Russell himself recalled it, "The postman, a jocular fellow with a somewhat sadistic sense of humor, arrived one morning saying in a loud voice, 'Heard the news? All London destroyed, not a house left standing!' And we could not know whether to believe him."

Fortunately, the other denizens of Fallen Leaf Lake were far more congenial. "I found in the Sierras," Russell reported later, "the only classless society that I have ever known. Practically all the houses were inhabited by university professors, and the necessary work was done by university students....There were also many students who had come merely for a holiday, which could be enjoyed very cheaply as everything was primitive and simple." Indeed, by some strange trick of fate, one of those Stanford student-workers, Nathaniel Lawrence, went on to become the chair of the philosophy department at Williams College, my undergraduate alma mater. In 1985 he and his wife, Mary (herself a professor of English), even paid me the compliment of a visit at Fallen Leaf Lake, where we hiked together up some of the very same trails that the Russell family had enjoyed forty-five years earlier.

Later I wrote to inquire if either of my mentors had ever met Lord Russell and his family while working at Fallen Leaf Lodge. "Yes," Mary responded warmly, "it was 1940 and we were there." Though by the time she wrote this response her husband had passed away, Mary Lawrence added some amusing memories of the Russell family to her letter:

> I do remember vividly the night the wiry little man in his sixties sat at dinner at the Lodge (I was hostess) with two adolescents [his children] both so brown I wondered if they were Navajos. I think that was the only time I saw Russell. He spent two or three months at one of the cottages with his third wife, who wanted to be addressed as Lady Russell, even if he had renounced his title.

In her letter, Mrs. Lawrence was also able to provide a few glimpses of the family's private life in that little rustic cabin by the lake (which included a living tree trunk built into one corner). She recalled one particularly amusing chance encounter with "Lady Russell":

> She did grocery shopping at the store—they must have had no car, because one of the boys in the store (where Nathaniel worked) always delivered them to the Russell house. One of them came back one day to report hearing her gently remonstrating with her little son, who was busy watering the parlor sofa cushions with the garden hose. They weren't to be watered, she told him, like the flowers—though they were similar colors. "One doesn't water cushions, Conrad," she remarked.

One does water ideas, however—especially at Lake Tahoe. So while Russell's son Conrad—later a noted British politician—played with his flower pots out on the porch, inside Lord Russell set to work on his new manuscript. With notes from his recent Chicago lectures to work from, the writing progressed quickly. By summer's end, the manuscript was already in the mail. Russell even felt proud enough of his handiwork at Lake Tahoe to have free copies mailed out to prominent philosophy departments across the United States. Thanks to his summer at the lake, Russell's plans for a comeback were fast becoming a reality.

And what a comeback it was: far from being finished or faded, Russell's career now entered a whole new phase, soon making his name virtually a household word via best-selling books such as *A History of Western Philosophy* (1946), further amplifying his longtime role as England's most prominent and passionate pacifist. Far from being his last resort, Tahoe turned out to be his new beginning. A Nobel Prize in Literature, awarded in 1950, seemed ample evidence that his comeback had succeeded. Indeed, by the time of his death in 1970—thirty years after his Tahoe retreat—Russell had published over sixty books, with a list of collected works that now runs to over sixteen volumes (and counting), not including more than thirty thousand private letters.

Viewed from the perspective of Lake Tahoe, one document in particular seems worth noting: in 1955, inside the living room of Albert Einstein's Princeton home, Russell and eleven of the world's top scientists signed a letter addressed to the world's political leaders urging an immediate ban on nuclear weapons worldwide. Today the Russell-Einstein Manifesto is still honored as the founding document in the antinuclear movement—a virtual declaration of interdependence. Ominously, that letter also turned out to be the last document that Albert Einstein would ever sign. But based in part on his signature (and Russell's), the worldwide antinuclear movement was born and President John F. Kennedy was convinced to sign the world's first Limited Nuclear Test Ban Treaty in 1963.

It would be an easy task to link Russell's work to the burgeoning "Deep Ecology" movement of the 1980s at Lake Tahoe—especially given that Tahoe's own Sierra College philosophy professor George Sessions coauthored that movement's manifesto. Titled *Deep Ecology: Living As If Nature Mattered*, published in 1985, Sessions's book explicitly names Bertrand Russell's work as one of the movement's inspirations. Much the same might be said of what University of Nevada, Reno, professor Cheryl Glotfelty calls "the literature of nuclear Nevada," with apocalyptic overtones often drawn more or less directly from the tone and content of the famous Russell-Einstein Manifesto, as well as a BBC speech broadcast by Russell worldwide.

"There lies before us if we choose," he begins optimistically, "continual progress in happiness, knowledge and wisdom." The alternative, he adds, is far worse than any future of ordinary human despair: "Shall we, instead, choose death," Russell asks his invisible radio audience worldwide, "because we cannot forget our quarrels?" Instead of responding to that question directly, Russell chooses instead to frame this human paradox with one final plea. "I appeal," the old philosopher concludes, "as a human being to human beings:

remember your humanity, and forget the rest. If you can do so, the way lies open to a new paradise; if you cannot, nothing lies before you but universal death."

Linking Kennedy's Limited Nuclear Test Ban Treaty of 1963 with Lake Tahoe might, at first glance, seem like overreaching. And yet several strange synchronicities suggest otherwise: on June 9, 1962, for example, a 20-kiloton nuclear device code-named "Truckee" was detonated by the U.S. military on Christmas Island in the South Pacific—just four months in advance of the Cuban Missile Crisis, and just one year before JFK finally signed off on the test ban treaty in Washington. The second such link involves the hidden ties between the Kennedy family and a notorious Mafia-controlled casino on Tahoe's north shore known as the Cal-Neva Resort—a casino co-owned by none other than Frank Sinatra.

Sinatraland, with silhouette of Cal-Neva Resort. Photograph by Scott Lankford

eleven

FRANK SINATRA

Tahoe's Sinatraland

" To say that he had worked hard to make Cal-Neva a success would not begin to approximate his efforts," remarked
Nancy Sinatra following her father's death in 1998, recalling the
exclusive resort her father had owned on the north shore of Lake
Tahoe between 1960 and 1963. "But it was worth it—a dream
come true," she added. For with every drop of sweat equity Sinatra
poured into his beloved Cal-Neva Resort Casino, she insisted, the
place became "a Sinatraland with bright lights, music, gambling. It
offered night life and razzle-dazzle juxtaposed with natural things:
clear water, clean air, giant trees, outdoor sports, and the purple
mountains." Not coincidentally, that's precisely the mix of mountains and magic that still brings most tourists up to Tahoe today.

Predictably, Sinatra's Tahoe years also capped the most creative
period in his long and tumultuous career—including the release
of five of America's top-ten albums for 1961, his epic film performance in *The Manchurian Candidate* in 1962, and his blossoming
friendship with the newly elected president of the United States,

John F. Kennedy. Financially, Sinatra's years at Lake Tahoe also helped to make him a true multimillionaire, a level of wealth he had always dreamed of. Meanwhile the array of world-class talent that trooped through the doors of the Cal-Neva's custom-built theater equaled anything on offer in Las Vegas or Hollywood then (or now)—from Sinatra's Rat Pack pals Sammy Davis Jr., Peter Lawford, and Dean Martin to sizzling international sex symbols such as Marilyn Monroe, a frequent Cal-Neva guest. Nowhere else in America did wealth, power, celebrity, mountain magic, and the Mafia mix as freely (or as catastrophically) as they did in Tahoe's Sinatraland.

Yet for all the success, wealth, and satisfaction that Sinatraland brought him, Sinatra's Tahoe years ultimately left him wounded, his reputation tainted by the Mafia associations that lay just beneath the surface of all that fresh air, razzle-dazzle, and ring-a-ding-ding. Arguably these inner struggles brought a new depth, maturity, and whiskey-soaked wisdom to The Voice—but at what cost? As his daughter Nancy later acknowledged in her 1998 interview:

> In my mind he never recovered from not being able to fight to save Cal-Neva—and his reputation....In burying his desire to make this a fight to the finish...he buried a lot of anger... Suddenly a new element was forced into his core—one with which he had great difficulty...it encouraged him to carry a grudge. It made him defensive...from this point on general statements were made—Frank Sinatra versus the American press—instead of small separate disputes with individuals.

Even today, more than forty years after Sinatra's departure from Tahoe and more than a decade after his death, a cloud of conspiracy theories still swirls around Sinatraland like a permanent fog. Did the lovesick singing superstar really attempt to commit suicide on the grounds of the Cal-Neva Resort? Was his financial stake in the Cal-Neva a direct payoff from the Kennedy family, or from the Mafia, or both? What role did President Kennedy's father,

Ambassador Joe Kennedy Sr.—a longtime Cal-Neva guest—play in this alleged association? Did Sinatra himself arrange secret trysts for the Kennedy brothers with Marilyn Monroe in the Cal-Neva's secret network of subterranean tunnels? Did Marilyn Monroe attempt suicide at the Cal-Neva only days before her death in Los Angeles in 1962? Or was it her murder? Most ominous of all, did the Cal-Neva's Mafia masters order a hit on President Kennedy in 1963—using a former Cal-Neva employee named Jack Ruby (the assassin of Kennedy's assassin) to help cover their tracks? And if so, what did Sinatra himself know of these machinations? Was the nature of America itself, not just Sinatra's own private psyche, permanently poisoned by Tahoe's Sinatraland?

Be forewarned: none of these questions can be answered completely. There is no Tahoe smoking gun (or if there was, it was long ago buried at the bottom of the lake). By the same token, none of these conspiracy theories can be easily dismissed, either. Like the ubiquitous images of Marilyn Monroe inside every Tahoe casino, like the Sinatra songs that flood the Tahoe airwaves each night, these conspiracy theories will soon present themselves to anyone who spends significant time at the lake—and Sinatraland is at the epicenter of every single theory.

For my own part, rather than attempt to sort out fact from fiction, my approach as a literary historian has been to catalog, combine, and savor all these various conflicting conspiracy theories as part of the wider literature of Lake Tahoe. Fact or fiction, fable or fantasy, these stories, like the Godfather series, collectively shed a lurid light on a chapter in Tahoe's hidden history (and on the hidden history of America itself in the 1960s).

To avoid a forest of footnotes, I've chosen to fold all the leading sources on Sinatraland together into a single, admittedly somewhat simplified history, relying on the half-dozen Sinatra biographies currently in print, including Nancy Sinatra's *Frank Sinatra: An American Legend*; Lee Server's *Ava Gardner: "Love Is Nothing"*; numerous biographies of Marilyn Monroe and Bobby Kennedy; Pulitzer Prize–winning journalist Seymour Hersh's

book *The Dark Side of Camelot*; veteran Las Vegas reporters Sally
Denton and Roger Morris's *The Money and the Power*; and the in-
depth research presented online by Mafia historian John William
Tuohy; not to mention a monograph titled *Cal-Neva Revealed*,
self-published in 2009 and based on Philip Weiss's survey of hundreds of digitally archived newspaper articles published in Reno
and Tahoe during the 1960s. Make no mistake: all of these sources
contradict each other—often fiercely. Those who hope to seek
the truth for themselves would do well to start reading here—and
then keep digging.

That said, many allegations that once seemed crazy have long
since been classified as verifiable facts by sober professional historians—including President Kennedy's dangerous drug use (to combat
his chronic back pain); his compulsive womanizing; even his midnight skinny-dipping parties in the White House pool—the merest
whispers of which could have brought his administration crash-
ing down in the years he was alive. And ever since the Church
Committee hearings of the 1970s, we've known all about the
CIA's shadowy liaisons with the Mafia, including various bungled
attempts to cooperate in the assassination of Fidel Castro. These
revelations, in turn, have spawned fresh new crops of conspiracy
theories each season, many linking the Kennedy assassinations to
the Mafia, to Castro, even to the CIA itself. More recently, Freedom of Information Act claims have pried loose many of the FBI's
previously top-secret files, including dozens which focused on the
Cal-Neva. In combination with other reputable sources, including
court documents, these FBI reports confirm beyond any shadow of a
doubt the presence of known Mafia kingpins on the Cal-Neva property during the Sinatra years. In the same files, dubious FBI infor-
mants repeated many of the most lurid, but inevitably less verifiable
claims surfacing elsewhere in tell-all Mafia confessions and Nancy
Sinatra's memoirs.

First some essential background: to understand Sinatra's presence
at Lake Tahoe in the first place, you have to begin with the three
great legislative pillars of modern Nevada's economy—legalized

gambling, streamlined divorce laws, and universal tax shelters. All three of these revolutionary legal reforms were enacted simultaneously by the Nevada legislature in 1931, back when a teenaged Frank Sinatra was first emerging as a singing sensation in his native New Jersey. By canceling all wealth taxes, legalizing gambling, and cutting the residency period for a quickie Nevada divorce down to just six weeks, Nevada provided the nation with a fast track to freedom that ultimately proved irresistible. At the time, these reforms seemed radical, perhaps even revolutionary. Today, with tax-cutting schemes, gambling, and no-fault divorce flourishing in all fifty states, it's no exaggeration to say that we're all living in Nevada now.

Back in 1931, one immediate result of Nevada's reforms was that the number of divorce cases filed there doubled the following year, filling Tahoe's plush hotels and dude ranches to overflowing with the eager (and often fabulously wealthy) divorced-to-be, soon to include Frank Sinatra—not to mention a fresh flood of gamblers. Meanwhile, more than eighty of America's wealthiest families immediately relocated to Nevada to avoid taxes, the vast majority settling down on Tahoe's north shore along a strip of beach still known today as Millionaire's Row. One eccentric multimillionaire, George Whittell, snapped up an astounding twenty-seven miles of continuous lakefront property along the Lake's east shore for just one or two dollars an acre, building his legendary Thunderbird Lodge on the cut-over forestlands abandoned by the old timber barons. With more than six hundred thousand contiguous acres under his exclusive control, Whittell had enough free space to let his menagerie of African lions and elephants run free during the summer as pets—and to invite Frank Sinatra over for a poker game from time to time.

To anchor his growing real estate empire, Millionaire's Row developer Norman Blitz acquired an interest in the nearby Cal-Neva Lodge, a longtime bootlegging and backroom gambling hide-out built directly on top of the Nevada/California state line. Sporting a white line (marking the border) running straight down the middle of its dining room, the notorious old lodge had long served as a hideout for legendary gangsters like Pretty Boy Floyd and Hollywood silent-film starlets like Clara Bowes. During Prohibition a series of tunnels was even constructed underneath the property to facilitate illegal transport of liquor and prostitutes across state lines. Just before Nevada re-legalized gambling in 1931, the original Cal-Neva Lodge mysteriously burned down. A new and improved Cal-Neva Resort rose from the ashes of what was almost certainly an arson-related fire, within a few short weeks. This was, of course, precisely the property which Frank Sinatra would someday come to think of as his own private Sinatraland.

Long before Sinatra himself arrived on the scene, however, numerous powerful Democratic Party politicians had made a habit of frequenting the Cal-Neva, most notably Ambassador Joseph P. Kennedy Sr.—the father of the future president. According to Denton, Morris, and Hersh, from the 1920s forward, Kennedy had spent increasing amounts of time vacationing at the lake each summer, even going so far as to send Tahoe Christmas trees home to Boston and New York each winter. All of Kennedy's children—Jack, Bobby, and Teddy included—opened their gifts under Tahoe-scented pines. Meanwhile, from the safety of his Cal-Neva retreat, Kennedy carried on an endless series of extramarital affairs with wealthy divorcées and Tahoe's notoriously ubiquitous prostitutes. Some sources also insist that Kennedy became a silent partner in the Cal-Neva Lodge in the years immediately prior to Frank Sinatra's arrival on the scene.

Into this cauldron of wealth, politics, booze, sex, crime, and scandal stepped Frank Sinatra, America's most famous crooner, seeking (what else?) a Nevada divorce. An impressive roster of Hollywood stars and hyper-wealthy divorcées had preceded him for decades, including Vanderbilts, Roosevelts, and Rockefellers, not to mention a future president of the United States named Ronald Reagan. All this helped make "going to Tahoe" or "going to Reno" synonymous in American slang with "getting a divorce." In effect, the Tahoe/Reno region became the epicenter of the American sexual revolution decades before the pill and *Playboy* swept the rest of the nation along with it.

Though he was still married to his high school sweetheart, Nancy Barbato, in 1951 the new object of Sinatra's philandering affections was Hollywood's hottest sex symbol, Ava Gardner, who was also seeking a Nevada divorce at the time. Their tumultuous twelve-year relationship, much of it played out at Lake Tahoe, would become the tragic love of a lifetime—and the most scandalous "tabloid marriage" of the 1950s, endlessly dissected by Hollywood gossip columnists in much the same way that the romantic fortunes of J-Lo or Brad Pitt dominate the pages of fanzines these days.

Hence Act One of our little Tahoe tragedy finds a lovesick Sinatra finalizing his Nevada divorce proceedings against his first wife in a Reno courthouse in 1951—and then immediately rushing off to marry the starlet Ava Gardner. Not surprisingly, their hyper-hasty remarriage provoked a furious backlash from the Catholic church, not to mention an increasingly hostile Hollywood press corps.

One of the super-couple's most vicious fights occurred on a twenty-four-foot cabin cruiser speeding across the surface of Lake Tahoe in 1951, shortly before Sinatra's divorce from Nancy Barbato was final. Frank and Ava had already downed copious amounts of champagne, with Sinatra's manager and best pal Hank Sanicola at the helm. When Gardner confessed that she had recently had a fling with the bullfighter Mario Cabré, her co-star in *Pandora and the Flying Dutchman*, Sinatra flew into a rage, and Sanicola raced the boat toward shore—only to run aground just off the Cal-Neva's pier, tearing a hole in the boat's hull. Enraged, Ava refused to get off the sinking vessel, hurling anything she could find, including toilet paper, at Sinatra—along with a healthy dose of her trademark invective. Eventually the boat sank, temporarily throwing cold water on her curses.

That night, high above the Cal-Neva Resort at the famous Christmas Tree Restaurant on Mount Rose, Sinatra and Gardner once again tore into each other, this time in public. In a fury, Ava drove back toward Los Angeles, leaving a despondent Sinatra to lick his wounds alone by the lake.

What happened next remains the source of much controversy. We know for a fact that a doctor was called in the wee hours of the morning to attend Sinatra at the Cal-Neva—and that sleeping pills were definitely involved. That much made the local news. We also know that Ava Gardner came rushing back from Los Angeles, alerted to the crisis by Sanicola (police records verify that she earned speeding tickets driving both to and from L.A.). Yet in a local news article entitled "Suicide Reports Denied by Sinatra," the star himself vehemently rejected any claims that he had attempted to take his own life at the Cal-Neva, offering slippery-sounding excuses about an "allergic reaction" to some sleeping pills he had "mistakenly" swallowed, and then lamely explaining that Gardner "found out the studio did not need her when she arrived in Hollywood the next day" and that she had returned immediately to the lake. Numerous other suicide attempts—none ever confirmed—have been reported over the years by various Sinatra biographers (each one triggered by bitter fights between Frank and Ava).

What seems indisputable is the fact that Frank Sinatra's devastating song "I'm a Fool to Want You" was written for Ava. Recorded mere weeks after the catastrophic boat-crash and sleeping-pill incident at Lake Tahoe in 1951, that landmark track literally helped to launch the second phase of Sinatra's career, debuting a deeper, darker, more brooding and mature sound than the skinny crooner had previously brought to his performances before screaming legions of teenaged bobby soxers. The take-me-back lyrics, penned by the singer himself, clearly deserve a place of honor within the larger literature of Lake Tahoe.

Act Two of our Tahoe tragedy opens three years later, in 1954, with Gardner seeking yet another Nevada divorce—this time from Sinatra himself. Smitten with love (or was it just lust?) for yet another matador, this time the world-famous Spanish icon Luis Miguel Dominguín, Gardner had once again taken up residence at Lake Tahoe—all at the expense of Howard Hughes, the eccentric megamillionaire who had been carrying a torch for her long before Sinatra ever came on the scene. "You let me take care of everything," Hughes had reputedly told her, sensing in her pending divorce from Sinatra an opening at last. "I own or lease half the houses on the lake anyway,'" he bragged. As was his habit, Hughes loaded the lavish Tahoe lodge at Zephyr Cove where Gardner stayed to the gills with secret listening devices. Just to be on the safe side, he assigned a twenty-four-hour detective to shadow her every move. Only boat trips out on Lake Tahoe promised any hope of privacy.

So began a series of voyages out on the lake worthy of a crazy romantic comedy script. First Sinatra himself showed up at Zephyr Cove, begging Ava to take him back. When Sinatra discovered that his boat was being shadowed by one of Hughes's, a crazed nautical chase ensued across the face of the lake, complete with Sinatra and Gardner screaming at each other at the top of their lungs (just for old times' sake). Safely back on shore, a defeated Sinatra departed in despair, no doubt humming "I'm a Fool to Want You" through gritted teeth.

Next in line for a Tahoe boat ride with Ava was her bullfighter and paramour Dominguín, but they too soon fell to fighting, and Ava was left to brood alone by the lake. Seizing his chance at last, Howard Hughes rushed up to Zephyr Cove, fell to his knees before the world's most beautiful woman, and coughed up a proposal of marriage (along with a suitably enormous ring). "You've been married three times already, don't you think it's my turn?" he reportedly pleaded. "You make it sound like I'm a pony ride at the county fair," Ava spat back. Needless to say, there would be no more boat rides for Ava that season.

With his divorce from Ava finalized in 1957, the bachelor Sinatra, now sporting a toupee, played out his midlife crisis amid a rogue's gallery of fellow Hollywood stars he dubbed the Rat Pack, including Sammy Davis Jr., Dean Martin, and Peter Lawford. It was Lawford, a B-level Hollywood star married to Patricia

Kennedy, who introduced Sinatra to his brother-in-law, Senator John F. Kennedy. Magnetized by their mutual charisma, the two became instant pals. Young Senator Kennedy was soon sighted partying publicly with the Rat Pack at Sinatra's Sands Casino in Las Vegas so frequently that Sinatra himself took to calling it the "Jack Pack" instead. Sinatra, for his own part, took the lead in introducing Kennedy to available females, including a former Hollywood showgirl named Judith Campbell with whom the future president had a longstanding affair (much to the alarm of FBI Director J. Edgar Hoover and Attorney General Bobby Kennedy). Allegedly Kennedy also launched a surreptitious affair with Sinatra's co-star and occasional paramour Marilyn Monroe (whose steamy rendition of "Happy Birthday, Mr. President" at Madison Square Garden in 1962 seemed to hint all too openly at a simmering sexual liaison).

Numerous sources, including Nancy Sinatra herself, have claimed that her father willingly functioned as a liaison between the Mafia and the Kennedy campaign. In some versions of this tale, the backroom deals went down inside the Cal-Neva itself, with Joseph Kennedy Sr. orchestrating every payoff in person. "The old man can't run my whole campaign sitting out in California," his son reportedly complained. Yet something close to that seems to have unfolded. Allegedly the Mafia's role was to tilt the West Virginia primary in Kennedy's direction. Next, Mafia muscle helped push the state of Illinois into Kennedy's column in the national election. Under this scenario, the Mafia clearly had reason to feel that they had delivered the presidency of the United States to the Kennedy clan—but for a price.

Coincidentally and disturbingly, Sinatra became part-owner of the Cal-Neva Resort on precisely the same day that John F. Kennedy happened to win the Democratic Party nomination in July of 1960—further fueling speculation that Sinatra's stake in the Cal-Neva was a direct payoff for his role as a go-between. On July 12, 1960, the *Reno Evening Gazette* ran a headline announcing, "Frank Sinatra Seeks Interest in the Cal-Neva." Exactly one day later, on

July 13, 1960, John F. Kennedy accepted the Democratic Party's nomination for President of the United States. As usual, Sinatra's timing seemed perfect.

Evidence of Mafia collusion doesn't stop there. As court documents, Nevada Gaming Commission investigations, FBI surveillance files, and reliable press reports all later revealed, Frank Sinatra's silent partner in the Cal-Neva deal was indisputably Sam Giancana, the notorious Chicago crime syndicate boss who had allegedly helped tip the election in Kennedy's favor. Of course under Nevada's recently strengthened gambling regulations, known gangsters such as Giancana should never have been able to set foot inside the Cal-Neva Casino, or any other. Instead they acted like they owned the joints—which they did.

By 1963, FBI reports and news clippings amply document Giancana's near-constant presence on the property. As San Francisco's legendary journalist Herb Caen once confessed, "I saw Sinatra at the Cal-Neva when Sam Giancana was there. In fact I met Giancana through Frank. He was a typical hood, didn't say much. He wore a hat at the lake, and sat in his little bungalow, receiving people." Clearly Giancana's presence at Lake Tahoe was an open secret—FBI surveillance notwithstanding. Indeed, the surveillance campaign mounted against Giancana grew so intense that the Chicago mobster actually sought—and won!—a court injunction claiming infringement of his constitutional right to privacy (an order upheld by the U.S. Supreme Court).

From day one as part-owner, Sinatra threw himself into management of his new "Sinatraland" with a passion. All the old lodge needed, Sinatra figured, was a brand new theater (complete with a helipad) plus a healthy dose of Rat Pack star power to assure sellout crowds all summer. Spending lavishly, Sinatra even had the Cal-Neva's network of underground tunnels expanded, including one running from backstage to Sinatra's private bungalow. Another new tunnel connected Sinatra's bungalow to the bungalow right next door—the one preferred, naturally, by Marilyn Monroe. It all paid off: on opening night, photographs show Monroe seated front row center, quaffing free champagne with her co-stars from the Hollywood film *The Misfits.*

Whether either of the Kennedy brothers were ever present backstage remains a mystery. For his part, Mob boss Giancana claimed that both Jack and Bobby participated in an underground orgy, complete with call girls. "The men," Giancana alleged, "had sex with prostitutes—sometimes two or more at a time—in bathtubs, hallways, closets, on floors, almost everywhere but the bed." Yet according to Nevada State Archivist Guy Rocha, the only *documented* visit of the president to Lake Tahoe came on a campaign swing through Reno in 1960 while he was still seeking the Democratic nomination for the presidency.

Yet another alleged link between Kennedy and the Cal-Neva sounds even more ominous. According to FBI files and the Warren Commission, during the Sinatra years one longtime Cal-Neva employee was named Jack Ruby: this was, of course, the same man who later murdered Lee Harvey Oswald (President Kennedy's assassin) in 1963.

So did Tahoe's mobsters have a hand in killing Kennedy? Lake legends, Mafia historians, and conspiracy theorists all say yes. The Warren Commission and Nevada State Archivist Guy Rocha both say no. Regardless of who is right, these colorful accusations help add new layers of intrigue to the ever-growing literature of Lake Tahoe. Consider the case of Marilyn Monroe's suicide, for example. FBI and press reports both confirm her frequent presence on the Cal-Neva property. Rumors even leave her former husband, baseball star Joe DiMaggio, snooping around the perimeter of the Cal-Neva, banned forever from entering the grounds by Sinatra himself. We also know for a fact that Marilyn Monroe's death in Los Angeles on August 5, 1962, occurred mere days after her last visit to the Cal-Neva, which was on July 27. Officially ruled a suicide, her sudden demise sent conspiracy theorists into a virtual feeding frenzy. Norman Mailer's 1973 *Marilyn* was among the first of many books to allege that Monroe was murdered by the FBI and the CIA. Several new books about Monroe continue to appear in print each year (and Frank Sinatra is near the center of most theories).

So did Tahoe's mobsters murder Marilyn, in addition to killing Jack Kennedy? And if so, did Sinatra have knowledge of these crimes? Worse yet, did both Sinatra and the Kennedys have a direct hand in Marilyn Monroe's untimely demise? Judging by the sheer number of books published on the subject each season, it's quite literally anyone's guess.

Summing up the long list of conspiracy theories succinctly, Guy Rocha skeptically concludes:

> The events surrounding Monroe's [final] short stay at Sinatra's Cal-Neva Lodge are controversial, confusing and contested, making it very hard to separate fact from fiction. We know that she met Dean Martin briefly to discuss a movie project. Joe DiMaggio, her second husband, was there, and according to one account, there was a reconciliation and talk of marriage. Still other accounts have Peter Lawford telling Monroe that all communication with John and Bobby Kennedy was cut off. There even have been unsubstantiated claims that Monroe tried to commit suicide or was drugged while staying at the Cal-Neva.

As Rocha himself admits at the end of his Nevada State Archives "Historical Myth of the Month" post on Marilyn Monroe, where the above comments appeared, "The entire truth about the John Kennedy–Marilyn Monroe affair most likely never will be known." Yet fact or fable, these stories incontestably form part of the bedrock lore of Lake Tahoe.

Following Monroe's mysterious death her co-star Frank Sinatra's own days at the Cal-Neva were numbered. Indeed, Sinatra seems to have become increasingly self-destructive. First he got himself into a very public fistfight with a local sheriff's deputy whose wife he had once dated. According to multiple accounts, Sinatra caught the deputy in the Cal-Neva's kitchen and screamed, "What the fuck are you doing here?" In response Deputy Anderson punched Sinatra in the face so hard that he couldn't perform on stage for a week. Soon thereafter the deputy and his wife were killed in a car accident. The family still blames Sinatra.

Next, Mob boss Giancana got into a disastrous fistfight right in the middle of the Cal-Neva's dining room. In the ensuing chaos, FBI agents photographed Giancana inside the casino and forwarded their evidence immediately to Nevada's Gaming Control Board. Later an account of the fight was published by Giancana's attacker. True or false, it captured the atmosphere of naked violence and bravado that heralded Sinatraland's decline and fall: locked in a death-grip struggle, Giancana's adversary reports, "blood from my eye was running all over his suit. I had a hold of him by the testicles and the collar and he couldn't move; that's when Sinatra came in." That was also the moment when Old Blue Eyes was doomed to leave Lake Tahoe.

When an unrelated murder was committed right at the Cal-Neva's front door just a few days later, even the notoriously com-promised Nevada Gaming Commission could no longer afford to wink and look the other way. Something had to give. So Nevada's gaming commissioner phoned Sinatra and demanded an explana-tion. According to the commissioner's own published account, an hour later Sinatra phoned him back, ranting: "You listen to me Ed…You're acting like a fucking cop, I just want to talk to you off the record.…This is Frank Sinatra, you fucking Asshole! F-R-A-N-K Sinatra.….I don't have to take this kind of shit from anybody in the country and I'm not going to take it from you people…Don't fuck with me. Don't fuck with me, just don't fuck with me!"

"Are you threatening me?" the commissioner inquired.

Within weeks Sinatra had lost his license, officially forfeiting not only his 50 percent stake in the Cal-Neva but his 9 percent stake in the Sands Casino down in Las Vegas, together worth some $3.5 million.

Yet as Philip Weiss concludes in *Cal-Neva Revealed*, Sinatra did not actually sell his interest in the Cal-Neva resort after all, despite appearances to the contrary. Instead the singer quietly retained a direct financial interest in the hotel—allowing others to "lease" the rights to operate the casino until Sinatra and his silent partners could find a suitable buyer. That didn't happen until 1968, more than five years after Sinatra first lost his license. Once again the coincidences sound suspicious: on the same day that the Washoe County Commissioners finally approved a controversial ten-story high-rise addition to the Cal-Neva complex, thereby doubling its value, Sinatra's sale of the property was completed.

Today a ten-story high-rise hotel still overshadows the old Cal-Neva lodge, Sinatra's last erection. Fortunately for lake lovers, a host of similar sixties-era development schemes were stopped. Had Sinatra and other developers had their way, today's North Shore might well be a carbon copy of the heavily urbanized South Shore high-rise casino corridor—with disastrous results for the lake. As the website of the League to Save Lake Tahoe (keeptahoeblue.org) brags, "One of our earliest victories was the defeat of a development plan in the 1960s which…included a high-speed freeway circling the lake, a bridge over beautiful Emerald Bay, additional casino districts, and heavily populated urban centers around the lake."

Admittedly, none of these stories casts Sinatra in a flattering light. Yet together they help to reveal the complex human being behind The Voice. As bandleader Tommy Dorsey once confessed, "He's the most fascinating man in the world, but don't stick your hands in the cage." Or as screenwriter David Thompson once observed, "That ruined look, vengeful, thrown back over his shoulder at the dark of the audience…was self-pity vindicated. For Frankie Sinatra was always playing a very nasty guy nursing that thing about respect." Even so, his Sinatraland dreams seem to conceal something hidden beneath the surface of all that brawling, bravado, brooding, and bitterness: the innocence of a happy-go-lucky kid from New Jersey with a golden voice. Perhaps it's that same bittersweet combination of nastiness and naiveté that still gives Sinatra's sound its timeless edge, with a swinging snarl that some have dubbed "white blues." Or is it really just the Tahoe blues we're hearing after all?

In the end Old Blue Eyes seems to have eluded us completely: no one really knows who he was. Sure, we've all heard about Sinatra's Mafia connections; his violent temper; his boozing; his womanizing; his vendettas; his toupee. Yet we know next to nothing about the true origins of The Voice. In a rare candid interview, Sinatra himself theorized that "being an 18-carat manic depressive and having lived a life of violent emotional contradictions, I have an acute capacity for sadness as well as elation." Notoriously difficult to unmask, Sinatra would typically turn away all questions about his personal life, telling reporters with a Whitmanesque snarl, "If you want to know who I really am inside, just listen to the songs."

So let's listen.

Hearing Sinatra's voice crackle in over my car radio while driving back to Tahoe one night from the Nevada desert under a moonlit sky, I hear his rendition of "East of the Sun, West of the Moon" as if for the first time. Even more than "I'm a Fool to Want You," his 1951 anthem to Ava, Sinatra's gently swinging cover of that old 1930s standard—which he re-recorded in 1957, and then again in 1961, at the very height of his Cal-Neva capers—seems to capture the deepest longings of his Tahoe years in a way that nothing else can touch. Yearning for a place "up in the sky," the song speaks of a "dream house" where love never dies—a sad requiem for Sinatra's own paradise lost at the Lake of the Sky.

So did Sinatra's time at Tahoe truly deepen his life or his art? Looking back from a distance of fifty years, the answer seems an emphatic yes: even a cursory glance at Sinatra's artistic output during his Cal-Neva years (1960–1963) seems to underscore Tahoe's role in a whole new series of artistic triumphs. In 1961 alone, Sinatra released no fewer than six albums recorded after the purchase of the Cal-Neva property. Five of those albums landed among the top ten for that year, including *Sinatra Swings, Come Swing with Me, Sinatra's Swingin' Session, All the Way*, and the notorious

Ring-A-Ding Ding. During that same year Sinatra recorded a total of seventy-one songs working with five different arrangers. Clearly something in that Sinatraland dream unleashed a new wave of his creativity. Ain't that a kick in the head?

True, Sinatra released only one film in 1961, *The Devil at 4 O'Clock* with co-star Spencer Tracy—to whom Sinatra respectfully ceded top billing. Coming on the heels of lighter fare, such as *Ocean's Eleven* and *Pepe* (both released in 1960), it might tempt you to argue that the Cal-Neva had become a distraction. But then came the release of *The Manchurian Candidate* in 1962, universally hailed by critics as perhaps Sinatra's greatest cinematic performance.

Finally, there's the greatest film that Sinatra never made, *The Execution of Private Slovik*. Based on the trial of the only U.S. soldier ever executed for desertion by the U.S. Army in WWII, the plot was a red flag waved in the face of the right wing—especially when Sinatra insisted on hiring blacklisted Hollywood writer Albert Maltz to do the screenplay. Battling a brutal backlash of negative publicity, Sinatra initially dug in his heels courageously, fiercely defending his freedom of speech under the Constitution. Eventually forced to back down—New York's Cardinal Cushing whispered it could cost Jack the election—Sinatra nevertheless showed his fighting best during this incident. "I do not ask the advice of Senator Kennedy on whom I should hire. Senator Kennedy does not ask me how he should vote in the Senate," he insisted. Had Sinatra succeeded in completing *Slovik*, we might be able to add movie producer to his already-extraordinary list of singing, songwriting, and acting credits during the prolific Cal-Neva period.

Even leaving *Slovik* out of the equation, it's hard to walk away from Sinatra's body of work between 1960 and 1963 without simply shaking your head in wonder. To quote Sinatra biographer Tom Santopietro's assessment of *The Manchurian Candidate*, "Sinatra is so good that his terrific performance registers as a feat akin to Marlon Brando having followed up his beautiful performance in *On the Waterfront* by recording *Only the Lonely*."

Surprisingly, much the same might be said for Sinatra's business success during the Cal-Neva era. Despite the obvious short-term financial catastrophe which losing his license inflicted, Sinatra hauled in a cool $80 million in 1964 solely from the sale of his Reprise label alone. That's to say nothing of the millions Sinatra received for every movie he starred in during the Cal-Neva years. By 1965 the Sinatra empire included everything from a film-production company called Artanis Productions (Sinatra spelled backwards) to a charter airplane business to an aerospace parts manufacturer called Titanium Metal. No wonder they call Sinatra "The Chairman of the Board."

Is the Cal-Neva haunted? Several high-profile television specials have been made on that premise, including an A&E episode of *Dead Famous* wherein the ghosts of Old Blue Eyes and Marilyn Monroe were both summoned from beyond the grave. Personally I find the case for a "Curse of the Cal-Neva" far more compelling: first came Marilyn's suicide; then the Kennedy assassination; then Sinatra's nineteen-year-old son was kidnapped and ransomed from a South Lake Tahoe casino the following year. A decade later Mob boss Sam Giancana would be shot through the head mere days before being called to testify before a Senate select committee investigating CIA-Mafia connections. And the list goes on. Few seem to have walked away from the Cal-Neva unharmed—least of all Frank Sinatra.

Indeed it often seems in retrospect as if a curse descended over America as a whole in the wake of President Kennedy's assassination. In the words of screenwriter David Thompson, "You don't have to cry for Marilyn, who was, at best, a cunning victim, one who engineered a lot of what happened to her. But America is another matter, and the terrible intimacy of Jack Kennedy and Frank Sinatra and the suspicion it fostered are cultural fallout, of which we are all downwinders now."

Curse or no curse, these days the popular Cal-Neva Tunnel Tour ends with dramatic displays of alleged spirit auras captured on cellphone cameras, combined with spooky tales of mediums speaking in tongues from the stage of the Frank Sinatra Theater. But it isn't Sinatra's voice they're channeling—or Marilyn's either. Instead, listening to the tapes, elders of the Washoe tribe instantly identified the unknown language as Washoe, the unknown speakers as their own ancient ancestors. "Well, what are the ancestors saying, then? Why are they so angry?" the TV producers allegedly demanded. "Trust us," the elders replied, "you don't want to know."

As of this writing, the Cal-Neva is once again on the auction block, skirting bankruptcy. As Sinatra himself once quipped at a gala performance for the United Nations in September of 1963, shortly after losing his gambling license and just a few weeks shy of the Kennedy assassination, "It's essential to relax, with the stress and the hot spots around the world—Viet Nam, Congo, Lake Tahoe. Anybody want to buy a casino?"

Lorne Greene, Pernell Roberts, Dan Blocker, and Michael Landon as the four Cartwrights of Bonanza, posing on their mounts at Borne Meadow in front of Lake Tahoe in the spring of 1961. Courtesy of Bonanza Ventures/Andrew J. Klyde Collection

twelve

THE CARTWRIGHT CRUSADERS

Tahoe's *Bonanza*

In the fall of 1959, the National Broadcasting Company premiered its first television series aired exclusively in Living Color, opening each new episode with a spectacular wide-angle shot of Lake Tahoe bursting out from behind a flaming map emblazoned with the word "Bonanza." Throughout much of the 1960s, Sunday nights around the family TV set would begin with a crudely pixilated glimpse of Tahoe Blue ringed in flames.

Headquartered on the fictional Ponderosa Ranch on Tahoe's east shore in the 1860s (the same era when the real Mark Twain roamed these shores), the Cartwright clan went on to dominate television ratings in a way which few shows have before or since. Today, with literally hundreds of satellite channels at our command, it's hard to fathom the pure hypnotic fascination—and money—a mega-hit television drama like *Bonanza* could unleash. Back then most Americans had access to just three channels: NBC, ABC, and CBS. Measured purely in audience share, this meant that every Sunday, a new episode of *Bonanza* generated a viewership roughly equivalent to a Super Bowl. In a very real sense, Americans of my generation grew up on the Ponderosa.

Even today, from Russia to Brazil and from Austria to Mexico, the Ponderosa Ranch remains a household name—and Tahoe Blue still blazes across television screens in endless reruns worldwide. Rodrigo Garcia, one of my former students, recalls that "My brothers in Mexico used to watch every single episode. Those were the reruns in Spanish in the late 1970s. At that time it was common to see carnicerías in Mexico named La Ponderosa after the Rancho of the Cartwrights." No doubt similar tidbits of Tahoe Blue seeped into cultures worldwide.

According to *Bonanza*'s backstory, patriarch Ben Cartwright had fathered three sons by three different wives (each of whom died young, leaving him a very busy widower). Hence each one-hour drama revolved around the romantic escapades of Ben and his three grown boys, Adam, Hoss, and Little Joe. Women, too, paraded through the Ponderosa's pines, in gaudy cowgirl array, but not a single one ever survived for more than a few episodes—prompting actor Michael Landon (Little Joe) to quip that you had to be darn careful when riding at the Ponderosa, or your horse might trip over the grave of one of the Cartwrights' dead girlfriends.

Living Color was only the first of many breakthroughs *Bonanza* pioneered: for in addition to a skilled cast and that alluring full-color format, *Bonanza* was blessed from the very beginning with cutting-edge content, years ahead of its time. No topic, it seemed, was too sensitive for *Bonanza* to tackle: from race relations to abortion, *Bonanza*'s screenwriters consistently pushed the boundaries of what would be considered presentable in a family-oriented American TV drama in the 1960s. In so doing they redefined the genre.

This, then, is the part of the *Bonanza* saga—and the saga of Lake Tahoe—that's remained strangely hidden from history (despite the long-term, popular survival of the show in reruns worldwide). Beneath all those quavering pixilated shots of Tahoe Blue, a quiet social revolution of sorts was brewing.

That's because from that first pioneering season forward, *Bonanza* deliberately set out to challenge the disturbing undercurrent of racism that underpinned so much of Hollywood's mythic Old West. Admittedly, episode one was fairly conventional horse opera fare. But in episode two, "Death on Sun Mountain," Ben discovers white swindlers selling antelope meat to Virginia City miners at inflated prices. Offering his own beef at a fair market rate, Ben breaks the back of the meat monopoly—only to have the white swindlers retaliate by framing the Indians for attacks on the miners (by dressing themselves up as Paiutes, no less). Here for perhaps the first time in U.S. television history, American Indians are portrayed as the victims of treachery—not as savages or sops. Likewise, in *Bonanza's* episode four, "The Paiute War," the Paiutes are falsely accused of attacks on white settlers. Soon the local militia is summoned to retaliate. Caught in the crossfire, Adam Cartwright is taken hostage—only to end up siding with the Paiutes *against* both the U.S. Army and the surrounding white settlers. In America nothing like this had ever been seen in television land before.

Season after season, *Bonanza's* writers continued to take careful aim at typical cowboys-versus-Indians plotlines—quickly establishing *Bonanza* as a socially conscious, crusading family TV drama, years before the more explicitly controversial sitcoms of the 1970s came along, such as *All in the Family*, *The Mary Tyler Moore Show*, and M*A*S*H.

Nor did it stop there: in their second season *Bonanza's* writers seemed determined to challenge virtually every sexual and racial taboo they could muster. In episode six, for example, Little Joe falls in love with a female saloon owner twice his age—pretty strong stuff for family television in the 1960s. By episode nine, the ever-lusty Little Joe is back at it again—but this time pursuing none other than "the daughter of Chief Winnemucca."

What? Interracial romance on American TV in the 1960s? Unthinkable. Remember that in 1961 miscegenation (to use Twain's term) was still illegal in most states—and would remain so until the 1967 *Loving v. Virginia* Supreme Court decision. Yet up at

Lake Tahoe on *Bonanza*, sparks flew between the Cartwright boys and women of color nearly every season. The public certainly didn't seem to mind: *Bonanza's* ratings continued to climb sky-high.

In fact several more *Bonanza* episodes revolve around romances between white men and Indian women. In episode fifteen, for example, "The Last Hunt," a pregnant Shoshone woman is brought home by Hoss and Little Joe so she can have her baby on the Ponderosa. Much to everyone's surprise—including the mother's—the new baby turns out to have blue eyes. Finally we discover that both the woman's family and her white lover have been searching desperately to find her. In the end the happy couple is reunited, and domestic tranquility reigns supreme.

Similarly, in episode thirty-nine Ben Cartwright's life is saved by Matsou, an outcast Indian. In gratitude, Cartwright gives Matsou legal ownership of some land carved out of his own Ponderosa Ranch (hence the title of this episode, "The Gift"). Predictably, the Cartwrights' Indian-hating neighbors are outraged by this gift. When a neighbor's wife is killed in a nighttime raid, they ignorantly blame Matsou—the "friendly" Indian—for the crime. Oh well, there goes the neighborhood. But here once again, as always, the Cartwright boys step in and justice returns to Lake Tahoe.

In later years, *Bonanza's* writers added yet more layers of social complexity to their episodes. In episode forty-four, "The Savage," Adam Cartwright comes across a Shoshone woman threatened by her own tribe for falsely claiming spiritual powers. Shot in the leg trying to help her, Adam must rely on White Buffalo Woman for survival—once more turning the tables on the usual cowboy-versus-Indian plotlines.

By the time episode sixty-nine was broadcast in October 1961, even the much-demonized Apaches had made a sympathetic appearance on the show. Traveling in Arizona, the Cartwrights rally to the defense of a U.S. Cavalry captain under attack by a band of Apaches—only to learn from the Apache chief that his tribe had been lured in for peace talks, then poisoned (a not infrequent tactic in American military history, in fact). Here again the moral of the story is crystal clear: simply by listening to both sides, it seems, the Cartwrights have blazed a path to justice for all Americans. In this way *Bonanza* both mirrored and shaped America's emerging idealism in the 1960s. Given the enormous size of its weekly viewing audience, this placed the Ponderosa—and Tahoe with it—at the center of interracial dialogues normally associated with a major metropolis, not with Tahoe territory.

With riveting plotlines and controversial content, the *Bonanza* formula transfixed American audiences for more than a decade—touching an emotional chord that is hard to explain otherwise. Indeed, year by year the focus of *Bonanza's* socially conscious critique gradually widened. By 1963 the show's antiracist plotlines included Mexicans, Chinese, Basques, and even Gypsies. By recreating the world of Lake Tahoe in the 1860s, *Bonanza* helped shape the civil rights movement of the 1960s.

Take episode twenty-one, "The Spanish Grant," for example. Here a woman claiming to be Isabella Marie Inez de la Cuesta claims legal ownership of the Ponderosa Ranch under an old Spanish land grant title. Although her claim to the land is eventually proven false, the plot at least manages to hint (albeit obliquely) that Anglo-Americans like the Cartwrights were far from the first to colonize the greater Lake Tahoe region—and that both California and Nevada were once officially Mexican land. Yes, there are Mexican stereotypes aplenty to contend with—including a bizarre Spanish flamenco dance sequence set in a Nevada cantina. Yet there is also real respect for Mexicans' legitimate claims to the land, especially as voiced by Ben Cartwright himself, and backed up by none other than the sheriff of Virginia City.

Anti-Chinese prejudice played a surprising role in one of *Bonanza's* earliest episodes. In "The Fear Merchants"—first aired on January 30, 1960, as if to herald the dawn of the civil rights decade—an American-born Chinese teenager stands falsely accused of both miscegenation and murder. "'America for Americans!'...It's a pretty tired platform," Ben Cartwright concludes, fighting bravely to quell the flames of race-based bigotry fanned by the local demagogue, who's running for mayor. That's a story eerily reminiscent of the real-life politician who once made Tahoe the epicenter of anti-Chinese violence nationwide, as we shall see in a subsequent chapter.

Admittedly *Bonanza's* portrayal of the Cartwrights' Chinese cook, Hop Sing, was problematic, to say the least. In an era when Asian Americans were scarcely ever portrayed on television—and then often only in the most humiliating roles—*Bonanza's* writers surely deserve at least some credit for including a Chinese character in the Cartwright home. Cast in the role of the "good Oriental" from Hollywood's *The Good Earth* (1937) to TV's *Kung Fu* (1972) to John Steinbeck's *The Red Pony* (1973), veteran actor Victor Sen Yung of San Francisco inevitably landed the role of Hop Sing. Yet for all his cringing and occasional clowning, Yung's Hop Sing does become a full-fledged member of the Cartwright clan, serving as a surrogate mother to those three orphaned boys who never had a real mother of their own.

Indeed, to call Hop Sing's role "feminized" would not be far from the historical truth. In the words of Jean Pfaelzer, a professor of American studies at the University of Delaware, "Images and fears of homoeroticism run through the journals, cartoons, and letters" of white settlers and newspaper editorialists in their descriptions of Chinese immigrants throughout the 1860s, especially in railroad towns like Tahoe's Truckee. Why all the xenophobia, if not outright homophobia? According to Pfaelzer, the Chinese man was feminized in the 1860s "because he was short, because he wore his hair in a queue, because he had less body hair than Caucasian men did, because he lived among men. These fantasies shaped the era's ideas of race." A full century later, at the time of *Bonanza's* debut, these same fantasies seemed to shape Hop Sing's implicitly feminized role on TV. Yet it was also Hop Sing who became the truth-teller on the Ponderosa Ranch, as in one of *Bonanza's* several cross-dressing comedy plots: "Him not boy! Him girl!" an outraged Hop Sing screams at the bewildered Cartwright clan.

In later years, *Bonanza's* socially conscious plotlines also reached into realms of working-class conflict and even disability rights.

One early episode broached the topic of mine-worker safety (a hot-button political issue in the early 1960s). Likewise, Americans with disabilities found themselves welcomed on the Ponderosa. In episode forty-five, "Silent Thunder," *Bonanza*'s screenwriters craft a sympathetic portrayal of a young deaf girl who is befriended by Little Joe. Compassionately, Little Joe tries to teach her sign language (and later relies on her silent courage to rescue him from danger). More than forty years later, that episode still earns favorable mention on websites run by disability rights advocates worldwide.

Political controversy was another frequent focus of the show. In episode eighteen, "House Divided," Little Joe's friend turns out to be an outspoken supporter of the Confederacy (a "Copperhead"). In episode twenty-four, Ben Cartwright finds himself running for governor of Nevada, only to find himself falsely accused of hiding a dark criminal past. Other notable *Bonanza* episodes deal with everything from police brutality and coerced confessions to the difficulties faced by ex-convicts trying to reestablish a place in society.

Part of *Bonanza*'s crusading social conscience may have come at the behest of the many distinguished directors who begged for a chance to shoot their own signature episodes. Robert Altman and John Cassavetes, among others, occupied *Bonanza*'s guest-director chair. The series also hosted legions of guest stars over the years, including James Coburn, Jack Lord, Adam West, and Leonard Nimoy—who still owns a home in North Tahoe today, just down the road from the shuttered theme park once dedicated to the fictional Ponderosa Ranch. Live long and prosper.

That now-shuttered theme park brings to light a whole new side of the Tahoe *Bonanza* story: surprisingly, little of the original series was actually filmed on location at Lake Tahoe. Instead, a mock-up of the Ponderosa ranch-house set was constructed on a sunny backlot down in Hollywood. With few exceptions, only the Ponderosa's outbuildings and roads were ever filmed with real Tahoe Blue in the background. That, in turn, left a bevy of bewildered tourists circling Lake Tahoe in search of the "real" Ponderosa Ranch. To placate these legions of loyal fans, a Lake Tahoe contractor named

Bill Anderson finally asked NBC for permission to construct a life-like replica of the original Hollywood Ponderosa ranch house right next to Lake Tahoe's north shore. The result, the Ponderosa Ranch theme park, came complete with pony rides and chuck wagon cookouts—and soon became a much-beloved Tahoe tradition, visited by some three hundred thousand eager tourists each year. The demise of the theme park, which closed its gates for good in September of 2004, followed the 1973 cancellation of the *Bonanza* series by thirty years.

Today the old Ponderosa Ranch theme park has become an eerie ghost town of sorts, hidden forlornly beside the Incline Village garbage dump and Millionaire's Row. On one side of the property lies the vast and extraordinary Lake Tahoe–Nevada State Park, spanning all of Tahoe's as yet undeveloped east shore. Arguably the most beautiful state park in America, it embodies a compelling vision of one possible future for Lake Tahoe. On the other side of the old Ponderosa lies one of America's wealthiest resort communities. Once derisively dubbed "Income Village" by the *New York Times*, Incline Village today is a densely suburbanized "planned community" complete with championship golf courses and its own high-rise Hyatt casino. Just beyond the Hyatt's tower lie the storied shores of Millionaire's Row, where the gated mansions built by Depression-era plutocrats are now owned by billionaire bad-boys such as former junk bond king (turned Tahoe philanthropist) Michael Milken and casino czar (turned Tahoe environmentalist) Steve Wynn. No doubt their good deeds prove that Tahoe still harbors some mystic healing powers after all.

I don't want to overstate the Ponderosa's own healing powers, however. Looking back now from a distance of fifty years, the same plotlines that once made *Bonanza* seem pioneering can seem painfully patronizing. Nor is it clear that Hollywood ever managed to move much beyond the white-heroes-on-white-horses story lines first pioneered by the Cartwrights and their TV kinsmen on *Gunsmoke* or *The Rifleman*. In his much-praised Academy Award–winning 1990 film *Dances with Wolves*, for example, Hollywood star

Kevin Costner claimed center stage throughout the film—while his noble-savage Indian allies, played by white actors, seemed doomed to eventual annihilation, picturesquely frozen in time. In this sense *Dances with Wolves* might just as well be titled *Dances with Hoss*.

Other equally famous White/Indian romances, such as Robert Redford's 1972 classic *Jeremiah Johnson* or Disney's 1995 animated *Pocahontas*, continue to recycle the tired fantasy of white explorers rescued by ravishing Indian "princesses" not unlike Little Joe's all-too-numerous dusky paramours on the Ponderosa, including "the daughter of Chief Winnemucca." Not until 1996, with HBO's breakthrough made-for-television movie *Grand Avenue* (written and directed by California Native American author Greg Sarris) did Hollywood finally manage to shatter its glass-teepee taboos in order to produce an accurate portrayal of Native Americans as integral members of contemporary urban society (and one absent the omnipresent focus on heroic white-hatted movie stars). Yet despite its record-breaking viewership ratings, few feature films with a similar focus on modern Native American life have been made in the fifteen years since *Grand Avenue* was first released. Even in the twenty-first century, it seems, Americans are still stuck living on the Ponderosa.

So what kind of future, I wonder, will the next great Tahoe bonanza bring? Hike the trails around the old Ponderosa Ranch theme park today and you'll find omens aplenty to ponder. For starters there are Tahoe's dense second-growth forests, including all those trademark ponderosa pines, which are suffering so severely from drought and disease and climate change that up to 50 percent of the existing trees on the mountainside directly above the theme park have died, left standing like ghostlike sentinels of an impending conflagration. Viewed in that light, the familiar opening credits of *Bonanza*—wherein flames burst through the map of the Ponderosa—seem strangely prophetic, if not downright terrifying. "On this land we put our brand," the theme song lyrics twang. But what will the next episode reveal?

"Across the Continent: The Snow Sheds on the Central Pacific Railroad, in the Sierra Nevada Mountains," by Joseph Becker. *Courtesy of California Historical Society, FN-28150*

thirteen

MAXINE HONG KINGSTON

The Truckee Method

Remember that famous painting of Governor Leland Stanford driving the Golden Spike? May 10, 1869, marked the historic completion of the world's first transcontinental railroad line, straight through the heart of Tahoe territory. A two-thousand-mile journey that had once cost the Donner Party twelve months and more than a dozen lives—laid out along a route first mapped for the U.S. government by John Frémont—could now be traversed in complete luxury in just a few days' time. That same moment also marked what was arguably the world's first fully globalized telecommunications media coverage: telegraph wires laid beside the rails flashed the news instantaneously to New York and San Francisco (and beyond that to the world at large). Yet like countless photo ops before and since, much of what happened that day was actually a fake—including the famous Golden Spike itself (there were two of them, one of which remained stashed away in a secret family collection until 2005). After the Golden Spike and then a Silver Spike were ceremoniously tapped into a predrilled hole with a special little silver hammer, Governor Stanford smiled for the cameras and took a swing at the real iron spike which replaced them—and missed. Even so, the single word "Done" was simultaneously flashed across the continent to an anxiously waiting nation.

Behind the scenes, the real story was far less picturesque. On the Union Pacific side, labor disputes with Irish rail workers had already delayed the event. Days earlier, a gang of eight Chinese workers had laid the last rail for the Central Pacific from the Western side of the continent (just as the Chinese had built virtually every mile of track from California to Utah). At least three of these men (Lee Shao, Ging Cui, and Wong Fook) survived long enough to attend the fiftieth anniversary ceremony in 1919. Yet the violence and persecution these same immigrants had suffered in the intervening fifty years has for the most part been airbrushed out of American history, hidden behind a Gilded Age frame. Far from being rewarded or honored for their amazing feats of endurance, eleven thousand Chinese workers lost their jobs the very next day after the Golden Spike was driven. Outcast and unemployed, banned by law from most ordinary forms of employment, within a decade these same Chinese workers were physically driven out of towns and cities across the West under a slick new form of domestic terrorism known to the world as the "Truckee method." In this tragic sense the little Tahoe railroad town of Truckee still provides a fiery lens through which to view the entire hidden history of Chinese immigration (and survival).

More recently, twentieth-century authors such as Maxine Hong Kingston have forged their own alternative representations of Tahoe's history, hoping to help redefine the very essence of what it means to be an American. As Kingston once told *The New York Times* in reference to her fictionalized historical memoir, *China Men*, "What I am doing in this book is claiming America."

In an era of global air travel and robot rovers on Mars, we tend to forget that construction of the transcontinental railroad was once considered an engineering accomplishment as improbable as putting a man on the moon. Indeed, the whole endeavor was widely mocked as insane. Fortunately, that didn't stop the dreamers from dreaming. Many of Frémont's expeditions were, in fact, explicitly funded with the search for a future transcontinental railroad route in mind. In the midst of the Civil War, Lincoln paused long enough to push through legislation promising untold riches to any company bold enough—or crazy enough—to push a rail line through from St. Louis to San Francisco. Though Lincoln himself never lived to see its completion, the dream of a transcontinental rail link did become a reality in less than a decade—but only because American engineers somehow found a way to run a railroad straight through the granite heart of Tahoe territory.

Pushing a route through the Tahoe Sierra indeed turned out to be by far the most treacherous part of the entire operation. At first, plans were laid to run the rails along the route of present-day U.S. Highway 50 toward the south shore of Lake Tahoe, the so-called Main Street of the West during the Silver Bonanza. Had such plans succeeded, the whole history of Lake Tahoe might have been different. Instead a visionary engineer named Theodore Judah—or "Crazy Judah," as he was derisively called—somehow convinced four prominent Sacramento Gold Rush merchants (Collis Huntington, Leland Stanford, Charles Crocker, and Mark Hopkins, better known to history as the "Big Four"), to build a railroad line straight across the abandoned immigrant route where so many of the Donner Party had died.

As Leland Stanford and his Big Four partners all knew, the completion of Crazy Judah's scheme could make them wealthy beyond imagining. But it could also bankrupt them—requiring construction techniques untested elsewhere, including the use of dangerous new explosives only just then being invented, such as nitroglycerin and dynamite.

In a world where pickaxes, horses, and human muscles were still the main source of motive power, the work of building a railroad across the Sierra's granite walls would also require vast armies of willing workers—because for all practical purposes, the world's first transcontinental railroad would literally have to be built "by hand."

With most of California's able-bodied men flocked to the mining fields, where on earth were the Big Four to find enough contract labor for such a massive endeavor?

In desperation, Charles Crocker eventually turned to Chinese labor (in stark contrast to the largely Irish immigrant workforce employed by the Union Pacific railroad barons back east).

Fleeing civil war and famine in China, from 1849 forward thousands of Chinese had already come to California, which they called "Gold Mountain." Within mere weeks of statehood, however, the California legislature had laid outrageously heavy taxes on Chinese and other nonwhite miners. Simultaneously, the legislature and the U.S. Supreme Court began systematically denying Chinese miners citizenship or legal standing of any kind in American courts. Indeed, for the first ten years of the Golden State's existence, fully two-thirds of California's annual state revenue was derived directly from taxes imposed on Chinese miners, despite the fact that the Chinese could neither vote nor testify in a court of law.

From a contemporary perspective this all sounds like sheer madness. But viewed within the context of the times, such laws seemed to make perfect sense, at least to the vast majority of California's white miners, and few challenged them. In the wake of the recent U.S. military conquest of California, gold and silver were simply viewed as the spoils of war—and hence no Asians, Mexicans, South Americans, or any other group could be allowed to lay claim to them. Clearly such laws were also driven by naked racism and xenophobia: the Chinese, other settlers argued, were irremediably foreign and "heathen," and hence could never be successfully assimilated into true "American" society, no matter how long they stayed.

Several prominent American authors, Mark Twain included, took courageous stands against this growing tide of anti-Chinese hatred. As we saw earlier, Twain penned several editorials in defense of the Chinese "Celestials" in Nevada (providing a welcome counterpoint to his sneers at "Diggers," "niggers," and "miscegenation"). In 1870 Twain's colleague, the frontier humorist Bret

Harte, took the fight one step farther by penning a brutally sarcastic poem which openly mocked the ignorance of anti-Chinese stereotypes. Alas, Harte's poetic prank backfired badly: readers embraced the same stereotypes he had so eagerly sought to lampoon, declaring his work to be a true masterpiece of frontier realism. Retitled "The Heathen Chinee," it remained a perennial favorite well into the next century. Appalled, Harte himself ruefully declared it "the worst poem I ever wrote, possibly the worst poem anyone ever wrote." But the damage was done.

Stung by such stereotypes, the Chinese miners faced economic blackmail as well. Eventually the taxes, the violence, and the flagrant claim jumping drove them from the goldfields completely—leaving anxious legions of unemployed Chinese laborers searching desperately for work elsewhere. Enter Charles Crocker, the Big Four's chief foreman. Fearing the growing efforts of Irish Americans to organize strikes against railroad owners back east, not to mention the Irish reputation for alcoholism, Crocker also feared that it would prove excessively difficult, expensive, and slow to import sufficient numbers of Irish laborers to distant California—or to keep them from running off to the mines once they had arrived. Why not use Chinese labor to build the rails here in California? Not surprisingly, given the vicious anti-Chinese prejudice Harte and Twain had battled, Crocker's plan was initially mocked and derided. Outraged editorials even labeled the new Chinese railroad workers "Crocker's Pets." But the strength and success of the new Chinese workers soon silenced the doubters.

"Who said laborers have to be white to build railroads?" Crocker angrily demanded when his white managers refused to work with the Chinese. "They built the Great Wall of China, didn't they?" And indeed, the American transcontinental railroad soon became the rough equivalent of China's Great Wall, the eighth wonder of the modern world.

Today you won't find any towering thirty-foot-high brass monuments in California dedicated to Chinese workers, although the Donner Party monument still stands directly in the shadows of rail lines the Chinese carved out of solid granite. Instead the railroad itself must stand as the sole monument to their sacrifices, triumphs, and struggles.

Arguably the greatest engineering feat of the nineteenth century, the road's completion radically transformed the very nature of America. As historian Stephen Ambrose reminds us in his Pulitzer Prize–winning history, there was indeed *Nothing Like It in the World.* "Not until the completion of the Panama Canal in the early twentieth century," Ambrose asserts, "was it rivaled as an engineering feat." Nor was the world's first transcontinental railroad primarily the work of any one individual or group: politicians and visionary planners, engineers and bankers, entrepreneurs and ordinary foremen all played pivotal roles in its construction. But above all, Ambrose argues, this revolutionary railroad could never have been built "without those who came over to America in the thousands from China, seeking a fortune."

In *China Men*, published in 1980, Maxine Hong Kingston recreates the world of these anonymous Chinese railroad workers through the eyes of her paternal grandfather, an immigrant laborer from Canton named Ah Goong. Together with her first book, *The Woman Warrior* (1976), *China Men* earned Kingston the National Book Award in 1981—and it has remained a favorite in American literature courses ever since.

In the culminating chapter of *China Men*, titled "The Grandfather of the Sierra Nevada Mountains," Kingston describes the dangerous process of carving out the railroad's path through solid granite. It's an astonishing tale. As Ah Goong himself reminds us, only the lightest and strongest of the Chinese laborers were selected for the dangerous task of setting dynamite charges into the vertical granite walls. The men were first carefully lowered down the sheer faces of the cliffs in woven wicker baskets, something like human Spidermen suspended at the ends of long ropes. Dangling wildly out over empty space, they would light long fuses to set off the explosive charges they had carried down the cliff face with them, thereby blasting out a thin shelf across the vertical walls of granite for the iron rails to cling to. As soon as the fuses were lit, the basketmen would signal those waiting to haul them back up the cliff to safety. At least that was the plan.

Inevitably many of these basketmen died when the charges they had set exploded prematurely, or when the ropes broke, or both. Elsewhere along the railroad, literally thousands of Chinese workers died in routine work-related accidents and avalanches, some of which swept away whole tent villages filled with Chinese workers.

For Maxine Hong Kingston, it is these Chinese railroad workers—not the Donner Party—whose heroism and sacrifice best embody the concept of American Manifest Destiny. The famous story of the Donner Party's cannibalism warrants only passing mention in *China Men*. Turnabout is fair play: "A party of snowbound barbarians," Ah Goong recalls vaguely, "had eaten the dead. Cannibals, thought Ah Goong, and looked around." In Ah Goong's eyes, it isn't the Chinese who are acting like "barbarians"—and it certainly isn't the Native Americans either. Instead it is the railroad bosses.

Describing the process of setting explosive charges on sheer granite faces, Kingston writes of "cliffs, sheer drops under impossible overhangs" where the men "lowered one another down in wicker baskets made stronger by the lucky words they had painted on four sides." Among these brave basketmen, Kingston's grandfather Ah Goong "saw the world sweep underneath him." Intoxicated by a feeling close to flying, he glimpsed "men like ants changing the face of the world" from on high. "Godlike," Kingston imagines, "he watched men whose faces he could not see and whose screams he did not hear roll and bounce and slide like a handful of sprinkled gravel." Through Ah Goong's eyes, it seems, human beings increasingly appear as insignificant as ants. Ironically, the Chinese themselves were often treated as such by their employers: swarming armies of faceless laborers sacrificed as needed to get the railroad built on time. Indeed, if anyone was acting "godlike" in their arrogant indifference to real human suffering, it was the Big Four themselves.

Later still, Ah Goong finds himself working with another gang of Chinese laborers, this one assigned to excavate one of a dozen great tunnels hewn straight through the heart of the Tahoe Sierra's solid granite battlements. In an era before power tools or heavy earthmoving equipment, excavating tunnels was almost unimaginably slow work. The longest of these tunnels, the notorious Number 6, still stands, empty, at the crest of Donner Pass today. (It was replaced by a larger, wider tunnel during the twentieth century.) Sneak a peek inside and you can feel the weight of the mountains, indeed of history itself, pressing down upon you in the darkness. At 1,659 feet long, the shaft lies as much as 124 feet beneath the surface of the earth. Daily progress in excavation was literally measured in inches, not feet. To speed the work, Crocker sent the crews working from both directions, twenty-four hours a day, seven days a week, throughout the brutal Tahoe Sierra winter. Squeezed together in the dark, one man would hold the rock drill square against the face of the granite, with two others swinging eighteen-pound sledgehammers to drive it in. In *China Men*, one of those men is Ah Goong.

Inch by inch, each newly drilled hole was packed with powder, lit with a fuse, and exploded in a deadly shower of stone. Often the fuses misfired. Dozens of Chinese workers died. As usual, Crocker and his partners shrugged it all off as the cost of doing business. After all, they reasoned, financially the tunnels were killing them too, costing well in excess of $50,000 per month to excavate.

Despite this creeping pace, the railroads themselves had already revolutionized humanity's concept of time and space completely—and this concept too plays a central role in Kingston's book. To quote historian Stephen Ambrose once more, "The locomotive was the greatest thing of the age. With it man conquered space and time." Laboring deep within the earth for three solid years, Ah Goong comes to an opposite set of conclusions, confronting what he calls "Stone Time": "Men change, men die, weather changes, but a mountain is the same as permanence and time…time unmoving," he muses. In essence, what Ah Goong has encountered head-on is what geologists call "deep time"— the vast sweep of time on a scale that makes the Western railroads' "conquest" of time seem puny by comparison. "Tell the foreigners that," Ah Goong asks the translators.

On a far less abstract level, Kingston's story culminates in the unsuccessful labor strike which Chinese rail workers launched in a desperate bid to win higher wages and better working conditions. "This is the hardest blow we have had," Crocker complained, confronted with the Chinese demand for a raise of five dollars per month and even an eight-hour workday. Yet wages and hours were not the sole issue at stake here. As the *Sacramento Union* reported, the Chinese also wanted to block "the right of the overseers of the company to either whip them or restrain them from leaving the road when they desire to seek other employment." Ultimately the strike was brutally crushed when the railroad bosses cut off all food supplies to the isolated Chinese camps. Starved into submission, the Chinese reluctantly returned to the brutal work of carving a railroad through the Tahoe Sierra.

Even in the face of broken strikes and starvation, however, Kingston's own "Grandfather of the Sierra Nevada" somehow retains his lust for life—sometimes literally. In one passage, Ah Goong even engages in an onanistic ritual he calls "fucking the world." "One beautiful day," Kingston explains, "dangling in the sun above a new valley, not the desire to urinate but sexual desire clutched him so hard he bent over in the basket. He curled up, overcome by beauty and fear, which shot to his penis...he fucked the world." To be honest, my own interpretation of this controversial passage is far more ecological than erotic. "Nowhere," the historian Rebecca Solnit points out, "is naming as a form of sexual possession more evident than in the West. Invasion was described in highly erotic terms. The land was virgin, untouched, undiscovered, unspoiled, and its discoverer penetrated the wilderness, conquered it, set his mark upon it, took possession of it with the planting of his flag or with the plough." In short, despite his lowly position as a laborer, Ah Goong responds directly to the erotic charge behind the railroads' "conquest" of time and space. Viewed in this light, his sexual antics symbolize the implicit rape of the virgin wilderness itself. Perhaps, Kingston implies, we are still "fucking with" the world even now.

What happened to men like Ah Goong after the railroad was completed? Kingston herself answers that question in two ways: first by tracing the lives and legacies of other males in her family, including her own father (Ah Goong's son); and second by tracing the equally tangled legacy of the Chinese exclusion laws, which prevented father and son from ever seeing one another again in America. Indeed, one section of *China Men* lists these laws in agonizing detail, from the Gold Rush era all the way forward to the Second World War (when America's notorious anti-Asian immigration laws were finally loosened in deference to our wartime ally China).

In effect it has taken several more decades for professional historians to catch up with Kingston's vision. First published in 2007, Professor Jean Pfaelzer's book *Driven Out: The Forgotten War against Chinese Americans* chronicles the Chinese exclusion laws in meticulous detail. Painfully, much of Pfaelzer's narrative revolves in a shockingly persistent way around events in Truckee.

As Kingston emphasizes, and as Pfaelzer's work verifies, the full saga of the Chinese exclusion laws took many decades, not just years, to unfold. Following the completion of the railroad in 1869, thousands of unemployed Chinese workers arrived in Truckee searching for whatever work they could find, arguably making Truckee's Chinatown the largest in America. Banned from working in the mines, and now unable to find work with the railroads either, many of these itinerant Chinese found jobs in fields deemed too low-paying (or simply too lowly) for other workers to pursue, working as laundrymen, cooks, and domestic servants (not unlike *Bonanza*'s Hop Sing, who performed all three of these tasks on Tahoe's fictional Ponderosa Ranch). Hundreds of others found work as lumberjacks, stripping Tahoe's forests to shore the tunnels or fuel the railroads or build the cities of America's frontier. During the winter hundreds more Chinese were put to work sawing blocks of ice from the rivers and ponds near Lake Tahoe to help ship the tens of thousands of pounds of fresh trout which Chinese fishermen were harvesting from Tahoe itself. As long as the silver mines of Nevada kept pumping out their bonanza, such menial jobs were widely considered too difficult or too low-paying for anyone but the Chinese to take. But as soon as the crushing economic Panic of 1873 struck the nation, such "menial" jobs suddenly seemed precious. The result was a brutal backlash against Chinese labor by various working-class whites—including the Irish, their old competitors in building the railroad lines. Attacked and burned out repeatedly, Truckee's Chinatown would be repeatedly besieged by violent mobs screaming, "The Chinese must go!"

When the Chinese refused to leave their homes, a vigilante group was formed, loosely modeled on the South's emerging Ku Klux Klan. In Truckee as elsewhere in the West, this group called itself the 601 (signifying "six feet under, zero trial, and one bullet"). Leading citizens also formed a white supremacist group called the Caucasian League. Faced with these new forms of domestic terrorism, the Chinese leaders in Truckee initially compromised by moving their dwellings to the far side of the Truckee River. Less than a year later, beginning in 1875, this brand-new Chinatown was repeatedly burned to the ground as well.

A decade later, in 1885, Charles F. McGlashan, the editor and publisher of Tahoe's leading newspaper, the *Truckee Republican*, stepped forward to harness the fires of anti-Chinese hatred for his own private gain. Coincidentally, it was McGlashan who had first made the saga of the Donner Party famous by compiling and republishing their diaries, along with new testimony by the aging survivors, some thirty years after the original tragedy occurred. Based in part on the immense fame his saga of the Donner party generated, McGlashan set out to run for governor of California, loosely modeling his campaign on the platform of our old friend Governor John Bigler. But whereas Bigler lumped Indians, blacks, and Chinese together as targets in order to win more votes, McGlashan focused solely on the Chinese, blaming them for virtually all of California's social ills, from prostitution to drug use to venereal disease and unemployment.

Rejecting outright violence—he was, after all, still running as a Lincoln Republican—McGlashan lobbied Truckee's Caucasian League to boycott any white businessman who hired Chinese labor. This became the core of McGlashan's "Truckee method." In essence, instead of simply burning the Chinese out or menacing them with murderous mob violence, as the residents of Tacoma and other coastal cities had recently done, McGlashan declared instead that Truckee would simply starve them out—along with anyone who dared to support them.

This was frontier fascism with a vengeance. To their enduring credit, the Chinese in Truckee and elsewhere across the West fought back bravely against such tactics, using everything from lawsuits to firearms to defend themselves. In the long run, however, McGlashan's boycott proved all too successful. So successful, in fact, that cities across the nation openly debated the choice between the so-called Tacoma method (using murderous mob violence to drive out the Chinese) and McGlashan's more indirect and supposedly gentler Truckee method.

In truth, the secret behind the Truckee method's success was the implicit threat of violence should the terms of the boycott be broken. In essence this made the Tacoma and Truckee methods two sides of the same murderous coin. In Truckee itself, for example, behind the screen of McGlashan's more temperate nonviolent rhetoric, the Chinese and their employers were surreptitiously threatened with death, arson, rape, and other forms of terror.

Granted, some of Truckee's white citizens did attempt to defy the boycott, at least at first. Several prominent business owners even declared they could not survive without Chinese labor. These included the former railroad magnate Charles Crocker, by now heavily invested in Tahoe timber. Just as he had during his days with the Central Pacific, Crocker fought the boycott with all the considerable political firepower at his command. Yet eventually even the great Charles Crocker caved in. Stoking the fires of anti-Chinese hatred ever higher by means of his syndicated statewide newspaper columns, McGlashan gloated openly when Crocker was forced, in order to stay in business, to fire hundreds of his Chinese lumberjacks.

Damning as they sound today, surprisingly few of these indictments against McGlashan's conduct remain open to serious question. His own public statements on "the Chinese Question" are simply too voluminous, too detailed, and too explicit to admit any other conclusion. As the elected leader of Truckee's Caucasian League, for example, McGlashan personally issued an ultimatum that "all individuals, companies, and corporations…discharge any and all Chinamen by January 1, 1886, and refuse to give them work of any kind." Soon white mobs were wandering Truckee's streets carrying banners declaring "The Chinese must go" and "Success to Anti-Coolie." Warned that the Chinese were arming themselves for a fight, McGlashan responded coldly that "if force is necessary…it will be used." Meanwhile anyone brave enough to stand up against the boycott would be slandered as a "China lover" and boycotted himself. In one especially virulent editorial, McGlashan predicted "a bitter, relentless warfare unto the death."

Faced with such naked threats of violence on all fronts, even the U.S. Marshal sent from San Francisco to defend the Chinese fled town. Inspired by Truckee's example, towns across the American West were soon waging similar boycotts and battles—with McGlashan always at their epicenter. Elected as Truckee's representative to the state convention of the Anti-Chinese League held in San Jose the following summer, McGlashan maneuvered to become a nationwide leader of the anti-Chinese movement, noisily demanding that the U.S. cancel its treaties with China and strengthen the laws barring Asian immigration. Like any good demagogue, he bitterly scorned all who opposed him. Nor did he ever shrink from mixing Christian doctrine with his own peculiar brand of hatred. In one column laced with Christian imagery, he even went so far as to brand the Chinese as biblical sons of Cain.

Women and even children were enlisted in this sordid campaign: "Let our mothers, wives and sisters draw their skirts as they pass them on the street," he wrote. "Let them teach the little ones to abhor a Chinaman or his upholder. Let the little fingers be pointed at them, and the first words that fall from their baby lips be 'Shame, you China lover.'"

The longevity of these racist curses in California's culture is amply demonstrated by John Steinbeck in his classic novella *Cannery Row*, published in 1945. Recalling boyhood tales of a lone, ghostly, old "Chinaman" who wanders the streets of Monterey late at night, Steinbeck's story tells of a little boy named Andy "singing in a shrill falsetto, 'Ching-Chong Chinaman sitting on a rail—Long came a white man an' chopped off his tail.'" What makes Steinbeck's little vignette so haunting is the bizarre survival of McGlashan's trademark stereotypes among California's school-children some six decades later. The wounds of hatred Tahoe had inflicted on the nation took several generations to heal.

But let's step back once more to the original source of the trouble: the first spasm of anti-Asian violence in Truckee—including riots and burnings—had come in the wake of the Panic of 1873. Now, more than a decade later, as the February 15, 1886, deadline McGlashan had set for the Chinese to leave Truckee came and went, bonfires and midnight torchlight rallies burned in towns up and down the spine of the Sierra. Just to make sure this message was crystal clear, the Truckee Hose and Engine Company flew one banner reading, "ORGANIZED TO PROTECT WHITE MEN'S PROPERTY" and another hailing "OUR NEXT GOVERNOR, C. F. MCGLASHAN, WHITE LABOR'S CHAMPION." To signal their solidarity with the angry male mobs outside, the wives of Truckee's white citizens even burned candles in every window.

Having been attacked many times before, armed groups of Chinese men organized to guard the bridges and river crossings. Others fled back to San Francisco in terror; some all the way back to China. A few even accepted offers to work on the new railroad connecting Mexico City with the Pacific—only to be confronted by more racist violence there. Then on June 17, 1886, the final Truckee firestorm burst, this time wiping out Truckee's Chinatown once and for all. "The greasy shanties," McGlashan's *Republican* crowed, were quickly enveloped in "one mass of flames." Sounding the alarm, the Truckee Hose and Engine Company rushed into action—not to protect the Chinese, of course, but instead to save the bridge across the Truckee River to Tahoe. The town of Truckee, McGlashan concluded, "has been cleansed and purged of its disease breeding nastiness."

"The present struggle," he added darkly, "is a final one."

"Cleansed" once and for all of its Chinese population, Truckee did not exactly become a model of moral propriety (as McGlashan vainly promised that it would). Instead the little Tahoe town once again became notorious coast to coast, now as a national headquarters for brewing bootleg whiskey. With its mining, fishing, and timber industries now in sharp decline—and with doorstep access to the nation's railways—Truckee's citizens increasingly turned to brewing booze to survive, much like the impoverished populations further east, in Appalachia. When Prohibition took effect in the 1920s, new speakeasies popped up along Truckee's backstreets like mushrooms.

Accounts of this era provide a vivid window into yet another chapter of Tahoe's hidden history. Most speakeasies could only be accessed via doors armed with peepholes and barred entry cages. Others were connected to Truckee's ever-notorious red-light district. If a saloonkeeper was arrested, a stand-in was sent to jail instead. Murder was commonplace—with bodies frequently dumped in the cemetery for disposal, as were hundreds of gallons of excess liquor. One year Truckee's storm drains became so clogged that the entire sewer system shut down. "After two days of digging," McGlashan's *Truckee Republican* chuckled, "an investigation showed that the stoppage was due to large quantities of corn mash being dumped into the system." In one raid, seventy-five gallons of wine and four stills were seized, along with "15 gallons of Jackass Brandy and 350 gallons of mash." Gambling dens of all kinds also remained rampant. So much for McGlashan's promises of "cleaning up" Truckee.

Ironically, gambling also provided the means for Maxine Hong Kingston's family's survival. Shut out from most forms of legal employment by McGlashan's Truckee method boycotts, many Chinese families across California struggled to support themselves by any means necessary—including underground gambling. Hence by the time Maxine Hong Kingston herself was born in 1940, her father (Ah Goong's son) owned an illegal casino in Stockton, 150 miles west of Lake Tahoe. Having planned to name his first son after a lucky local gambler known as Max, Tom Hong simply changed the name to "Maxine" when a daughter arrived instead. Judging by the long list of literary awards Maxine Hong Kingston has brought home, Max must have been a very auspicious name indeed.

Alas for Kingston's "Grandfather of the Sierra Nevada," the man she named Ah Goong, he never succeeded in being united with his son—nor did he live to meet Maxine. In her *Fifth Book of Peace*, published in 2003, Kingston asks her mother, "How is it that my father and grandfather didn't meet?" "By the time your father got to Cuba," her mother explains, "your grandfather left for California. They missed each other." But this "missing" is more than just a matter of random fate. Instead it was those notorious Chinese exclusion laws championed by Tahoe's McGlashan, among others, which ultimately succeeded in separating father and son forever. "Your father was caught twice by Immigration in New York," Kingston's mother explains, "put in jail, and deported back to Cuba....by the time he settled in New York, your grandfather was at the other side of America and leaving for China." Separated by an ocean, Kingston reports, father and son never even exchanged letters— only poems.

These days Truckee is a different world entirely. Within restored Victorian buildings that once housed brothels and whiskey stills, boutique restaurants, upscale shops, and classy ski chalets now thrive. Even the old Chinese medicinal herb shop, built from brick to resist arson, has been lovingly restored by the local historical association. A few miles further upstream toward Tahoe, Amy Tan, one of America's best-known authors, owns a cabin. "What Walden once was for Thoreau," Tan jokes, "perhaps Tahoe can be for Tan."

The only official monument dedicated to the Chinese railroad workers lies some ten thousand miles away from Tahoe, on the far side of the Pacific Ocean. Set amid the shimmering skyscrapers of modern Shanghai, the monument consists of an abstract pyramid some thirty feet tall composed entirely of iron railroad spikes. In both Chinese and English, a simple brass plaque speaks eloquently of the thousands of Chinese who journeyed out from this port in search of Gold Mountain. Not one of the spikes in that pyramid is golden.

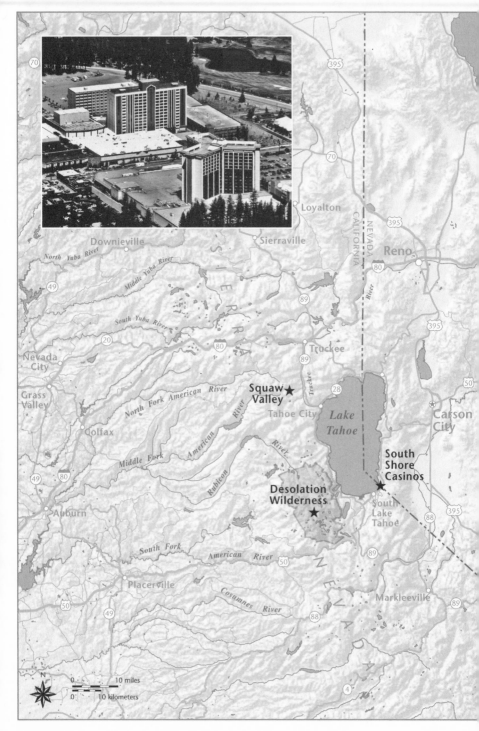

South Lake Tahoe. Photograph by Scott Lankford

fourteen

MICHAEL ONDAATJE *and* GARY SNYDER

Déjà Blue

So far our journey beneath the surface of Lake Tahoe has focused on the past. But what about Tahoe's future (and our own)? What changes will the next one hundred years—or even the next one thousand years, or ten thousand years—bring to the Lake of the Sky? What prophesies, what promises, what perils does the increasingly murky crystal ball of Lake Tahoe's literature reveal to those who dare to stare beneath its surface? Is there a new generation of Steinbecks and Winnemuccas lurking out there in the woods, working on the next great American novel?

To date, only two authors writing about Tahoe in the twenty-first century already enjoy truly global reputations. They represent starkly contrasting visions of the lake and its landscape, virtual opposites on the spectrum of possible Tahoe futures: the one dystopian, the other utopian. Which, then, of these two contrasting futures will we ourselves choose to embrace?

In his novel *Divisadero*, published in 2008, Michael Ondaatje conjures a dark underworld of professional gambling, deception, amnesia, and brutal violence in which the natural beauty of Lake Tahoe itself disappears completely, eclipsed by human illusions. By contrast, poet and essayist Gary Snyder has long argued for a radical reconnection to the natural world of the Sierra Nevada—creating a human community rooted in respect for Native cultures and local ecosystems. Viewed through the watery blue lens of Lake Tahoe, the contrast could not be more striking: where Ondaatje's characters struggle against a dark undercurrent of alienation and despair, Snyder's work remains optimistic, joyful, playful, sensuous, gently humorous, and deeply healing.

Born in Sri Lanka but educated in England and Quebec, Canada's Michael Ondaatje first came to fame with his Booker Prize–winning novel *The English Patient*, subsequently a hit Hollywood film. In *Divisadero* Ondaatje weaves together three apparently separate landscapes: coastal California, southern France, and Lake Tahoe. Similarly, his plot revolves around the separate lives of adoptive siblings—Coop, Anna, and Claire—whose idyllic family life is shattered during their teenage years by violence and incest. Fleeing for their lives, the three never meet again—except, and then only briefly, at Lake Tahoe.

At the center of his novel Ondaatje presents a detailed portrait of the professional poker players who inhabit the South Shore Tahoe casinos. Into this eerie underworld steps one of the three siblings, Coop. A close-knit circle of professional Tahoe gamblers take this lost young man under their wing as a willing apprentice. Something in the churning vortex of risk and deceit at the Tahoe tables calls out to Coop. In Ondaatje's words, "When he saw drunks steer themselves uncertainly between the card tables in Tahoe, as if avoiding whirlpools, he recognized the same look that had been on him and other fooled youths." In effect Tahoe becomes Coop's second adopted home; this loose group of professional card sharks his new makeshift family.

By sheer coincidence Coop and his long-lost adopted sister Claire meet in a Tahoe diner. Yet their reunion immediately turns bloody when Coop suffers a near-fatal beating at the hands of rival gamblers. In scenes reminiscent of *The English Patient*, Claire nurses her critically wounded brother back to health in a rented chalet. But much as in *The English Patient*, the trauma of his wounds has left Coop with near-complete amnesia. Unable to recognize Claire, Coop briefly mistakes her for their sister Anna (his adopted father's child, with whom Coop once shared a stormy incestuous affair). Intrigued by this unexpected chance to "be Anna," Claire does not attempt to correct Coop's mistake. Lost in a maze of false memories and unrecognized mirages, all three siblings are, in a sense, finally reunited at Lake Tahoe.

Of course their fleeting reunion is little more than a tangled illusion brought on by Coop's amnesia and Claire's acquiescence to her new role as Anna: a mask of intimacy born of lost identity, violence, and erotic confusion. In the end Coop and Claire part, returning to their separate lives, never to meet again—and never to meet Anna again either. Tahoe alone, it seems, had the power to unite them—and then only briefly, based on a delusion.

Without delving further into the intricacies of Ondaatje's notoriously complex plot, we can now begin to ask what role, if any, Lake Tahoe itself plays in this strange novel. The answer is none. Instead the natural landscape of Lake Tahoe outside the casino walls disappears from *Divisadero* completely, providing a crucial symbolic key to the novel's hidden moral depths. For although Ondaatje never says so outright, the utter absence of any natural description of the Lake Tahoe landscape is clearly designed to shock us into some kind of new awareness—and so it does. This is in sharp contrast to the hundreds of pages of lush prose Ondaatje lavishes on landscapes elsewhere in the novel, from coastal California to the South of France. That's the point: lost in this murky moral wasteland, Claire and Coop seem as emotionally distant from each other as they are from the lake.

When Ondaatje finally does mention Tahoe directly, several dozen pages of prose have flown by. Even then, Tahoe makes its first appearance only briefly, and only in the context of absence, death, and emotional trauma. As Coop and his circle of gamblers mourn the sudden death of one of their pals, a professional poker player nicknamed "the Dauphin," Ondaatje speaks of how the men "watched in silence, remembered anecdotes about the Dauphin, then got in the car and took a drive around the lake." That's it. No dialog. No description. No scenic detail. No interior monologues. Nothing. Only the choked silence of an unspoken grief, with the mute circle of "the lake" at its unspoken center.

Claire's relationship to the natural world of Lake Tahoe seems, if anything, even more remote than her adopted brother's. Earlier in the novel Claire literally revels in the rolling rural landscape of coastal California, wandering for days on end on horseback through the open countryside. By contrast, at Tahoe she drifts immediately into a drug-infested nightclub and shuts herself up inside. Cocooned for hours, perhaps even days, within the club's windowless confines, she stares blankly at mute television screens where the bloody murder scene from Hitchcock's *Psycho* loops ominously over and over. Then "at some point during her evening," Ondaatje reveals, "someone offered Claire a tablet." Stoned to the gills and now dancing limply, "jammed up against several bodies moving together like particles of a wave," Claire muses groggily to herself that "she was in Tahoe for something, but she could no longer remember what." Whatever "it" is, she certainly won't be going outside to search. Instead, "she would go into the silent room, behind thick pneumatic doors, and work it out there. The reason for being in Tahoe would then roll in her direction like a marble."

And so it does.

In a wild-card plot twist, "Somewhere during this somnambulistic walk she saw someone who looked like Coop..." Their utterly unexpected reunion stuns them both. Here the lake itself makes a brief appearance, but glimpsed as through a glass darkly. Returning with Claire to her hotel room, "Coop walked over to the window that showed the still-pulsing lights of Tahoe." Here the lights do not so much embody the lake as define its absence: ringed by the flickering windows of the South Shore casinos, the water itself remains an inky absence. Tahoe Blue fades to Tahoe Black.

Then through a series of flashbacks Coop's fatal attraction to a femme fatale named Bridget is revealed: Bridget, we learn, has gradually seduced Coop. He has returned to Lake Tahoe despite threats to his life—only to discover, in a classic film noir reversal, that she has consciously deceived and betrayed him; his decision to return at Bridget's behest has led him straight into a trap. After the near-fatal beating at the hands of Bridget's compatriots that induces his amnesia, he literally loses himself completely.

Clearly it is no accident that Ondaatje titles the Tahoe section of his novel "Out of the Past"—thereby invoking the 1947 black-and-white film noir classic shot on location at Lake Tahoe. Long hailed as among the most influential Hollywood films of all time, *Out of the Past* launched the career of a young Robert Mitchum (who plays a former detective seeking to escape his sordid past). It also helped launch the career of a young Kirk Douglas (who plays the grinning mobster whose stone estate overlooks Tahoe's Emerald Bay) and made a sinister sex symbol out of Jane Greer (who inspired every Hollywood femme fatale from that point forward).

Framed amid smoky interior scenes of murder and deceit, the fevered black-and-white close-ups first featured in *Out of the Past* set the tone for a whole genre of Hollywood whodunits, now loosely grouped as film noir. Yet in the original film version of *Out of the Past* all is not smoke and mirrors after all: instead the cinematic backdrop of *Out of the Past* also features some of the most stunning wide-angle shots of Lake Tahoe ever to grace the silver screen. Here the lake itself provides a crucial visual counterpoint to the murderous plotline, symbolically framing the detective's quest to escape his violent past even while he discovers he has been literally "framed" by his lover.

In Ondaatje's novel, Coop too struggles to rebuild his life at Lake Tahoe yet finds himself brutally "framed" as a result. In a classic film noir reversal, he realizes only too late that "Bridget was there only to bring him to Tahoe, with the crook of her finger, with a swirl from her sea-green skirt." In a rare flash of self-awareness, Coop "saw himself in the frame, surrounded by the con."

Here, then, we encounter a crucial difference between the film *Out of the Past* and Ondaatje's novel *Divisadero*: in the film, Tahoe itself vividly embodies an older, simpler, purer, uncorrupted America. In *Divisadero*, by contrast, Lake Tahoe no longer offers any hope of redemption. In an opening sequence from *Out of the Past*, for example, the former detective and his new Tahoe girlfriend enjoy a perfect picnic (and an innocent kiss) framed against the world-famous background of Emerald Bay, often cited as among the most frequently photographed landscapes on Earth. For a brief moment their world seems drenched in sunlight and joy, the detective's escape from his sordid past complete. Within mere seconds this idyll is shattered by the sudden arrival of an unwelcome messenger from—where else?—"out of the past." Yet even then Tahoe shimmers on unperturbed and unbloodied. Later the blood of a man murdered at Emerald Bay is even literally washed away by the rushing current of Eagle Falls, the symbolic sanctity of Lake Tahoe still unsullied.

Of course *Out of the Past* was hardly the first, much less the last, Hollywood epic to use Tahoe as a backdrop for cinematic drama. From the earliest days of silent film forward, Tahoe had hosted Hollywood's elite—including Charlie Chaplin, Clark Gable, and Elizabeth Taylor. A few years after *Out of the Past* came out, in the 1951 film *A Place in the Sun* (which garnered eight Academy Awards), a stunning eighteen-year-old Elizabeth Taylor embraces Montgomery Clift against a flaming Technicolor Tahoe sunset. That kiss became one of the most iconic and influential film close-ups of all time. Yet just as in earlier film noir formulas, sex and betrayal drive the plot of *A Place in the Sun* relentlessly forward: scheming to escape his working-class origins, the up-and-coming young man murders his pregnant girlfriend to salvage his chance of marrying a debutante. The crux of the film even features a murder staged on a boat floating out on Lake Tahoe (or "Loon Lake," as it appears in the script).

Perhaps the most famous Lake Tahoe murder scene ever captured on film came several decades later at the climax of *The Godfather: Part II*, in 1971. Here again the cinematic influence of *Out of the Past* is unmistakable, from the smiling gangland godfather with his lakeside mansion to the inevitable murder scene in a boat out on the lake. When the Godfather's brother Fredo is quietly murdered, once again on a boat on the lake, Tahoe Blue literally floods the screen.

In all these Tahoe film classics, then, the implicit subtext is that big-city corruption threatens small-town values (with Tahoe standing in for old-fashioned American purity). Hence when Michael Ondaatje suddenly erases the natural world of Lake Tahoe from his novel altogether, all the while explicitly invoking the iconic film *Out of the Past*, he is clearly aiming for a contrast—and a subtext of a sharply different sort. This time, in Ondaatje's indictment, instead of being washed away by Tahoe Blue, American morality is literally splashed like blood across a bank of mute TV screens locked inside the casinos, with Lake Tahoe itself nowhere to be seen. Indeed, right at the crux of Coop's poker-playing con game inside the casino, the crucial distraction Coop needs to disguise his "corrupt shuffle" takes the form of Operation Desert Storm, brazenly beamed into the casino's cavernous interior by means of satellite downlink and then brought deviously into the conversation by Coop's card-sharking accomplice. In effect, Ondaatje implies, America's weapons of mass destruction have become weapons of mass distraction (not just here inside the casino but worldwide). Viewed from within the closed confines of this video-saturated, greed-infested world, war itself has become just another mirage. Here, then, is Ondaatje's description of the Gulf War as viewed from inside the casinos of Lake Tahoe.

> The Gulf War begins at 2:35 a.m. during the early hours of January 17, 1991. But it is just another late afternoon in the casinos of Nevada. The television sets hanging in mid-air that normally replay horse races or football games are running animated illustrations of the American attack. For the three thousand gamblers inhaling piped-in oxygen...the war is already a video game, taking place on a fictional planet.

Amid this mazelike world of man-made mirages, Lake Tahoe itself is simply nowhere to be seen. Clearly Ondaatje's core message here is that the casinos and the killing fields are linked. To double-emphasize this connection, in the same paragraph Ondaatje immediately follows up his catalog of "floor shows, cell-phone hookers, masseurs at work..." with an equally detailed catalog of the digitally enhanced weapons of postmodern warfare:

> Simultaneously, in the other desert's night, orange-white explosions and fireballs light up the horizon. By 2:38 U.S. helicopters and stealth bombers are firing missiles and dropping penetration bombs into the city. During the next four days, one of the great high-tech massacres of the modern era takes place. The Cobra helicopter, the Warthog, the Spectre, and its twin, the Spooky, loiter over the desert highway and the retreating Iraqi troops, pouring down thermobaric fuel, volatile gasses, and finely powdered explosives, to consume all oxygen so that the bodies below them implode, crushing into themselves.

What in the world does the bombing of Baghdad have to do with Lake Tahoe? Everything—at least in Ondaatje's bleak fiction. Even the legendary oxygen piped into the casinos (rumored to make gamblers feel giddy) mirrors the oxygen-starved implosion of charred bodies back in Iraq. Deep beneath the surface, Ondaatje implies, these two apparently separate worlds are in fact one. Cut off from nature, cut off from each other, this is what happens to the human spirit: souls implode like rootless plants in a withering drought—a warning heightened, not diminished, by Lake Tahoe's own darkly implicit yet still invisible presence just outside the casino's windowless walls. If we continue to cut ourselves off from the natural world in this way, Ondaatje warns us, this too may become our future.

Set against the lurid gloom of Ondaatje's dystopian nightmares, Gary Snyder's poetry does indeed sound utopian—although he himself would simply see it as realistic. For more than fifty years Snyder has urged Americans to reconnect with the natural world, and with each other: to "become Native to this place" within the physical and spiritual watershed boundaries of the local, the regional, and the earthy. Hence for Snyder nature is no empty "blank space" or even a "virgin" wilderness waiting to be exploited, much less a violent video game. Instead the Sierra Nevada becomes a place of grace gifted with an ancient healing power. Indeed, in Snyder's work it is the human-made world of the casinos which disappears from view—eclipsed by what he calls (in his signature work of poetry) *Mountains and Rivers Without End.*

Above all it is Snyder's overflowing sense of joy that distinguishes his work from Ondaatje's seething despair. In the words of literary critic Greg Garrard, Snyder's doctrine is "part deep ecology, part Beat Generation hedonism, and all gentle, humane injunction." As Snyder himself insists:

We can enjoy our humanity with its flashy brains and sexual buzz, its social cravings and stubborn tantrums, and take ourselves as no more and no less than another being in the Big Watershed. We can accept each other all as barefoot equals sleeping on the same ground. We can give up hoping to be eternal and quit fighting dirt. We can chase off mosquitoes and fence out varmints without hating them...The wild requires that we learn the terrain, nod to all the plants and animals and birds, ford the streams and cross the ridges, and tell a good story when we get back home.

For more than forty years Snyder has told his own Sierra homecoming story in both essays and poems. Born in San Francisco in 1930, he was raised on a family farm in rural Washington, attending Oregon's Reed College and the University of California at Berkeley to study anthropology, literature, and linguistics (all lifelong passions). Later he spent years studying Zen Buddhism in China and Japan. He now has a mountain of literary awards to his credit, beginning with a Pulitzer Prize for Poetry in 1975, but his rise to fame began during the legendary San Francisco Renaissance of the 1950s. Portrayed as Japhy Ryder in Jack Kerouac's iconic Beat generation novel *The Dharma Bums*, he began building his rustic home in the Yuba River Valley, just outside the boundaries of the Tahoe National Forest, in 1971. There he has emphatically remained rooted ever since.

As a Tahoe-area writer, Snyder's credentials are impressive. For several years he taught at the celebrated Squaw Valley Community of Writers workshops. More recently he became a founding member of the newly created Tahoe Environmental Research Center. Two of his most recent books include the Tahoe watershed within their wider range of concerns: *The High Sierra of California,* published in 2005, includes excerpts from journals Snyder penned in the Desolation Wilderness, at the highest reaches of the Tahoe watershed; *Back on the Fire*, a collection of essays published in 2008, features Snyder's thoughts on fire ecology in the Tahoe National Forest.

In effect, Snyder has made it his life's work to "reinhabit" the Tahoe Sierra by becoming "native to this place" in the spirit of the Native American tribes who have already lived here for countless generations. As for newcomers (like himself), Snyder quips, "We are going to stay right here for the next 3000 years and learn how to do it right." As the Harvard ethnologist Wade Davis explains, "When the American poet Gary Snyder was once asked to discuss at length how individuals could best help resolve the environmental crisis, he responded with two words: 'Stay put.' Only by rediscovering a sense of place, he suggested, a commitment to a particular piece of ground, will we be able to redefine our relationship to the planet." This makes searching beneath the surface of the Sierra Snyder's medium, not just his message. It also makes Snyder the best-known exponent of bioregionalism and deep ecology in the American West. Daunting as these terms might sound at first, the essence of Snyder's environmental philosophy can be neatly summed up in the commonsense concept of a watershed: in essence, the spiritual and political boundaries of any human community, including Tahoe's, are best defined by the rivers and ridges and physical watersheds which form the biological boundaries of the places we inhabit, in stark opposition to the often-arbitrary boundaries etched on a map. Hence it is Snyder's hope "that we may see ourselves more accurately on this continent of watersheds and life-communities—plant zones, physiographic provinces, culture areas; following natural boundaries."

Straddling five counties, two states, and a dozen overlapping and sometimes conflicting forest jurisdictions, the Lake Tahoe watershed makes an ideal example of what Snyder has in mind, beginning with the Nevada/California state line that runs straight through the heart of the lake. What could be more artificial, more arbitrary, than an invisible line that splits a living lake in half? But that's just the beginning, not the end, of the political fragmentation of the wider Lake Tahoe region viewed from Snyder's bioregional perspective. "The Sierra counties are a mess," he complains. "A string of them lap over the mountain crest, and the roads between the two sides are often closed in winter. A sensible redrawing of lines here would put eastern Sierra, eastern Nevada, and eastern Placer counties together in a new 'Truckee River County" and the seat could be in Truckee." In short, the Tahoe watershed's political boundaries as Snyder envisions them should mirror the biological and geological realities on the ground, not some abstruse set of antique political abstractions imposed from afar. Unlike the invisible borders of most political entities, in fact, watersheds define purely physical boundaries you can literally see, hear, feel, touch, and smell: "I never drive over the Donner Pass without, just cresting the summit, saying to myself, 'aha, the Great Basin,'" Snyder muses. "That is the bioregional boundary—and where the Truckee River heads on out to rest in Pyramid Lake. Whatever California really is," he adds, "it fades away when you cross the Sierra crest and get those vanilla- or caramel-smelling Jeffrey pines."

Snyder's larger vision, like his poetry, also includes a global context. Hence at Tahoe his vision embraces not just the "little watershed of northern California," or even the "Greater Sierra watershed," but rather "the big watershed of the planet" as a whole. Similarly Snyder's own work constantly incorporates layered allusions to far-flung cultures. As a voracious scholar and award-winning translator of Japanese and Chinese classical texts, Snyder typically weaves references into each poem or passage he crafts that range from ancient Buddhist texts to contemporary American pop culture icons (as in his lighthearted mock-epic "Smoky the Bear Sutra" republished in *Back on the Fire*).

Snyder's favorite themes also recapitulate many of the core insights we've encountered in our own journey beneath the surface of Lake Tahoe's long history. Reaching all the way back to Spirit Cave Man, for example, Snyder often reflects on the stark ecological changes which have swept through the Tahoe region in the last ten thousand years, since the retreat of the great glaciers. In one recent essay in *Back on the Fire*, for example, he reminds his neighbors, "There are paleo-Indian sites in this county that indicate human presence from eight thousand years ago." Similarly, his poem "Finding the Space in the Heart" speaks of "Faint shorelines seen high on these slopes" where one can still trace the shape of "long forgotten Lake Lahontan" and find "Columbian Mammoth bones / four hundred feet up on the wave etched beach ledge." Here too he finds human petroglyphs depicting "curly-horned / desert sheep outlines pecked into the rock." Finally, at the exact opposite extreme of the Tahoe watershed, his Desolation Wilderness journals note the traces of the great glaciers' passing etched on the granite bedrock high above the lake. "Walking across the broken rock bottom of an old glacier—through the ghost of a glacier—each sweep of bedrock [whispers] 'it touched me here.'" This free-flowing sense of writing as "clear water on clean rock" infuses every page and paragraph of Snyder's work. Time out of mind, through endless volcanic cycles of mountain building, we are all thrown *Back on the Fire*.

Leaping forward from the ice ages to the arrival of European explorers, Snyder is fully aware of the oft-destructive tide of ecological changes which have swept through the region. Repeatedly

Snyder underlines the fact that local Native American tribes practiced seasonal burning: "The 'pre-contact' forest was apparently a mosaic of various different forest stages," he reports, "from brush fields to many broad and open forest stands." Even the reproductive cycles of the native plants, Snyder emphasizes, were fully adapted to survive periodic bouts of drought, flood, and fire. The seeds of the common manzanita brush, he reminds us, open *only after* a fire has swept through (or after passing through the guts of a bear, he adds with a wink). In short, what Snyder means by becoming "native to this place" involves learning to listen to the indigenous plant life, wildlife, and human wisdom rooted within each living watershed.

Reminiscent of Datsolalee, who wove her dreams into memory baskets, Snyder often refers to his work as word-weaving. In a poem entitled "Word-Basket Woman," he literally takes on the voice of a timeless Indian weaver: "I dwell / in a house on the long west slope / of Sierra Nevada, two hundred mile / swell of granite," the poem begins, where "…the heart / words are Pomo, Miwok, Nisenan." Hence poetry itself requires weaving indigenous languages, sacred myths, and stories together such that "the small poem word baskets / stretch to the heft of their burden."

This does not mean that Snyder believes nature in the Tahoe Sierra is in any way innocent, harmless, or gentle. On the contrary, much like John Muir, in both his poetry and his prose Snyder shows a healthy respect for the stormy cycles of destruction and disruption that sweep through the Sierra forests at regular intervals. "A great Sierra-wide fire will come," he warns his neighbors in one recent essay, "and so will the flood that will make the Great Central Valley into a lake again, as it was during one winter in Sutter's time, when everything from mountain lions to rattlesnakes retreated up into the Sierra Buttes." Not unlike Muir, Snyder is unafraid to reach for biblical metaphors in defense of the wild. "If God hadn't wanted all these critters to be around, including rattlesnakes and cougars, he wouldn't have put them on the Ark," he opines. "The high country and the forests are the twenty-first century Ark of the Sierra,"

Snyder concludes, "an Ark even for all of California. Let's be sure it's an ark that stays afloat. Let's not try to second-guess God."

In some cases his literary influences are equally explicit: in one recent interview, for example, Snyder credits his early reading of John Muir's journals with shaping his own worldview. In other cases the influence of Tahoe-area authors seems, at best, implicit: like John Steinbeck's, for example, Snyder's work reveals a life-long fascination with biology. Like Bertrand Russell, he has long denounced nuclear weapons as the ultimate insanity. In George Sessions's *Deep Ecology: Living As If Earth Mattered*, Snyder's work is cited more frequently than that of any other American author.

Yet Snyder sees himself as standing outside, and in some cases standing against, the typical tradition of "American nature writing" as it is usually presented by professors of American literature such as myself. In 1992, invited to give the keynote lecture at the opening of the first "Art of the Wild" Squaw Valley Nature Writing Conference, he immediately launched into a critique of the word "Squaw," suggesting (only half-jokingly) that the conference be renamed the "*Brodiaea*-Harvester's Valley Conference" instead. But that was just the beginning, not the end, of his critique. By the end of his lecture, Snyder had also rejected the term "nature writing" completely, replacing it with a concept he himself calls "unnatural writing." Hence in Snyder's half-joking, half-serious opinion, the Squaw Valley Nature Writing Conference really ought to be called the "*Brodiaea*-Harvester's Valley Conference on Unnatural Writing."

So what does "unnatural writing" consist of? In part Snyder simply insists that a more inclusive, more culturally diverse range of works be added to the familiar list of Anglo-American "nature writers" from Thoreau and Muir to, well, Gary Snyder—including everything from Old Norse sagas to ancient Chinese poetry. But in the final analysis Snyder's critique reaches all the way down to the very roots of human language itself. In *Riprap and Cold Mountain Poems* (1990) Snyder explains, "There are poets who claim that their poems are made to show the world through the prism of language. Their project is worthy. There is also the work of seeing the world *without* any prism of language, and to bring that seeing *into* language."

In simple human terms, what Snyder's vision demands is that we remember to touch the waters of Lake Tahoe directly, even nakedly, unfettered by the intervening cultural clothing of science, literature, or even language itself: that we dive beneath the surface; that we plunge in raw.

All of which brings us back to the contrast between Michael Ondaatje's denatured vision in *Divisadero* and Gary Snyder's Sierran ecotopia. Beneath all that apparent complexity, their difference of perspective boils down to a simple distinction between absence and presence. In Ondaatje's *Divisadero*, in short, Coop's crisis of alienation is triggered by amnesia and the sheer absence of any human connection to nature, to history, or to the people whom he loves—as symbolically embodied by the absence of the lake in his life. In Snyder's *High Sierra*, by contrast, nature, history, and human community are always present. Even the past is literally *present* not just in memory but in every breath, in every sentence, in every line. There is no separation, no disconnect, no casino wall between us and the world outside. In this sense there is indeed "no nature"—at least insofar as the word "nature" implies an opposition or separation between human and nonhuman worlds. For Snyder, past, present, and future always flow together and merge as one—just as they do within the wider waters of Lake Tahoe itself.

"We do not easily *know* nature, or even know ourselves," Snyder observes in his preface to the book *No Nature*. "Whatever it actually is, it will not fulfill our conception or assumptions. It will dodge our expectations and theoretical models. There is no single or set 'nature' either as 'the natural world' or 'the nature of things.' The greatest respect we can pay to nature is not to trap it, but to acknowledge that it eludes us and that our own nature is also fluid, open and conditional." So too with Daowaga/Lake Bigler/Lake Tahoe—or whatever names we choose to call it. Regardless of our puny human efforts to contain or comprehend it, the deeper reality of the lake itself runs like water through our hands.

As for more specific visions of Lake Tahoe's future, utopian or otherwise, Snyder's closest approach to prophecy comes in his recent essay titled "Thinking Toward the Thousand-Year Forest Plan." Here his timeline suits Tahoe to a tee, given that the lake's own waters will take at least the next seven hundred years to fully cycle through. That same timeframe suits the ancient ways as well; the Iroquois law calling for the consequences of each decision to be considered by thinking at least seven generations into the future is a well-known example, though it is a perspective most Americans seem to confront only when planning nuclear waste storage facilities. Hence in Snyder's essay, past and future merge as one. We are not really living at the dawn of the twenty-first century, Snyder argues, but rather the dawn of the fifty thousandth century since the birth of the first recognizable human arts. Clearly, such a deeply rooted view of the human past also contains the seeds of an unshakeable optimism toward the future. If only we can remember how to stay rooted, the future (much like the planet) will take care of itself.

Which of these two contrasting visions of the future—the one dystopian, the other utopian—will we ourselves finally choose to embrace? Here at Lake Tahoe the truth is that we have already embraced them both. For Tahoe today already embodies all the deepest contradictions in the American spirit, from our gambler's fondness for wild-card wagers to our equally powerful desire to strip ourselves spiritually naked, to plunge back into some kind of primal relationship with nature itself. Yes, we really do want it all—and so far we've got it.

Then again, the future might surprise us. It always has before. If our voyage beneath the surface of Tahoe's history teaches anything, it should be that the future is always deeply, decisively, deceptively unpredictable. This need not be disturbing. It might even be a source of hope. For like the future landscape of Lake Tahoe, the nature of America itself is still taking shape before our very eyes. Perhaps that's even the message our ancient ancestors journeyed through ten thousand years of continuous Tahoe Time to tell us. As Yogi Berra once said, "The future ain't what it used to be." Viewed through the watery lens of Lake Tahoe, it's déjà blue all over again.

Twister II, by Gary Kaufman: a waterspout on Lake Tahoe, September 26, 1998.
Reprinted with the artist's permission

fifteen

THE WEASEL BROTHERS

Waterspouts and Water Babies

Anyone who wants to repeat Jacques Cousteau's journey beneath the surface of Lake Tahoe these days has something akin to magic at their command. No, I'm not talking about twenty-first-century SCUBA gear, or even those new privately owned submersibles just now coming out on the market. Instead I'm describing the Tahoe Environmental Research Center's state-of-the-art 3-D diving simulator. Slide on some plastic 3-D glasses—green lens on one side, blue lens on the other—and then sit back for the dive of a lifetime. At the helm of your simulated sub, a docent-guide pushes the joystick forward, and together you soar off into the virtual universe beneath the surface of Lake Tahoe. Millions of digitized data points recreate the exact topography of Tahoe in full-color plasma-screen high-definition wonder. Before your eyes underwater canyons, submerged mountains, and even the tracks of Tahoe's vast underwater landslides go swimming by smoothly in all their three-dimensional, lifelike glory. Call it depth perception.

Right next to this simulated submarine ride is another high-tech simulator with an equally powerful, if opposite, perspective on offer. There, suspended before your eyes, spins a huge plastic globe some five feet in diameter—representing the earth, of course, but made with a skin of transparent plastic so that you can literally see beneath the surface of continents and oceans. This time the principal purpose of the exhibit is to display real-time earthquake data projected on a global scale, thereby allowing you to watch swarms of tiny tremors swimming across the surface of the planet like shimmering schools of subterranean fish. Not surprisingly, most of the earthquakes are clustered along the edges of colliding tectonic plates, especially at the edge of the Pacific Rim, the so-called Ring of Fire (of which Tahoe is but a tiny part). Here then, at last, is Tahoe viewed in macrocosm and microcosm simultaneously, and in not just three but four dimensions: Lake Tahoe turned inside out.

At least on the surface, the lesson these exhibits all seek to embody is one and the same. Just as the First Rule of Ecology states, "Everything is connected to everything else." Or as John Muir expressed it far more elegantly decades ago, "Whenever we try to pick out anything by itself, we find it hitched to everything else in the universe." Tahoe included.

Nearby you'll find an array of microscopes and illuminated test tubes which invite visitors to examine some of the lake's smallest multicellular life forms. These include several invasive species only introduced into the lake's ecosystem within the last few years and now swarming throughout its waters in countless profusion. At the center of the whole exhibit "floats" a full-sized model of the modified fishing trawler that Tahoe scientists use to make annual measurements of the lake's clarity—with visibility currently holding steady, thanks to our longstanding battle to Keep Tahoe Blue. This same vessel is also used to dredge up mud core samples from the deepest reaches of the lake (artfully arranged like layer-cake slices of Tahoe's ancient memory in miniature).

Admittedly our own journey beneath the surface has focused more on literature than limnology (the scientific study of lakes and rivers). Yet several recent scientific discoveries still merit mention within these pages, if only for the poetry they seem to embody. The first such finding recently revealed that the entire body of water we now call Lake Tahoe is constantly vibrating like a huge blue bell, traversed by massive ultra-low-frequency subsurface waves which ebb and flow like the breathing of an enormous organism.

Simultaneously, humans have only recently become aware of the existence a "deep hot biosphere" extending at least one mile beneath the earth's surface—not just here at Lake Tahoe, but literally everywhere on Earth. Reaching down as far as the molten mantle, this newly discovered earthly ecosystem contains a total biomass far in excess of all the forests and fields and fisheries here on the surface, oceans included. Deep beneath the surface, in short, lurk silent legions of our most ancient ancestors: bacteria from the newly recognized phylum Archaea, feeding not on sunlight or carbon, as most surface plants do, but instead on a seething satanic soup of fiery subterranean substances like sulfur and phosphorus. Truly then, there is a vast lake of life right beneath our feet, fully as deep and fertile and fantastic as anything Lake Tahoe itself has on offer.

Which leaves us at last with that living "lake of the sky" above our heads to consider—an ocean of air filled to overflowing with still more forms of life we've only recently discovered. For as it turns out, even the most extreme reaches of the earth's outermost atmosphere contain life in abundance (bombarded by radiation so intense scientists formerly considered it fatal). Like the tiniest of Tahoe's crustaceans, we too find ourselves floating within a vast seething lake of life, suspended midway between Earth and sky.

That's surely one assertion that, as lifelong science lovers, Muir, Russell, Steinbeck, and Snyder would all agree on. Of course not all scientific insights depend on high-tech gadgetry for their magical appeal: take, for example, that magic moment when Tahoe's most famous scientist, Dr. Charles Goldman, danced in an ancient circle ceremony with the assembled elders of the Washoe tribe at the dedication of the new Tahoe Environmental Research Center in 2006.

Rarely if ever have past, present, and future flowed together quite so smoothly at Lake Tahoe.

Of course the Washoe have their own explanations of Tahoe's natural wonders to offer. Consider, for example, the mysterious case of the great "Tahoe Twister." As described by Tahoe photographer Gary Kaufman (who somehow captured this exceedingly rare meteorological event on film), "On September 26, 1998 at approximately nine o'clock in the morning, a huge waterspout rose from the mysteriously calm waters of Lake Tahoe like a waterfall in reverse, rising in a spiraling column to the stormy sky above." In essence what Kaufman had witnessed was a mountain tornado—a Tahoe Twister—but one in which the spiral funnel of the tornado touched down directly on the surface of the lake, filling the sky with a shimmering cloud of whirling water. According to Kaufman's account:

> Scientists who arrived later in Tahoe from the National Oceanic and Atmospheric Administration (NOAA) to study this phenomenon reported that the twister rotated in a clockwise direction—something that occurs approximately once in a thousand events. Stranger still, one of the spouts was of unusual size: approximately 250 feet in diameter. In fact, according to the scientists this was one of the largest waterspouts ever seen documented anywhere in the world.

In fact the waterspout first rose up from the lake's surface not far from Cave Rock—the legendary home of the mysterious Water Babies of Washoe legend. So were those waterspouts just Water Babies made manifest, as Kaufman himself has dared to assert?

For answers we can only turn to the ancient legends, myths, and stories of the Washoe tribe itself. At least one ancient Washoe legend describes a fierce struggle between the Water Babies and the ever-mischievous Weasel Brothers—a struggle that gave rise to all the smaller lakes within the Tahoe Basin. Since the literature of Lake Tahoe literally begins with these same ancient Washoe legends, it seems only natural that the Washoe should have the last word here as well. What follows, then, is JoAnn Nevers's English version of an ancient Washoe tale, handed down across countless generations by Daowaga's timeless shores, as recorded in the book *Wa She Shu: A Washo Tribal History*:

Pawetsile [Weasel] had just killed a deer. He told his brother *Damollale* [Squirrel], the mischievous one, to fetch some water from Lake Tahoe while he built a fire. When *Damollale* reached the Lake, he saw a young water baby combing her long, beautiful hair. Looking at the water baby sitting on Cave Rock, he thought, "My brother always wanted beautiful hair like that." The water baby, who knew what he was thinking, said to him, "If you try to take my hair, the Lake will swallow you." Then *Damollale* began to wrestle with the water baby. They rolled around the Lake to the place on the south shore where the Little Truckee runs into the Lake. There, *Damollale* killed the water baby. That is why the creek is always red.

When *Damollale* killed the water baby, the Lake began to boil. As *Damollale* started up the mountain to escape, he pulled a strand of hair from the water baby's scalp. The Lake advanced behind him; each time he plucked a hair it rose up and then receded. Finally *Damollale* reached Job's Peak, where his brother was. *Pawetsile* told him to give the water baby's hair back to the lake before the water swallowed them. *Damollale* protested, "But I thought you wanted her hair." Since by this time the water had reached their necks, *Pawetsile* insisted that his brother throw the hair back. Finally, he convinced his younger brother, who did what he was told. Then the Lake returned to its original bed, but as it retreated it left water in all the depressions in the area. That is why there are many small lakes in the mountains near Lake Tahoe.

So are waterspouts really just Water Babies made visible at last, their legendary long hair twisting toward the sky? I for one would love to think so. In a circular watershed as big and beautiful as this one, a place where literally everything living flows together as one, why *shouldn't* poetry and science, dream and reality, magic and mystery sometimes mingle and merge? Haven't they always? Clearly one lesson this ancient story teaches is a deep humility when faced with the hidden powers of the wider world. Clever as they are, the Weasel Brothers steal what is not theirs to take. Transfixed by beauty, blinded by desire, they almost destroy the same beauty they hoped to possess. The results are catastrophic—and not just for themselves. Yet not until they are quite literally up to their necks in troubles do the Weasel Brothers undo their mistake.

Since we're now up to our necks in troubles ourselves, it might well be time to heed this ancient warning. It's no longer something we can simply weasel out of or afford to ignore. The most recent findings posted on the Tahoe Environmental Research Center's website sound genuinely alarming: "UC Davis researchers at Lake Tahoe," the website reports, "this week published the first evidence that climate change alters the makeup of tiny plant communities called algae, which are the very foundation of the web of life in freshwater lakes." As one of the study's principal authors, Monika Winder, warns, "It is inconceivable that you could alter the base of the food web and not have other things start changing. What those changes will be, we don't know yet." My own guess is that, come hell or high water, we'll need these ancient stories to survive.

Acknowledgments

I have often joked that this book is simply "my Stanford dissertation translated into English." Hence I want to thank my dissertation committee mentors—Professors David Halliburton, Mary Pratt, and Greg Sarris—for many years of encouragement, advice, and support (as well as Stanford University and the Whiting Foundation, for crucial funding). Students at Foothill College slogged bravely through an early draft during an Honors Institute Seminar on Lake Tahoe I taught in 2005. Their advice helped transform a book for Tahoe aficionados into something accessible to everyone. Foothill College generously granted not one, but two sabbaticals during which I completed this project. Back in Colorado, my extended family put up with long absences from the Rockies and my deeply misguided preference for the Tahoe Sierra.

Without the contributions of previous generations of Tahoe historians, this book would not have been possible. I have relied especially on Edward B. Scott's *The Saga of Lake Tahoe* (1957), Douglas H. Strong's *Tahoe: From Timber Barons to Ecologists* (1984), and Lyndall Baker Landauer's *The Mountain Sea: A History of Lake Tahoe* (1996) every step of the way. I'm also deeply indebted to JoAnn Nevers and her Washoe collaborators for the book *Wa She Shu: A Washo Tribal History* (1976). David Beesley's *Crow's Range: An Environmental History of the Sierra Nevada* (2004) proved invaluable for its in-depth discussions of early human history in the Lake Tahoe region.

In my bookcase crowded with Tahoe titles, there are several more worthy of special mention—not just for the information but for the precious inspiration they provided. The first is Rebecca Solnit's *Savage Dreams: A Journey into the Landscape Wars of the American West* (1994), which first sparked my own investigations into the hidden history of the Donner Party. The second was Jean Pfaelzer's *Driven Out: The Forgotten War against Chinese Americans* (2007), which not only confirmed but explained much that other historians, myself included, had merely hinted at.

Finally there are countless Tahoe friends whose help and support was instrumental to this book's creation. Chief among them is Stanford Sierra Camp Director Dave Bunnett, who gave me the keys to his Fallen Leaf Lake cabin during the winter of 1999 so I could write the first draft of this book. Barbara Price Craven and her husband, Bill Craven, at the Fallen Leaf Lodge are my living link to the lake's own Greatest Generation, and their early enthusiasm for this project meant more than I can say. Jacquie Chandler and Chuck Greene on Tahoe's North Shore were especially generous in cheering me on. In San Diego my friend Tim Chan helped me find the heart of what I had to say. There is no greater gift.

Finding a home at Heyday has made my journey complete. For forty years publisher Malcolm Margolin, the essence of a true California intellectual and an ally to Native Americans—has built a publishing house whose books have informed my own. My editor at Heyday, Gayle Wattawa, read the last few drafts with the kind of care, insight, and patience that most writers only dream of. Jeannine Gendar sanded and smoothed my rough sentences even further and saved me from the embarrassment of a dozen glaring inaccuracies. Every chapter of this book was shaped, sharpened, and improved by their touch. At Sierra College Press our copublisher, Gary Noy, has helped bring the book full circle back to Lake Tahoe—a dream come true. Tom Killion's inspired image of Lake Tahoe viewed from Maggies Peaks, which appears on the cover, captures depths and dimensions of Tahoe's luminous, numinous beauty that no words of mine can possibly match.

About the Author

Raised in Colorado, Scott Lankford got lost en route to Stanford University and spent much of the next ten years as a maintenance man, musician, and mountaineering guide at Lake Tahoe. After joining the 1985 American Everest West Ridge Expedition, he completed a PhD in Modern Thought and Literature with a dissertation on John Muir. Currently a professor of English at Foothill College in California's Silicon Valley, he has previously served as Foothill's dean of Language Arts as well as codirector of the Foothill College Cultural Diversity Center.

Photo by Kevin Wayland

SIERRA COLLEGE PRESS

In 2002, the Sierra College Press was formed to publish *Standing Guard: Telling Our Stories* as part of the Standing Guard Project's examination of Japanese-American internment during World War II. Since then Sierra College Press has grown into the first complete academic press operated by a community college in the United States.

The mission of the Sierra College Press is to inform and inspire scholars, students, and general readers by disseminating ideas, knowledge, and academic scholarship of value concerning the Sierra Nevada region. The Sierra College Press endeavors to reach beyond the library, laboratory, and classroom to promote and examine this unique geography.

For more information, please visit www.sierracollegepress.edu/press.

Editor-in-Chief: Gary Noy
Board of Directors: Bright Rope, Rebecca Bocchicchio, Julie Bruno, Keely Carroll, Kerrie Cassidy, Charles Dailey, Frank DeCourten, Daniel DeFoe, Danielle DeFoe, Tom Fillebrown, Brian Haley, Robert Hanna, Rick Heide, Jay Hester, Joe Medeiros, Lynn Medeiros, Sue Michaels, Mike Price, Randy Snook, Barbara Vineyard
Editorial Advisory Board: Terry Beers, David Beesley, Patrick Ettinger, Janice Forbes, Tom Killion, Tom Knudson, Gary Kurutz, John Muir Laws, Beverly Lewis, Roger Lokey, Malcolm Margolin, Mark McLaughlin, jesikah maria ross, Michael Sanford, Lee Stetson, Catherine Stifter

Special thanks to our major financial supporters: Sierra College Friends of the Library, Rocklin Historical Society, Sierra College Natural History Museum

HEYDAY

into California

About Heyday

Heyday is an independent, nonprofit publisher and unique cultural institution. We promote widespread awareness and celebration of California's many cultures, landscapes, and boundary-breaking ideas. Through our well-crafted books, public events, and innovative outreach programs we are building a vibrant community of readers, writers, and thinkers.

Thank You

It takes the collective effort of many to create a thriving literary culture. We are thankful to all the thoughtful people we have the privilege to engage with. Cheers to our writers, artists, editors, storytellers, designers, printers, bookstores, critics, cultural organizations, readers, and book lovers everywhere!

We are especially grateful for the generous funding we've received for our publications and programs during the past year from foundations and hundreds of individual donors. Major supporters include:

Anonymous; Audubon California; Barona Band of Mission Indians; B.C.W. Trust III; S. D. Bechtel, Jr. Foundation; Barbara and Fred Berensmeier; Berkeley Civic Arts Program and Civic Arts Commission; Joan Berman; Lewis and Sheana Butler; Butler Koshland Fund; California Council for the Humanities; California State Coastal Conservancy; California State Library; California Wildlife Foundation / California Oak Foundation; Joanne Campbell; Keith Campbell Foundation; Candelaria Fund; John and Nancy Cassidy Family Foundation, through Silicon Valley Community Foundation; Christensen Fund; Creative Work Fund; The Community Action Fund; Community Futures Collective; Compton Foundation, Inc.; Lawrence Crooks; Ida Rae Egli; Donald and Janice Elliott, in honor of David Elliott, through Silicon Valley Community Foundation; Evergreen Foundation; Federated Indians of Graton Rancheria; Mark and Tracy Ferron; Furthur Foundation; George Gamble; Wallace Alexander Gerbode Foundation; Richard & Rhoda Goldman Fund; Evelyn & Walter Haas, Jr. Fund; Walter & Elise Haas Fund; James and Coke Hallowell; Sandra and Chuck Hobson; James Irvine Foundation; JiJi Foundation; Marty and Pamela Krasney; Robert and Karen Kustel, in honor of Bruce Kelley; Guy Lampard and Suzanne Badenhoop; LEF Foundation; Michael McCone; Moore Family Foundation; National Endowment for the Arts; National Park Service; Organize Training Center; David and Lucile Packard Foundation; Patagonia; Pease Family Fund, in honor of Bruce Kelley; Resources Legacy Fund; Alan Rosenus; Rosie the Riveter/WWII Home Front NHP; San Francisco Foundation; San Manuel Band of Mission Indians; Deborah Sanchez; Savory Thymes; Hans Schoepflin; Contee and Maggie Seely; James B. Swinerton; Swinerton Family Fund; Taproot Foundation; Thendara Foundation; TomKat Charitable Trust; Lisa Van Cleef and Mark Gunson; Marion Weber; John Wiley & Sons; Peter Booth Wiley; and Yocha Dehe Wintun Nation.

Getting Involved

To learn more about our publications, events, membership club, and other ways you can participate, please visit: www.heydaybooks.com.

green press
I N I T I A T I V E

Heyday is committed to preserving ancient forests and natural resources. We elected to print this title on 30% post consumer recycled paper, processed chlorine free. As a result, for this printing, we have saved:

10 Trees (40' tall and 6-8" diameter)
3 Million BTUs of Total Energy
951 Pounds of Greenhouse Gases
4,580 Gallons of Wastewater
278 Pounds of Solid Waste

Heyday made this paper choice because our printer, Thomson-Shore, Inc., is a member of Green Press Initiative, a nonprofit program dedicated to supporting authors, publishers, and suppliers in their efforts to reduce their use of fiber obtained from endangered forests.

For more information, visit www.greenpressinitiative.org

Environmental impact estimates were made using the Environmental Defense Paper Calculator. For more information visit: www.papercalculator.org.